European Integration, Regional Policy, and Growth

Edited by Bernard Funck and Lodovico Pizzati

THE WORLD BANK
Washington, D.C.

Contents

FIGURES

Foreword

The European Union (EU) stands out internationally as one of the political units that has most explicitly and deliberately attempted to reduce regional disparities among its constituents. How effective this effort has been, and continues to be, is a matter of open debate. The current enlargement of the EU to less affluent new members gives rise to a fresh set of questions. First, how can the objective of cohesion best be advanced in a context in which initial income disparities among the members of the enlarged EU will be greater? Will the accession cause the income of the poorer regions to converge toward EU standards, or, on the contrary, will prevailing disparities be exacerbated? What, if anything, can the new members do, and how should the expected EU structural funds be applied to maximize the cohesion objective? How can a new concept of solidarity for the enlarged Union be developed? Enlargement will present new challenges and raise questions as to whether the existing system of mutual support through structural and cohesion funds can be financed in the future, at least at current levels.

To elucidate these questions, the World Bank, the Bertelsmann Foundation, and the CIDOB Foundation (Barcelona) brought together leading scholars, senior policymakers, and practitioners from existing and new EU member countries, as well as representatives from the European Commission, to a conference in Barcelona in October 2002. This book presents the results of their discussions. Opinions presented by participants have in most cases been made in their personal capacity and do not necessarily reflect the institutions they represent. Drawing on the experience of existing EU members and the latest developments in growth theory and economic geography, the authors highlight the potential trade-off between promoting national growth and reducing relative disparities within countries rather than within the EU as a whole. This book also emphasizes the role of growth poles on the one hand, and investment climate (at the macro and micro levels) and labor market flexibility on the other, in furthering regional income convergence at the European level. In addition, it evaluates the potential role of EU structural funds either as mere income transfer mechanisms or as key ingredients of growth-enhancing fiscal strategies. Finally, it discusses the nature of institutional arrangements that can help bring about one or the other outcome, as well as the challenges that enlargement (and the ever deeper integration of EU factor and product markets) may bring to EU regional policy.

In addition to the papers presented in this volume, the conference drew inspiration from speeches and remarks by the following:

Narcís Serra i Serra
President, Fundació CIDOB, Barcelona, Spain

Joaquim Llimona
Secretary-General, General Secretariat of the Presidential Department, Generalitat of Catalonia, Barcelona, Spain

Lluis Riera
Director, ISPA and Pre-Accession Measures, DG Regional Policy, European Commission, Brussels, Belgium

József Veress
Deputy Commissioner, Office for the National Development Plan and EU Funds, Office of the Prime Minister, Budapest, Hungary

Much of the success of the conference is due to the effective session chairmanship provided by the following:

Martin Brusis
Senior Researcher, Bertelsmann Group for Policy Research, Center for Applied Policy Research, Munich, Germany

Bernard Funck
Sector Manager, Central and Eastern Europe, World Bank, Washington, D.C., United States

Roger Grawe
Country Director, Central and Eastern Europe, World Bank, Warsaw, Poland

Franz Kaps
Senior Advisor, Aid Coordination and Partnerships, World Bank, Budapest,
Hungary

Cornelius Ochmann
Director, Central and Eastern Europe, Bertelsmann Foundation, Guetersloh,
Germany

Finally, we would like to acknowledge the World Bank Publications team in managing the production of this volume.

Johannes Linn	*Narcís Serra i Serra*	*Werner Weidenfeld*
Vice President,	President,	Member of the Board,
Europe and	Fundació CIDOB	Bertelsmann
Central Asia,		Foundation
World Bank		

Contributors

Fabrizio Barca
Director General in Charge of Regional Policy, Ministry for Economic and Financial Affairs, Rome, Italy

Frank Barry
Lecturer, Economics Department, University College, Dublin, Ireland

Jiří Blažek
Lecturer, Department of Social Geography and Regional Development, Charles University, Prague, Czech Republic

Michele Boldrin
Professor, Department of Economics, University of Minnesota, Minneapolis, United States; Research Fellow, Centre for Economic Policy Research (CEPR), London, United Kingdom

Martin Bruncko
Director, Foreign Policy Studies, Institute for Public Affairs, Bratislava, Slovak Republic

Vasco Cal
General Coordinator of the Cohesion Report, DG Regional Policy, European Commission, Brussels, Belgium

Fabio Canova
Professor, Department of Economics, Universitad Pompeu Fabra, Barcelona, Spain; Research Fellow, Centre for Economic Policy Research (CEPR), London, United Kingdom

Antoni Castells
Professor, Department of Public Finance, University of Barcelona, Spain; Carles Pi i Sunyer Foundation, Barcelona, Spain

Angel de la Fuente
Researcher, Institute of Economic Analyses, Barcelona, Spain

Marta Espasa
Professor, Department of Public Finance, University of Barcelona, Spain

Bernard Funck
Sector Manager, Central and Eastern Europe, World Bank, Washington, D.C., United States

Carole Garnier
Director, Structural Funds and CAP, DG Economic and Financial Affairs, European Commission, Brussels, Belgium

Janis Kruminš
Minister of Public Administration Reform of the Republic of Latvia, Riga, Latvia

Luis Madureira Pires
Calouste Gulbenkian Foundation, Lisbon, Portugal

Philippe Martin
Researcher, Center of Education and Research in Socio-Economic Analysis (CERAS), Paris, France

Alexandre Muns
Lecturer of International Economic Institutions and European Integration, Escola Superior de Comerć International, Pompeu Fabra University, Barcelona, Spain

Vitalis Nakrosis
Deputy Director General, National Regional Development Agency, Vilnius, Lithuania

Lodovico Pizzati
Economist, Central and Eastern Europe, World Bank, Washington, D.C., United States

Alfred Steinherr
Chief Economist, European Investment Bank, Luxembourg

Igor Strmšnik
Secretary of State for Regional Development, Ministry of the Economy, Ljubljana, Slovenia

Jan Szomburg
Head of the Board, Gdansk Institute for Market Economics, Gdansk, Poland

Christian Weise
Senior Expert, German Institute for Economic Research, Berlin, Germany

CHAPTER 1

Overview

Bernard Funck, Lodovico Pizzati, and Martin Bruncko

In the 2000–2006 fiscal framework, the European Union (EU) has allocated €213 billion (about one-third of the EU budget) to transfers for regional policy. These transfers amount to €30.4 billion per year, about 0.35 percent of Europe's gross domestic product (GDP) and roughly 3.2 percent of the beneficiary regions' GDP. The EU regional policy was formally established with the purpose of reducing disparities among European regions. Funding under this policy comes from a panoply of EU funds, collectively known as "structural funds," some of which predate the policy itself. Regions with GDP per capita below 75 percent of the EU average are the main beneficiaries. (See the annex to this chapter.)

As the European Union enlarges eastward and southward, it will absorb a population of more than 100 million people with an average income that is roughly half of the previous EU level. This enlargement will test existing regional policy frameworks in two different ways. First, it will raise the question of how to ensure cohesion in a Union with such vastly disparate initial conditions between regions and countries and, if this objective is to be maintained, what instruments are available to achieve it. Second, enlargement will raise the question of how EU funding can best be applied in light of a surge in the number of claimants and how funding mechanisms should be adjusted to achieve that effect.

Will enlargement narrow or widen initial disparities between European regions? What (if any) policy instruments do national governments, regions, and the EU have at their disposal to achieve regional growth? And what is the role of the European regional policy, alongside other instruments, in stimulating convergence and mitigating potentially negative effects of integration? Can the existing system of mutual support through structural funds be financed at current levels? If not, how can a new concept of solidarity for the enlarged Union be developed?

These are some of the questions that the participants at a conference held in Barcelona in October 2002, "Income Convergence and European Regional Policy," sought to address. It should be remembered that the conference took place prior to the completion of the accession negotiations and raised some topics that have subsequently been resolved. This publication contains the papers presented at that conference. The volume is organized in four parts. The first two parts discuss the impact of economic integration on the disparity of income across regions and the role of regional transfers in that context, from a theoretical and empirical perspective; that is, based on the latest insights coming from economic theories as well as on the recent experience of EU members themselves (in contrast, for instance, to that of the United States).

The first part looks at these issues from a global perspective, providing theoretical arguments and empirical evidence regarding the effects of economic integration on the geographical dispersion of economic activity and on regional growth performance at the European level, and the role of EU structural funds in that process. In doing so, this part raises the fundamental questions that will permeate the rest of the book: Are the structural funds developmental in nature (do they serve to enhance productivity), or are they merely redistributive (do they simply reallocate disposable income between contributing and beneficiary regions)? A consensus emerges around two propositions: (1) that regional policy in the EU sense is to a large extent a second-best substitute for labor mobility (and a potentially self-defeating one, if regional interventions further weaken the incentive for labor to move); and (2) that a trade-off exists between these two objectives (developmental and redistributive) both at the EU level and in the circumstances of each particular country.

The second part of the volume looks at the same questions on the basis of the specific experience of some current EU members. The examples of Spain, Italy, and Ireland are presented in detail. National officials and academics discuss how they have judged the growth/redistribution arbitrage in their own countries and regions and how the EU framework may have helped make the best of it.

The third part of the book focuses on the regional policy prospects in the new EU member countries. In this part, experts and national officials from the Slovak Republic, Slovenia, Lithuania, Poland, and Latvia discuss how they are approaching the same arbitrage, how they are planning to implement regional policy and the allocation of structural funds in response, and how they are setting up their institutional framework for the task. The final part of the book discusses the future of the EU regional policy. A key question is whether, within a given resource envelope, structural funds should be redirected toward the newer members or spread thinner across new and current beneficiaries, or whether the envelope itself should be expanded to accommodate all.

What Is a Region?

Before getting into the heart of the matter, however, we must clarify how "regional disparities" are defined. Regional statistics in Europe follow the *Nomenclature des Unités Territoriales Statistiques* (NUTS) classification (see map 1-1). What level of territorial aggregation should be a matter of concern to the policymaker? In order to make an assessment of regional inequalities tractable, the European Commission has chosen the NUTS-2 level of disaggregation rather than the more aggregated NUTS-1 or the more disaggregated NUTS-3, and it is at this level that the largest amount of structural funds is being allocated. The choice of a particular level of disaggregation has great relevance for the view one can form of regional disparities. As Alfred Steinherr points out, at the NUTS-2 level, the United Kingdom presents the largest regional income disparity among current members, while France shows a very homogeneous distribution. At the NUTS-3 level, however, it is France that exhibits the widest variation.

Why should we be concerned with one measure of regional inequality (NUTS-2) more than another (NUTS-1 or NUTS-3)? One reason, explain Michele Boldrin and Fabio Canova, is that idiosyncratic differences between small, undifferentiated geographical entities are unavoidable, and that the matter of regional disparity becomes significant only when regions are large enough (and thus, presumably, have a minimal degree of internal differentiation) to become objects of meaningful macroeconomic inquiry. At a higher level of disaggregation, we will find large discrepancies in output per capita. However, they would be quite normal, simply reflecting the differences in local natural endowments: for instance, a district that, thanks to its ideal soil, specializes in agricultural production would not generate as much output per capita as a neighboring district with a heavy concentration of capital-intensive industries, even though living standards might be identical. In this respect, Boldrin and Canova call attention to the large differences that exist even between NUTS-2 regions, which range from 100,000 to 10 million inhabitants. They argue that economic convergence should be targeted for larger areas, if any. This would suggest that the NUTS-1 level might be the only one that is pertinent for policy and planning purposes, and in the case of the smaller countries (such as Ireland, Portugal, and many Central and Eastern European candidates), it would even correspond to the national boundaries.

The Impact of Regional Policy on Income Convergence

This being posited, we note that the European Union has set itself the goal of promoting economic and social cohesion by reducing disparities between the levels of development of its various regions, however defined, and the backwardness of the least-favored regions. Why should this require regional transfers? After all, neoclassical models predict that increasing trade and economic integration should sponta-

MAP 1-1 EU REGIONS

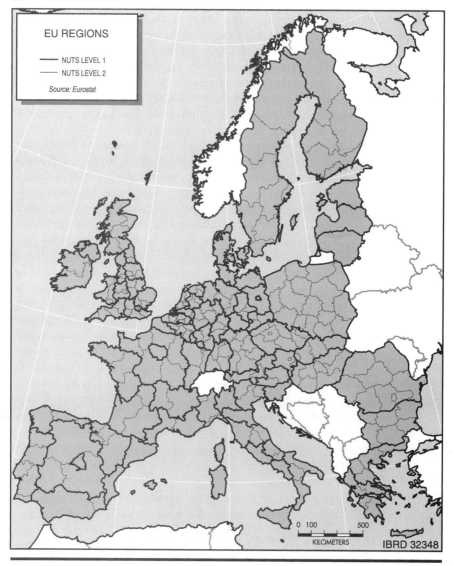

neously fuel convergence. In the presence of diminishing marginal returns on factor inputs, capital investment should flow to less developed countries, which tend to be relatively undercapitalized and where, consequently, capital can earn higher profits. Increased investment should translate into improved productivity, which should in turn lead to higher income levels and spontaneous real convergence to EU levels.

Still, we cannot fail to note that progress in EU integration has gone hand in hand with an increasing emphasis on interregional transfers. In fact, the fear that the advent of the Single Market and of the Economic and Monetary Union would exacerbate intra-European disparities contributed to the addition of a new transfer mechanism to the existing panoply of structural funds, the so-called Cohesion Fund.

Drawing on the tenets of "economic geography theory," Philippe Martin explains why this might be the case. Firms benefit from agglomeration effects (arising from the quality of infrastructures, concentration of human resources, etc.) and economies of scale. When markets open up and transaction costs are reduced, firms naturally tend to congregate in areas where such agglomeration effects are strongest or they can best exploit economies of scale (i.e., closer to main consuming markets).[1] If labor markets are rigid, concentration of activity may lead to greater disparities in unemployment across regions than is politically tolerable. Hence the role of regional policy: *to bring jobs to the people, if the people do not go the jobs.*

As Martin indicates, this pattern of activity concentration is not specific to Europe. In the case of the United States, economic activity is highly concentrated in a few regions, although much less than in past decades. Due to American labor mobility, concentration of production can more easily attract the bulk of the population. Therefore, when we look at income per capita, regions with high GDP are also very dense in population, and present GDP per capita is similar to that in regions with low GDP and low population. According to Martin, a process of regional concentration is under way in Europe today. However, Europe does not have the same labor mobility as the United States, and, therefore, economic integration may lead to increased regional discrepancy in per capita GDP. If there is underutilization of economic potential in the periphery because of labor market rigidity, structural funds may provide the incentive for firms to relocate enterprises to the depressed peripheral regions.

Martin adds, however, two important words of caution. First, attempting to counteract firms' natural tendency to concentrate (at least in the initial stages of integration) necessarily leads to a loss of efficiency, reducing the overall growth potential accordingly. Conversely, one can see that if labor-market concerns could be addressed differently, the scope would exist for maximizing growth by stimulating, rather than dampening, agglomeration effects, including, for instance, through a deliberate concentration of infrastructures within "growth poles." One example of this approach is the deliberate effort to improve transport infrastructure in the North of France, which made this region competitive with neighboring wealthy European regions, spurring a concentration of economic activity there.

Martin's second caveat is that investing, for example, in public infrastructure may have different effects in different regions. For instance, investments aiming to reduce trade costs, such as those in new highways, may have exactly the opposite effects. If economic integration has not advanced sufficiently, decreasing trade costs may not induce firms to establish their production in the economically disadvantaged regions—even if those regions may offer lower labor costs. In contrast to what happened in the North of France, highway construction in southern Italy may well have accentuated its decline by encouraging firms established in this region (or that would have otherwise located in it) to move (or keep) their production outside of it in order to benefit from economies of scale closer to larger markets.

Michele Boldrin and Fabio Canova challenge this view, calling into question whether the agglomeration effects Martin envisions exist at the macroeconomic level in the real world. According to their research, such effects are not observed empirically at any reasonable level of spatial disaggregation. They also argue that European structural funds have had no observable impact on regional growth and economic convergence. In the past 20 years, they claim, despite the significant increase in regional funds invested, there was no visible impact on economic convergence *within* countries. As to convergence across countries, Boldrin and Canova insist, it is national policies that reduce taxes and inefficient public spending, liberalize labor markets, attract foreign direct investments, and minimize income support transfers that have led to increased growth. After all, the authors stress, it is not high investment per se that causes growth. Rather, when policies create appropriate conditions for growth, investment follows. The most striking example the authors cite to support their argument is East Germany, which received €571 billion from the German government between 1991 and 1997. Despite having full access to the EU markets, East Germany has not converged. Other transition economies have fared better in the absence of regional transfers by undergoing the necessary structural change and having new investment directed toward productive sectors.

If this is the case, Boldrin and Canova note, EU regional policy can be rationalized only as an exercise in income redistribution or by political economy arguments pertaining to the need for EU-level politicians and bureaucrats to secure political support and legitimacy for the European enterprise, albeit at some efficiency cost—a motivation expressed unapologetically by Barca and Cal later in the volume.

Whatever the case might be, in the absence of economies of scale or the type of external effects described by Martin, efficiency considerations would argue in favor of reducing the scope of the related transfers as much as possible and targeting them to the lower-income region rather than toward potentially more affluent "growth poles," as earlier suggested. To the extent that they remain in place, income support programs should target job-seekers (as in the Netherlands), and structural funds should create employment opportunities to enlarge labor force participation (as in Ireland). In general, Boldrin and Canova suggest focusing regional funds on infrastructure (transport, communication, power, water, education) and not on subsidies to small business development, as that may create the wrong incentives. Instead, a favorable national policy framework should facilitate the business environment.

Carole Garnier retorts that Boldrin and Canova's policy recommendations are derived from excessively limited empirical data. Indeed, it is only since the late 1980s that structural funds have had an efficiency-oriented design. Because supply-side effects take time to materialize (as does investment in infrastructure aiming to spur productivity), it is too early to assess the impact of structural funds on long-term convergence. While regional policy based on the small and heterogeneous NUTS-2 is being criticized as a target for regional convergence, she submits that structural funds can make a positive contribution to *national convergence.* In line with Martin's thesis, she attributes this effect to a trade-off between national convergence (national GDP per capita catching up with EU average) and regional-level convergence (regional GDP per capita converging toward national averages).

Whether the trade-off identified by Martin and Garnier has actually been properly exploited is a different matter. A more recent paper, Midelfart-Knarvik and Overman (2002) suggests that Boldrin and Canova's findings (no empirical evidence of divergence) are not necessarily irreconcilable with the view that agglomeration effects exercise a powerful influence on firms' location decisions. Contrary to Boldrin and Canova, however, Midelfart-Knarvik and Overman (2002) finds that regional policy *has* been effective in shifting firms' location where it is less efficient, thereby potentially offsetting the impact of agglomeration effects (and explaining the lack of observable divergence). In other words, the regional policy's initial emphasis on dispersing economic activities would have "succeeded," but at the cost of overall growth.

This begs the question as to why regional transfers would be needed at all. Would there be a need to remedy a shortage of private investment due, for example, to national savings being insufficient or to limited access to foreign borrowing? Are there microeconomic constraints to "good projects," public or private, finding financing? Alfred Steinherr doubts that such macroeconomic or microeconomic constraints still exist now that EU capital markets have opened up—at least as far as the current members are concerned (the accession countries might present a different case).

Therefore, instead of a lack of public investment, Steinherr identifies three types of externalities and labor market rigidity as the main source of regional income differences. First, *technological externalities* lead firms to locate where there is already economic activity and a developed market (Martin's argument). Second, as a result of excessive movement of capital and labor to more productive areas, *pecuniary externalities* arise from falling wages and increasing consumer prices that may emerge from labor movements. Third, when a region does not reach a minimum threshold of economic activity, it lacks the required price information and business knowledge, and this leads to a *coordination problem* for the development of a network of services and intermediate goods suppliers. Finally, *labor market rigidity,* understood as low degree of labor mobility and skill differences, exacerbates those three factors of regional imbalances. Steinherr points to inflexible housing markets (high registration taxes and other transaction costs), lack of cross-regional job information, and language barriers as the main sources of a low degree of labor mobility. According to Steinherr, these, and not a lack of investable funds, are the problems that need a remedy.

That leaves us with only the political economy argument for "doing something" in the name of Europe to justify regional aid. Jiří Blažek concurs with Boldrin and Canova on the dangers of creating a "dependency mentality" and agrees with their insight on using larger territorial units for regional fund eligibility. However, Blažek warns against their nonintervention approach, given the risk that the potential frustration with limited opportunities on the part of the population in post-communist countries may put into question the market economy and parliamentary democracy. Regional "activism" would obviate this risk.

Country-Specific Experiences

In the chapters focusing on specific country experiences, we find our contributors generally more sanguine about the impact of EU regional aid than the previous discussion may have led us to believe. Overall, we can divide the impact of structural funds into demand- and supply-side effects. On the demand side, the increased spending will have a definite relevance for aggregate expenditures. Whether regional funds are serving a purely redistribution purpose or are efficiently invested, in the short run they will have a positive impact on aggregate demand. On the other hand, if these funds are successfully invested, they will increase the production potential of the recipient region irrespective of future funding. These are the supply-side effects that will increase income and employment levels in the long run as well, without necessitating the inflow of additional funding. Frank Barry makes the additional distinction between "direct" and "indirect" effects of regional funds. Besides directly adding to the productive capacity of the beneficiary economy, Barry suggests that the direct impact could be complemented by indirect supply-side effects if, past their initial impact, the investments lead to a sustained increase in the productivity growth *rate*. The magnitude of supply-side effects is hard to quantify and presumably initially much lower than that of the demand effects, which are close to the amount of actual spending. Without any supply-side effects whatsoever, the funds would de facto amount to a pure income transfer, increasing expenditures in beneficiary regions at the expense of contributing regions, and perhaps also of overall growth, if the related transfers are financed by distortionary taxes.

Most authors would agree that the demand-side effects are positive. Looking at a wide geographical coverage, Castells and Espasa find clear evidence of the redistribution effect of regional aid, as the demand-side effect of these transfers induces a short-term reduction in regional *income disparities*.

Positive as the demand-side effects may have been, has EU regional aid achieved supply-side effects on growth beyond the natural impact of redistribution? De la

Fuente contends that in Spain, direct supply-side effects of structural funds can also be observed. Barry's estimate of the impact of EU regional aid on the Irish convergence is also positive, though surprisingly modest, particularly on the supply side. Was the potential of the structural funds insufficiently carried out? De la Fuente's analysis indicates that, in the case of Spain, regional aid could have had much higher impact had the government attached a greater weight to efficiency considerations rather than to redistribution. It may be argued that this redistributive bias is actually preordained in the regional targeting of structural funds to selected NUTS-2 regions. Certainly, when relieved from that constraint and allowed to allocate regional aid irrespective of regional income, the Spanish government chose to prioritize very different regions. When it came to allocating the (regionally untargeted) Cohesion Fund resources, the comparatively more affluent Catalonia came first, followed by Andalusia and Madrid. Of course, some projects financed in Catalonia may be justified as having interregional benefits (e.g., the construction of a high-speed train route and the expansion of the port of Barcelona). But substantiating Steinherr's remarks on the risk of regional aid displacing private market-based financing, Alexandre Muns notes that many projects cofinanced with EU regional aid would have been undertaken even without EU regional funds.

This being said, a number of authors stress that the main benefits of the EU regional policy lie elsewhere. Fabrizio Barca, for instance, underscores the importance of the peer review/pressure it involves for improving *the quality of expenditure policies and institutions*. Regional policy puts a strong emphasis on planning, partnership, monitoring, evaluation, and control requirements in the use of EU funds. In order to draw upon these funds, national administrations must have a certain set of institutions and follow strictly defined policies at both national and regional levels. All these requirements are designed to ensure the effectiveness and efficiency of public interventions funded by EU money. Structural funds have thus been instrumental in increasing efficiency in public administration. Barca recounts, for instance, how the discipline created by the EU framework helped the Italian government deal with the notoriously inefficient Cassa del Mezzogiorno, a centralized Italian state agency that managed subsidies and infrastructure. Following decades of mismanagement, the agency was terminated in 1993. The results, Barca says, are plain to see: savings in southern Italy have increased, unemployment has dropped, and self-employment is surging.

Barry similarly suggests that the indirect impact of regional aid may have been the most important one, particularly its *contribution to the quality of Ireland's fiscal adjustment*. Up to the mid-1980s, the country had been struggling with a debt crisis resulting from pro-cyclical fiscal expansions. Financing rising public spending with high taxation had proved unsuccessful, as workers responded with higher wage demands. With the increase of structural funds in 1989, Ireland was able to bring down its deficit without compromising its public investment program. EU transfers helped relax the budget constraint and allowed lower tax rates, which in turn attracted foreign firms (primarily thanks to lower corporate taxes), with a direct impact on growth. According to Barry, the regional policy framework also proved instrumental in bringing about an improvement in the composition of Ireland's public expenditure, with greater emphasis on communication infrastructure and education.

Favorable labor market conditions, however, proved key to the success of the Irish formula. Barry emphasizes the importance of *labor market flexibility,* reminding us how Portugal, with a different industrial strategy focused on low-tech manufacturing (as opposed to the Irish high-tech), is also converging to EU standards. With flexible labor markets, new investment increases the demand for labor, which in turn translates into increased employment and income growth. Conversely, in labor markets more dominated by insiders, such as in Italy or Spain, the same labor demand increase will translate into higher wages (for insiders), and thus into less employment and growth. National policies, of course, "naturally" generate less rigidity in small and comparatively uniform countries like Portugal and Ireland than in larger, more differentiated ones like Spain and Italy. With similar national wage policies, and thus comparable labor costs in both rich and poor regions, it is hardly surprising that firms would locate production in industrialized areas, leaving the poorer regions with higher unemployment.

Lessons for Accession Countries

How does that experience apply to the countries that are now joining the EU? How should they spend the huge sums that will be coming from the structural funds? Should they target efficiency or redistribution goals in their allocation decisions? How should they manage the structural funds to maximize their intended impact? Two main messages come out of this book: First, regional policy should be used primarily according to efficiency criteria, with growth-oriented domestic policy ensuring the diffusion of convergence across regions. Second, if regional aid is to be disbursed, it should be used to finance essential infrastructure rather than for transfers to private and public enterprises in the name of attempting to support small business development. As for the institutional arrangements for managing structural funds, they may be more or less decentralized, according to the size and degree of decentralization of the recipient country itself; what is important is that they be firmly integrated as part of government's overall fiscal strategy (as described above in the case of Ireland) and in the mainstream of public resource management.

The first point is made by Martin Bruncko in the context of the Slovak Republic. While recognizing that substantial regional disparities exist, particularly between the booming capital of Bratislava and the eastern part of the country, Bruncko argues that these disparities are not particularly large by European standards, and the difference in regional output per capita is not widening. The truly worrisome disparity is in unemployment, as the growth pole of Bratislava, prospering with small and medium enterprises, is in direct contrast with the declining agriculture and collapsed military industry of the eastern part of the country. Bruncko also observes that regional wage variation is less pronounced than productivity variation would warrant. It is no surprise that wage/productivity ratios lead foreign investments to areas like Bratislava, which also happens to be closer to major European markets and transport arteries. It would be a mistake in this context to bypass the emerging Bratislava growth pole as recipient of structural funding (as the Slovak government proposes), since from an efficiency perspective it promises the highest return on investment, at least in the initial years of accession. What would facilitate the diffusion of investment and growth to more backward regions is not dispersing public spending efforts, Bruncko suggests, but improving wage competitiveness in poorer regions and reforming social welfare to stimulate labor mobility, while reducing trade costs over time in peripheral regions through a well-calibrated transportation infrastructure.

Even so, the magnitude of the investment required may sometimes exceed the financial capacity of the country alone. If the benefits of the proposed investments also accrue largely beyond a country's borders, there might be a good case, Strmšnik submits, for the international community (that is, the EU) to fund the investment, irrespective of narrowly defined national benefits and financial limitations. Slovenia's location makes it an important link for European infrastructure integration. While the interregional benefits might make the development of this infrastructure worthwhile for Slovenia's neighbors in the first place, the magnitude involved would strain budgetary resources and make it difficult for a country of Slovenia's size to meet the Maastricht criteria on fiscal deficits. Hence the need, according to Strmšnik, for the country to have access to structural funds, irrespective of its income level (which may exceed the eligibility threshold), not so much in consideration of Slovenia's priorities and requirements per se, but on the basis of larger cross-border returns.

In practice, the allocation of structural funds will be determined in part by the nature of the institutional arrangements set up for the tasks. Integrating structural funds in the overall management of national budgets would typically allow governments to deploy them better in the framework of a consistent fiscal strategy than an extra-budgetary operation would. On the continuum that links "redistribution-based" and "efficiency-based" investment decisions, a more decentralized setting is more likely to err on the redistributive side, while a more centralized one may be more adept at marshaling resources toward maximizing national growth. Conversely, a more decentralized approach might be more effective at mobilizing local partnerships. Vitalis Nakrosis outlines the pros and cons of the institutional choices involved: integrated versus unintegrated, centralized versus decentralized arrangements. After an initial hesitation, countries have generally adopted the integrated approach. As to the second alternative, Nakrosis concludes, in line with the argument made at the outset about the existence of a minimum size threshold for regional targeting, that an integrated-centralized system would be the most cost-effective option for a country the size of Lithuania.

In contrast, Janis Krumiņš defends the decentralized approach. Krumiņš argues that in the case of Latvia's national growth can currently be seen only in the biggest cities, while the rural areas are in continuous decline. In areas with no foreign investment and no job creation, the low income levels do not permit a large enough tax base to support the maintenance of essential infrastructure, much less its development. It is to these lagging and depressed territories that, in his view, regional aid should be directed. And the best way to make sure that this happens is to decentralize the funds away from the capital.

After considering the idea of decentralized management, Jan Szomburg explains, Poland has chosen a mixed approach, with about 80 percent of funds being managed under national programs and the remainder being allocated as follows: 80 percent allocated to all regions in proportion to their population, 10 percent to regions with GDP per capita below 80 percent of national average, and 10 percent to provinces with an unemployment rate 50 percent above the national average. Szomburg anticipates, however, that Poland will shift to a more fully decentralized approach in the next budget cycle (2007–2012).

Luis Madureira Pires observes that, although the range options available for managing regional aid varies a lot between large regionalized countries such as Poland, and smaller, more centralized ones, the European Commission has typically favored more centralized approaches—sometimes, in his view, to the detriment of local efforts to build more modern and more responsive governance frameworks. Similarly, while countries may take different views of the arbitrage they want to make between redistribution and efficiency considerations in utilizing regional aid, the Structural Funds philosophy has, since 1988, increasingly stressed the need to reduce the development gap between poor member states and the EU average rather than to decrease internal regional disparities, the latter being regarded more and more as a domestic issue.

The Future of EU Regional Policy

Arguing that structural funds have had no impact on growth but generate distorting effects, Boldrin and Canova, as we have seen, called for their termination at the end of the current EU budget cycle (in 2006), or at least for lowering eligibility to regions with 50 percent of EU average GDP per capita (which would leave out virtually all current beneficiaries in Western Europe, as well as Slovenia, the Czech Republic, and perhaps Hungary), with funding to be phased out by the next six-year budget cycle.

Christian Weise makes the case for reform, instead. In his view, reform will be needed to resolve two principal-agent problems embedded in the current regional policy framework. First, net paying countries do not directly control the allocation of transfers, relying on the European Commission to ensure the appropriate implementation of structural funds. Second, the European Commission is itself subject to a principal-agent problem, as it cannot implement the desired policy itself and must rely on the receiving countries, which may or may not pursue the same ultimate goals. With enlargement, Weise warns, these problems will worsen, as there will be more receiving countries to potentially take advantage of such principal-agent problem and the regional administrative structures in new member countries are likely to be weak.

Weise recommends, therefore, heightening the incentives for recipient countries to adhere to the spirit of a growth-oriented cohesion policy; for instance, through a higher degree of national cofinancing, a greater reliance on loans instead of grants, and perhaps even policy conditionality. Moreover, Weise favors leaving the current eligibility threshold for regional aid (expressed as a percentage of the average EU income) untouched after enlargement, even if that means weaning many current beneficiary regions in Western Europe from EU support (because the absolute level of the threshold would decline as new lower-income entrants bring down the average EU income). This would be in line, he says, with the fundamental rule of the EU cohesion policy, which is to concentrate support on the needy.

In his reply, Cal argues that this approach is politically impractical. Limiting funding to the extent proposed by Weise would undermine the political support for the entire idea of regional policy (as fewer would benefit from it), with the ultimate result that even the money for less developed areas would disappear. As part of the enlargement process, Cal highlights how EU regions will basically be divided into three groups: (1) per capita GDP below 45 percent of average (most of the Central European accession countries); (2) per capita GDP above 120 percent of average (most of the current member states); and (3) per capita GDP around 80 percent of average—previous cohesion member states (Spain, Portugal, and Greece) as well as some new entrants (Czech Republic, Slovenia, and Cyprus). With enlargement, EU regional policy will thus automatically focus more on less developed areas. But also as a result, regions encompassing as many as 18 million people may lose their previous eligibility, thereby potentially eroding the political constituency for the system. The best way to obviate this risk, Cal suggests, is for EU regional aid to continue to flow to the not-so-underdeveloped regions of the enlarged EU.

Conclusions

Summing up the proceedings, Carole Garnier stresses how limited our understanding of the determinants of long-term growth remains, particularly at the regional level. Therefore, our understanding of the potential and actual impact of EU regional policy in this process, particularly in the presence of such unquantifiable benefits as the improvement in public administration efficiency noted by some of the speakers, is also limited. What is clear, however, is that simply injecting resources is not sufficient to fuel sustained regional growth. What counts is the policy framework into which those resources are injected and the strategy applied in deploying them.

Garnier lists three essential ingredients to such a successful framework/strategy for regional convergence at the EU level. First, financial stability is a prerequisite for growth, and national-level macroeconomic policies need to be supportive of that objective. Second, convergence policies need to be pursued at the appropriate territorial level. A trade-off appears to exist between maximizing growth at the national level and reducing disparities between smaller territorial units within individual countries. This is not necessarily a zero-sum game, however. In the case of Ireland, for example, regional disparities actually increased during the economic takeoff, as some regions grew faster than others; even the lagging regions, however, converged to European averages. The third ingredient for a successful strategy concerns the specific types of investment to be supported. There is no formula for this. Investment strategies need to be grounded in a careful analysis of regional specificities, bottlenecks, and potential competitive advantages.

Annex: What is EU Regional Policy?

The European Union's regional policy is based on financial solidarity, inasmuch as part of member states' contributions to the Community budget goes to the less prosperous regions and social groups.[2] For the 2000–2006 period, these transfers will account for one-third of the Community budget, or €213 billion (see table 1-1 below):

TABLE 1-1 REGIONAL POLICY FUNDS IN EU-15, 2000–06 FISCAL CYCLE
(millions of €)

			Regional policy funds			
		Cohesion fund		Structural funds		
EU-15				Objective 1	Objective 2	Objective 3
Spain	56,205	11,160	45,045	38,096	2,651	140
Germany	29,764		29,764	19,958	3,510	4,581
Italy	29,656		29,656	22,122	2,522	3,744
Greece	25,000	3,060	21,940	21,000	0	0
Portugal	22,760	3,060	19,700	19,029	0	0
United Kingdom	16,596		16,596	6,251	4,695	4,568
France	15,666		15,666	3,805	6,050	4,540
Ireland	4,200	720	3,480	3,482	0	0
Netherlands	3,286		3,286	123	1,752	1,686
Sweden	2,186		2,186	722	406	720
Finland	2,090		2,090	913	489	403
Belgium	2,038		2,038	625	433	737
Austria	1,831		1,831	261	680	528

- €195 billion will be spent by the four structural funds (the European Regional Development Fund, the European Social Fund, the Financial Instrument for Fisheries Guidance, and the Guidance Section of the European Agricultural Guidance and Guarantee Fund);

- €18 billion will be spent by the Cohesion Fund.

The structural funds concentrate on clearly defined priorities:

- 70 percent of the funding goes to regions whose development is lagging behind. They are home to 22 percent of the population of the Union **(Objective 1)**.

- 11.5 percent of the funding assists economic and social conversion in areas experiencing structural difficulties. 18 percent of the population of the Union lives in such areas **(Objective 2)**.

- 12.3 percent of the funding promotes the modernization of training systems and the creation of employment **(Objective 3)** outside the Objective 1 regions, where such measures form part of the strategies for catching up.

There are also four **Community Initiatives** seeking common solutions to specific problems. They spend 5.35 percent of the funding for the Structural Funds on

- cross-border, transnational, and interregional cooperation **(Interreg III)**;

- sustainable development of cities and declining urban areas **(Urban II)**;

- rural development through local initiatives **(Leader +)**; and

- combating inequalities and discrimination in access to the labor market **(Equal)**.

There is a special allocation of funds for the adjustment of fisheries structures outside the Objective 1 regions (0.5 percent).

There are also provisions for innovative actions to promote and experiment with new ideas on development (0.51 percent).

The structural funds finance multiyear programs that constitute development strategies drawn up in a **partnership** associating the regions, the member states, and the European Commission, taking into account **guidelines** laid down by the Commission that apply throughout the Union. They act on economic and social structures to

- develop infrastructure, such as transport and energy;

- extend telecommunications services;

- help firms and provide training to workers;

- disseminate the tools and know-how of the information society.

Development initiatives financed by the structural funds must meet the specific needs identified on the ground by regions or member states. They form part of an approach to development that respects the environment and promotes equal opportunities. Implementation is decentralized, which means that it is mainly the responsibility of the national and regional authorities.

One particular fund, **the Cohesion Fund**, provides direct financing for specific projects relating to environmental and transport infrastructure in Spain, Greece, Ireland, and Portugal, as these are still inadequate. **The Instrument for Structural Policies for Pre-Accession** (ISPA) provides assistance along the same lines to the 10 Central and Eastern European countries that have applied for Union membership. (See table 1-2 below.)

Irrespective of the type of assistance, these instruments complement but do not replace national efforts.

TABLE 1-2 REGIONAL POLICY FUNDS IN ACCEDING COUNTRIES, 2004–06
(millions of €)

| | | | | Regional policy funds | | |
| | | Cohesion fund | | | Structural funds | |
Acceding countries				Objective 1	Objective 2	Objective 3
Poland	11,369	3,733	7,635	7,321	0	0
Hungary	2,847	994	1,853	1,765	0	0
Czech Republic	2,328	836	1,491	1,286	63	52
Slovak Republic	1,560	510	1,050	921	33	40
Lithuania	1,366	543	823	792	0	0
Latvia	1,036	461	575	554	0	0
Estonia	618	276	342	329	0	0
Slovenia	406	169	237	210	0	0

Notes

1. With high transaction costs (barriers to trade, transportation costs), it is more convenient to disperse production in each country (and be closer to consumers). With low transaction costs, it is preferable to produce in areas with access to larger markets, leading to a concentrated agglomeration of production.

2. The information in the annex is from the European Commission.

Bibliography

Midelfart-Knarvik, Karen H., and Henry G. Overman. 2002. "Delocation and European Integration: Is Structured Spending Justified?" *Economic Policy* 35(October):322–59.

CHAPTER 2

Public Policies and Economic Geography

Philippe Martin

Regional inequalities are an inescapable fact of Europe's economic geography. Close to one-fifth of Europeans live in regions eligible for aid under Objective 1 of the Structural Funds, the principal regional policy instrument of the European Union (EU). The criterion for receiving this aid is a per capita income 75 percent lower than the European average. If such a criterion were applied to the United States, only two states (Mississippi and West Virginia), representing less than 2 percent of the American population, would qualify. The disparities in the average unemployment rate are also very wide in Europe but practically nonexistent in the United States. They represent disparities not only between countries but also between regions within each country: for the five "big" countries (France, Germany, Great Britain, Italy, Spain), the unemployment rate in the most affected region is at least 7 points higher than in the least affected one.

As a reaction to these disparities, the EU has been devoting an increasing share of its budget to regional policies. The Structural Funds and the Cohesion Fund today represent over one-third of the community budget. These transfers are of considerable macroeconomic significance: over the period 1991–94 they represented 3.5 percent, 3.3 percent, 2.4 percent, and 1.5 percent of gross domestic product (GDP) for Greece, Portugal, Ireland, and Spain, respectively. For the period 2000–2006, their impact will be less, in particular for Ireland. In terms of investment, they play a decisive role: respectively for those four countries, 15 percent, 14 percent, 10 percent, and 6 percent of total investment is financed out of community resources.

Such intervention has had contrasting effects. Since 1989, there has certainly been convergence among the European countries, Ireland being the most successful and the most spectacular example. However, convergence among the regions within each country has not come about; indeed, in most countries, regional disparities have increased.

Regional Convergence and Divergence in Europe

A comparison between the economic geography of the EU and of the United States is instructive on more than one count. From the standpoint of regional income gaps, we have already noted that these are much wider in Europe than in the United States. But this larger disparity does not reflect a greater spatial concentration of economic activities: on the contrary, in Europe close to half of industrial employment is concentrated in 27 regions representing 17 percent of the continent's territory and 45 percent of its population. In the United States, half of industrial employment is concentrated in 14 states representing only 13 percent of the entire country and 21 percent of its population. Midelfart-Knarvik and others (2000) show that, even taking into account the fact that industry in Europe is less concentrated than in the United States, most of the sectors are more geographically dispersed in Europe than in the United States. However, over the past 20 years the European countries have become increasingly specialized, and the structures of their industries have become more and more different. The empirical studies performed by Brülhart (1998), Brülhart and Torstensson (1996), and Amiti (1998) strongly suggest that a process of spatial concentration is under way in Europe today, going back in particular to the 1980s, when good progress was made with trade integration.

Why has the greater spatial concentration of economic activities in the United States not engendered a larger income gap among the states? The first reason is the marked mobility of economic agents in the United States, a phenomenon that does not exist in Europe. In the United States, mobility among states is much greater than mobility not only among European countries themselves but also among the regions within each European country. This strong American mobility explains why the phenomenon of spatial concentration of economic activities in the United States has not been accompanied by a process of per capita income divergence among its states. The fact is, when workers follow mobile capital (physical or human) from regions in decline to regions experiencing growth, the problem of spatial equity becomes much less acute. Although certain regions are being emptied of their economic activities, per capita income does not diverge among the different regions. The emigration of workers from declining regions to growth regions makes it possible to reduce competition among workers in the former and to increase it in the latter. Such migrations are thus the principal force for adjusting regional inequalities in the United States. This certainly explains why, in the United States, the question of regional or spatial planning policies has never become as significant an issue as it is in Europe. To the contrary, it is because the workers (often the most disadvantaged) are also less mobile in Europe that economic geography has taken on a political dimension only in the old continent.

Another phenomenon noted in the introduction is the different way inequalities have developed among the European countries and among the countries' own internal regions. Table 2-1 illustrates the development of those disparities measured by the standard per capita GDP deviation for the Nomenclature des Unités Territoriales Statistiques (NUTS 2) regions. Only two countries, France and Germany, showed a lessening of inequalities over the period. In three countries—Austria, Belgium, and Portugal—they remained somewhat constant. In the seven other countries for which regional data are available, inequalities increased. The two last lines of the table also show that while inequalities among countries diminished, those among the countries' own internal regions on average increased.

Map 2-1 shows GDP growth rates per region and gives a clear picture: it is easy to recognize the areas that have "triggered" their country's growth. For Spain, Catalonia and Madrid; for Portugal, the Lisbon region; for England, the southeast; for Sweden, Stockholm; for Finland, Helsinki; and for the Netherlands, the Amsterdam region. More detailed studies (Duro 2001) have shown that up to the mid-1980s, income inequalities among member states represented half of the inequalities among the European regions, and inequalities among regions within each state represented the other half. Since then, inequalities among states have diminished by 25 percent, but regional inequalities within the states have increased by 10 percent. As a result, the majority

TABLE 2-1 REGIONAL DISPARITIES IN PER CAPITA GDP
WITHIN THE MEMBER STATES, 1994–98

Member state	1994	1995	1996	1997	1998
Austria	28.1	30.8	30.2	29.2	27.8
Belgium	25.9	25.3	25.7	25.7	25.7
Finland	17.1	18.3	21.2	22.0	24.6
France	30.8	28.2	28.2	27.0	26.5
Germany	31.3	26.7	26.7	26.5	26.8
Great Britain	18.3	31.4	31.7	33.4	33.9
Greece	7.8	10.4	10.2	10.1	10.2
Italy	25.5	28.6	28.7	27.8	27.6
Netherlands	10.8	13.4	14.3	15.4	15.8
Portugal	13.8	13.5	13.3	14.0	14.2
Spain	15.9	17.1	17.7	18.4	19.1
Sweden	11.0	13.1	14.0	16.2	17.1
EU15 (by member state)	12.7	12.5	11.9	11.5	11.2
EU15 (within member states)	23.0	24.5	24.7	24.8	25.0

Note: Standard deviation of index EU15 = 100.
Source: European Commission 2001.

MAP 2-1 CHANGE IN GDP PER HEAD (PPS), 1995–1999

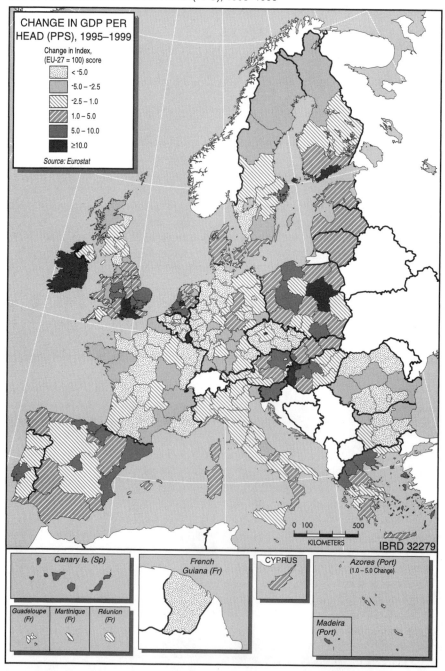

CHANGE IN GDP PER HEAD (PPS), 1995–1999

Change in Index,
(EU-27 = 100) score

< -5.0
-5.0 – -2.5
-2.5 – 1.0
1.0 – 5.0
5.0 – 10.0
≥10.0

Source: Eurostat

Canary Is. (Sp)

Guadeloupe (Fr)   Martinique (Fr)   Réunion (Fr)

French Guiana (Fr)

CYPRUS

Azores (Port)
(1.0 – 5.0 Change)

Madeira (Port)

0   100   500
KILOMETERS

IBRD 32279

of regional inequalities in Europe are explained by inequalities within the countries. Thus, Europe is experiencing a process of convergence among countries at the same time as a process of divergence among the countries' own regions: all of the convergence among the regions in Europe at the European level is thus explained by the convergence among countries.

A similar development in spatial polarization may be described for unemployment. Overman and Puga (2002) show that since the mid-1980s, regions starting out with a low or high unemployment rate have not shown much change in their relative situations. Regions with intermediate unemployment rates, on the other hand, have moved toward the extremes. The authors interpret this result as an effect of the spatial polarization of economic activities due to economic integration. They show that the fate of the regions in terms of unemployment is linked much more closely to the results of the neighboring regions (whether or not they belong to the same country) than to those of the respective country itself.

New Economic Geography

The introduction of economies of scale and of transaction costs may explain why regions with no obvious comparative advantage in certain activities can become centers of production of those activities. A model of the underlying mechanisms was introduced by Krugman (1991), who led the way for the so-called new economic geography. The central finding of this literature is that the diminution of transaction costs on trade may engender a concentration of economic activities in certain regions that have better access to the large markets even if they do not have the lowest production costs. This spatial concentration is advantageous because of the existence of economies of scale conducive to limiting production locations, and it is made possible by commercial integration, which, while reducing transaction costs, does not oblige enterprises to be located close to all their consumers.

The interaction of economies of scale and transaction costs may be understood on the basis of a numerical example. Let us assume that an industry can locate in three regions: the Ruhr, a rich and central region with high wages and hence high labor costs; Catalonia, a middle-income region close to the large European markets; and Andalusia, a peripheral region with low wages and hence low labor costs. Economies of scale play a major role in the sense that unit production costs increase with the number of locations. The firm can produce in all three regions, in two of them, or in only one. The choice of location is simply a minimization of the sum of production and transaction costs. The numerical example in table 2-2 assumes that (a) production costs are higher in the Ruhr than in Catalonia, and higher in Catalonia than in Andalusia; (b) it is less expensive to concentrate production in one location because of the economies of scale; and (c) ease of market access means that production in three locations minimizes transaction costs and that Andalusia is farther from the large markets than Catalonia, and Catalonia than the Ruhr.

TABLE 2-2 HYPOTHETICAL COSTS

		Transaction costs	
Assumption	Production costs	High	Low
Production in three locations	16	0	0
Production in Ruhr + Catalonia	15	3	1.5
Production in Ruhr + Andalusia	14	6	3
Production in Ruhr	13	4	2
Production in Catalonia	12	5	2.5
Production in Andalusia	11	16	8

What happens with the integration process in this numerical example when the transaction costs are cut by half? At first, it is easy to see that when transaction costs are high, it is profitable to produce in the three regions in order to minimize transaction costs. We thus have the situation of a geographically dispersed industry, since companies want to be located close to all their markets, both big and small.

When transaction costs are reduced, for example because of commercial and monetary integration or the integration of transport infrastructures, the firm may exploit the economies of scale and produce in only a single location. Which region is going to benefit from this concentration? In this example, we see that it is not the region with the lowest costs that benefits from relocation. Catalonia has higher costs than Andalusia but has better access to the large markets, not only its own but also those within the core of Europe.

Thus, in this example integration has a convergence effect, since Spain benefits from the relocation within its territory of activities that were at first partially located in a richer country. However, in Spain itself, activities are relocating from the poor and peripheral region to the wealthy region. Thus we have the phenomenon of local divergence.

It is clear, however, that if transaction costs were lower (for example, if they were close to zero) the region with the lowest costs would benefit from relocation. In theory, we have here a bell-shaped relationship between spatial concentration and transaction costs. This means that the poor and peripheral regions will attract enterprises for which the regional costs are relatively higher than the transaction costs, and for which the economies of scale are relatively small. On the other hand, the "core" regions will attract firms for which economies of scale and transaction costs are of prime importance. The study by Forslid, Haaland, and Midelfart-Knarvik (2002) shows that in Europe the location of industries seems to follow this pattern and that the relationship between concentration and commercial integration follows a different bell curve for each industry. Concentration is particularly strong when the firms involved belong to sectors with increasing returns, which seems to provide empirical confirmation of the studies on the new economic geography.

Recent literature using the term "new economic geography" exploits this interaction between economies of scale and transaction costs but goes further, analyzing the cumulative phenomena that can come about. These can culminate in agglomerations based on worker migration (American model) or on relocation of the enterprises (European model).

Let us take the example of the second agglomeration mode. An industry setting up in a region with few other businesses will need to import most of its inputs from other regions and will also have to sell most of its production in regions other than the one in which it is located. From that standpoint, it will be at a disadvantage compared with firms in other regions with high levels of industrial concentration. This will apply in particular to industries with strong economies of scale, namely those to which market size is decisive for their profits. These are in general firms from sectors where the fixed cost (for example, the amount assigned to research and development before the start of the production phase) is high. On the other hand, businesses locating in a low-concentration region will experience less competition in terms of attracting workers (and hence have lower wage costs).

We therefore see that industries with strong economies of scale, belonging to sectors with a high profit margin, will automatically be attracted to regions where other enterprises (both customers and suppliers) are already installed. In such regions a cumulative process is likely to be established, since the more a given region has been able to attract enterprises of one type, the more it will attract others. Conversely, the regions from which those businesses have fled will find it increasingly difficult to attract others. Such regions will be able to attract firms whose wage cost represents a large share of total costs, in sectors that are highly competitive and thus post low profit margins. But this cumulative process will mean a high level of specialization in regions with a heavy concentration of industries with high profit margins and wages as compared with regions that are able to attract only firms with low profit margins and wages. The former will specialize in high-technology goods that do not suffer much competition from the opening up of the low-wage countries to trade. The latter will be directly affected by trade globalization. This process of spatial concentration is not linear, given that the drop in transaction costs may have no impact at first. It is only when those costs have reached a critical level that the cumulative process takes shape. Once that process has started (once the former spatial equilibrium has been destabilized), it becomes self-maintaining and self-reinforcing.

Regional Policies—Trade-off between Equity and Efficiency

Equity is one of the traditional motivations of regional or spatial planning policies. Certain economic agents, be they workers or consumers, are not mobile and are therefore condemned to live in poor or declining regions from which the mobile factors (capital and highly skilled workers) have departed. Because of the lower labor demand in such regions, real wages will adjust downward, or, if real wages do not adjust because of labor market rigidities, unemployment will increase. In both cases, the welfare of the inhabitants will deteriorate. As consumers, those agents will also see their welfare deteriorate since certain goods and services will no longer be produced locally (the businesses will have left for more wealthy regions). In certain cases, in particular for certain services, the transaction cost will become so high that the agents will no longer be able to afford the services. Thus the diversity of consumable goods and services in the poor region will decline. Moreover, the most mobile agents are in general those with the highest level of human capital (education, experience, and so forth). Such agents, thanks to the possession of "positive externalities" in the form of localized social interactions, have a positive impact on the productivity and thus on the real wages of other workers. By leaving a region in decline, the most productive workers thus also have a negative impact on the productivity of the remaining workers—that is, those who are the most disadvantaged. There is, therefore, an absence of market coordination, given that when certain agents decide on their location, they do not take into account the effect of their choice on the other agents. From that standpoint, there is a real market failure, with the consequent increase in inequalities that is specific to the spatial dimension of the economy and may thus serve as motivation for public intervention.

There are several ways to analyze the impact of the agglomeration phenomenon on the least mobile agents. The first would be to refuse to see it as a problem of equity but to interpret it as coming from a specific market failure. This approach would find its origin exclusively in the lack of mobility of the most disadvantaged agents, something we have already noted as characteristic of the European countries relative to the United States.

In Europe, promoting the spatial mobility of workers is not considered a solution to the problems of regional inequality. This is legitimate, but only partially, since because of cultural and sociological obstacles, there will always be a substantial set of workers who will be harmed by geographic inequalities. Having regions empty both of inhabitants and of economic activities (such as the Dakotas in the United States) is unacceptable in Europe.

A further motivation for public intervention at the regional level, put forward by the Commission, is that of efficiency. It sees in geographic disequilibria "an underutilization of economic and social potentials and an inability to take advantage of opportunities that could be beneficial to the Union as a whole" (European Commission 1999).

This motivation is much less clear than the equity-based motivation. If the phenomena of spatial concentration are explained by the existence of economies of scale, this means that the spatial agglomeration is at the origin of economic gains. This will be the case if firms can benefit from the proximity of other enterprises in the same sector to diminish their costs (transport costs or fixed costs). It will also be the case if such concentration makes it possible to increase the firms' productivity through localized spillover effects—that is, if the firms can receive transfers of knowledge from other neighboring businesses. These localized spillovers have been documented in numerous studies (see, for example, Jaffe, Trajtenberg, and Henderson 1993). The example of Silicon Valley shows the advantage a country can obtain from a very heavy spatial concentration of activities with positive technological externalities. The stronger spatial concentration of innovation-based activities in relation to production activities thus has an economic rationale, and the benefits of this spatial concentration go beyond private gains.

The objective of policies promoting a greater dispersal of economic activities is based on the assumption that the economic geography produced by market forces alone is too concentrated. However, the efficiency argument may demand more or less spatial concentration: on the one hand the economic gains of spatial agglomeration, and on the other the effects of congestion (pollution, for example). The fact that in Europe the convergence of countries is accompanied by national divergence makes one think that the former type of argument, efficiency gains with spatial concentration, has pride of place. In this case, a trade-off between equity and spatial efficiency appears inevitable (see Martin 1999a, 1999b). Figure 2-1 shows the positive correlation between per capita income growth and growth in regional disparities over the five-year period 1994–98 and suggests the existence of such a trade-off.

FIGURE 2-1 GROWTH AND REGIONAL DISPARITIES, 1994–98

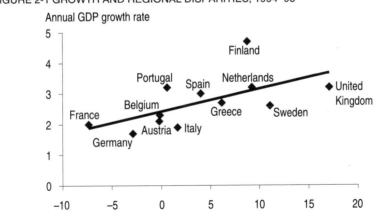

Difficulty of Assessing Regional Policies

One of the principal lessons from the studies on the effects of public policies on economic geography (see, for example, Puga 2002 and Baldwin and others 2002) is that
because of the cumulative, nonlinear processes under way it is very difficult to evaluate and anticipate the effect of public policies intended to offset tendencies toward
concentration. Thus, regional policies that, for example, finance transport infrastructure, have effects in terms of both supply and demand. The demand effects are
principally of a short-term, typically Keynesian nature: the construction of a highway increases the local demand for goods and labor and hence increases the incomes
available in the region. In turn, this increase generates expenditure on local goods (in
particular nonexchangeable services), and so on. In actuality, macroeconomic studies, such as those of the European Commission (1999), have found a positive effect
on regional growth over the short term—that is, over a five- or six-year period of
regional policies. But those macroeconomic studies look at the macroeconomic effect
at the country level only, not the regional level. This is a problem, since we have seen
that convergence exists among the European countries but not among regions in the
same country. Nothing is said about regional policies benefiting the poorest regions
of countries converging at a global level, but it is well known that the poor and rich
regions of those countries did not converge over the same period. The pertinent study
level is the region, not the country.

Other empirical studies have not been very encouraging for regional policies.
This is particularly the case for Boldrin and Canova (2001), who find no effect of
regional policies on regional convergence. Midelfart-Knarvik and Overman (2002)
find that regional policies have encouraged research and development–intensive
industries to locate in countries and regions that have low endowments of skilled
labor. From the standpoint of efficiency, it is not obvious whether this is a great
achievement.

More basically, it is essential to study the effects of these long-term policies—
that is to say, the effects on supply. Those effects, particularly as regards the location
choices of industries, are more complex and may even be the exact opposite of the
effects on short-term demand. This may be the case, for example, with transport
infrastructure, which has received preferential treatment within the framework of
European regional policies.

If we look at the case of industries with economies of scale, a policy to open up
peripheral regions may have a paradoxical effect. By reducing transaction costs for
interregional trade, such a policy may encourage firms to exploit their economies of
scale by concentrating production in a single location. For firms whose wage cost is
relatively low, this will mean concentrating production in the wealthy region, even
if it means exporting part of that production to the poor region at low cost, thanks to
the new transport infrastructures (see Martin 1999a; Martin and Rogers 1995). The
numerical example given in table 2-1 may be reinterpreted as an experiment to set up

transport infrastructure between the three regions, and it is easy to see that it culminates in the concentration of activities in one single region.

The recent study by Combes and Lafourcade (2001), suggesting that the drop in transportation costs in France over the past 20 years has resulted in an increased concentration of industries with strong economies of scale, shows that this result is not only theoretical. The example of Italy is also interesting: the construction of highways between north and south to open up the south does not appear to have had the expected effect and has perhaps even accentuated the decline of the south (see Faini 1983).

Of course, this outcome is not a widely generalized one. Martin and Rogers (1995) show that a transportation infrastructure that reduces transaction costs within a disadvantaged region will have a positive effect on that region, since it makes it possible to increase the effective size of the market in that region. The public infrastructure that has enabled the northern region of France to come close (in terms of transportation costs) to the most wealthy European regions is at least partially at the root of that region's renewed growth. In this case, transportation infrastructure has had the effect of making this a "core" region and has not simply served to open up a peripheral region. Thus, industries have been able to concentrate their production in a region that has grown close to the large markets and also benefits from relatively low wages or at least a labor market that is very favorable to businesses. This example shows that the same public infrastructure will have very different effects from one region to another.

While part of the phenomenon of concentration and regional inequality is due to processes of localized "technological spillovers" (that is, to the fact that enterprises located in the same region benefit, through social interaction, from a higher level of technological performance), the recommendations for public policies are very different. It is no longer a matter of reducing transaction costs on trade in goods among regions but of reducing transaction costs on the trading of "ideas." This involves a change in priorities: rather than financing highways (with positive Keynesian effects), it will be necessary to promote technological convergence among regions, which will involve public programs for telecommunications, the Internet, and training of human capital as well as policies aimed at increasing the productivity of poor regions and facilitating the transportation of people rather than goods. Martin (1999b) argues that such policies make it possible to achieve gains in both regional efficiency and regional equity, in contrast to the regional policies financing goods transportation infrastructure or transfers to the poor regions.

Another difficulty with regional policies is that the goal of reducing regional inequalities is often confused with that of reducing inequalities among individuals. The fact is that regional policies consisting of subsidizing industries to enable them to relocate in disadvantaged regions may have exactly the opposite effect. If the capital is mobile, subsidizing the return on that capital in one region amounts to increasing its return in all regions. Regional policies for subsidizing capital, even if they succeed in reducing regional inequalities, can thus end up increasing inequalities among individuals, since the first beneficiaries may be those who hold the capital.

Conclusions

The low mobility of Europeans—not only among countries, but, and more important, among regions of the same country—helps explain why the location of economic activities is a major political and social issue in Europe. On the one hand, it weakens the agglomeration process. Greater mobility would certainly involve the multiplication of regions devoid of both inhabitants and businesses. On the other hand, it is this low mobility that is at the root of the human cost of spatial concentration, in particular in terms of unemployment, since the departure of companies does not involve the departure of workers. In the United States there is more or less a pattern where the workers passively follow the businesses, while in Europe there is a demand for policies designed to encourage firms to follow the workers wherever they choose to live. Regional policies then appear as an alternative to human mobility: it is socially preferable to move activities to where the people are than to move people to activities.

In this chapter, I have reviewed some of the challenges faced by regional policies. I have done this using some of the insights provided by the new economic geography literature. I identified several main challenges. First, a trade-off may exist between spatial equity and spatial efficiency: the same economic forces, namely increasing returns, that explain spatial agglomeration are at the origins of economic gains. Second, policies that aim to reduce the peripherality of poor regions by reducing trade costs among poor and rich regions may lead economic activities to leave the poor regions. The long-term supply effect of these policies may be the opposite of the short-term demand effect. In theory, policies that promote technological convergence seem more appropriate. Third, reducing regional inequalities does not automatically reduce individual inequalities. The identification of these challenges is not meant to disqualify the legitimacy of regional policies in Europe but to underline simple rules of public economics that should apply to regional policies: it is essential to identify the market failures that legitimate public intervention, to pinpoint objectives (that is, which inequalities to reduce), and to recognize possible trade-offs between these objectives.

Bibliography

The word *processed* describes informally produced works that may not be commonly available through libraries.

Amiti, M. 1998. "New Trade Theory and Industry Location in the EU: A Survey of the Evidence." *Oxford Review of Economic Policy* 14(2).

Baldwin, Richard, Richard Forslid, Philippe Martin, Gianmarco Ottaviano, and Frederic Robert-Nicoud. 2002. Economic Geography and Public Policy. Princeton, N.J.: Princeton University Press.

Boldrin, Michele, and Fabio Canova. 2001. "Inequality and Convergence: Reconsidering European Regional Policies." *Economic Policy* 32:205–53.

Brülhart, Marius. 1998. "Trading Places: Industry Specialization in the EU." *Journal of Common Market Studies* 36(3):319–46.

Brülhart, Marius, and Johan Torstensson. 1996. *Regional Integration, Scale Economies and Industry Location in the EU*. CEPR Discussion Paper 1435. London: Centre for Economic Policy Research.

Combes, Pierre-Philippe, and Miren Lafourcade. 2001. *Transportation Costs Decline and Regional Inequalities: Evidence from France, 1978–1993*. CEPR Discussion Paper 2894. London: Centre for Economic Policy Research.

Duro, Juan Antonio. 2001. "Regional Income Inequalities in Europe: An Updated Measurement and Some Decomposition Results." Madrid: Instituto de Análisis Económico Consejo Superior de Investigaciones Sientíficas. Processed.

European Commission. 1999. *The European Regions: Sixth Periodic Report on Socio-Economic Situation in the Regions of the EU*. Luxembourg: Official Publications Office.

———. 2001. *Second Report on Social and Economic Cohesion*. Luxembourg: Official Publications Office.

Faini, Riccardo. 1983. "Cumulative Process of Deindustrialization in an Open Region: The Case of Southern Italy, 1951–1973." *Journal of Development Economics* 12(3):277–301.

Forslid, Richard, Jan Haaland, and Karen H. Midelfart-Knarvik. 2002. "A U-Shaped Europe? A Simulation Study of Industrial Location." *Journal of International Economics* 57:273–97.

Jaffe, Adam, Manuel Trajtenberg, and Rebecca Henderson. 1993. "Geographic Localization of Knowledge Spillovers as Evidenced by Patent Citations." *Quarterly Journal of Economics*. 108(3):557–98.

Krugman, Paul. 1991. *Geography and Trade*. Cambridge, Mass.: MIT Press.

Martin, Philippe. 1998. "Can Regional Policies Affect Growth and Geography in Europe?" *World Economy* 21:757–74.

———. 1999a. "Are European Regional Policies Delivering?" *European Investment Bank Papers* 4(2):10–23.

———. 1999b. "Public Policies, Regional Inequalities and Growth." *Journal of Public Economics* 73:85–105.

Martin, Phillipe, and Carol A. Rogers. 1995. "Industrial Location and Public Infrastructure." *Journal of International Economics* 39:335–51.

Midelfart-Knarvik, Karen H., and Henry Overman. 2002. "Delocation and European Integration: Is Structural Spending Justified?" *Economic Policy* (October).

Midelfart-Knarvik, K. H., H. Overman, S. Reading, and A. Venables. 2000. *The Location of European Industry.* Economic Papers 142. Luxembourg: European Commission.

Neven, Damien, and Claudine Gouyette. 1995. "Regional Convergence in the European Community." *Journal of Common Market Studies* 33:47–65.

Overman, Henry, and Diego Puga. 2002. "Unemployment Clusters across Europe's Regions and Countries." *Economic Policy: A European Forum.* 34:115–43.

Puga, Diego. 2002. "European Regional Policies in Light of Recent Location Theories." *Journal of Economic Geography* 2(4):373–406.

CHAPTER 3

Regional Policies and EU Enlargement

Michele Boldrin and Fabio Canova

The European Union (EU) is moving toward the sixth enlargement of its history. The process started in 1988, when the first Trade and Cooperation Agreement was signed with Hungary; took its main turn with the 1993 European Council of Copenhagen; and is supposed to come to its first completion with the Intergovernmental Conference of 2004. Candidates to enter the EU are 10 Central and Eastern European countries (CEECs) that were ruled by socialist regimes until about 1990—Bulgaria, the Czech Republic, Estonia, Hungary, Latvia, Lithuania, Poland, Romania, the Slovak Republic, and Slovenia. To this group (which we will refer to, collectively, as CEECs or the CEEC10) one should add Cyprus and Malta, for a total of 12 candidates. In 2000, the European Council of Nice established that negotiations with a first group of candidate countries about the exact timing of their accession should be completed by the end of 2002. Recent political signals from Brussels suggest that, roughly, the planned admission schedule should be followed, with Cyprus, the Czech Republic, Estonia, Hungary, Latvia, Lithuania, Malta, Poland, the Slovak Republic, and Slovenia gaining full admission in 2004, while Bulgaria and Romania should join about four years later. Given the very small size of Cyprus and Malta, our analysis concentrates on the CEEC10, and the term "enlargement" refers to the entrance in the EU of the CEEC10. We are interested in the following broad policy question: Taking both the enlargement process, as currently defined by the EU, and the Structural Funds as a given, what is the best way for candidate countries to fuel real convergence at the national and regional levels?

To put it differently, assume that the ongoing admission process is completed by 2004. What changes, if any, in the principles and methodologies underlying current EU structural policies should be recommended to foster fast and homogeneous growth among the new members, at both the national and the regional levels? What role should national and supranational policies play in this process? The word "regional" here means Nomenclature des Unités Territoriales Statistiques (NUTS) 2 territorial units or lower, as this is the level at which EU structural policies are designed and evaluated. We pointed out elsewhere (for example, Boldrin and Canova 2001) that the NUTS 2 regions are highly heterogeneous and that pursuing economic convergence at such a territorial level makes little sense. We argue later that this is even less sensible for most CEECs. Nevertheless, taking this policy objective at face value, we ask how Structural and Cohesion Funds and their allocation should be modified to reach it, and what kinds of national policies may create an environment conducive to growth. Our attention concentrates on the twin issues of economic run growth and convergence for the CEEC10 after joining the EU.

In the second section of this chapter, Initial Conditions in the Enlargement Countries, we quantify the extent to which enlargement countries are economically backward with respect to the EU15. We document the evolution of the main macroeconomic indicators since the transition from socialism began, and we find that, despite the fact that the process began to bear fruit in the mid-1990s, the average CEEC is still where it was 10 years ago relative to the average EU15 country. Heterogeneity across CEECs, measured either in levels or in rates of change, is probably more substantial than the regional differences within each country. Some countries (Hungary, Slovenia, and, depending on the indicators, Poland or the Czech Republic) appear to be ahead of the rest. We document that, with the current investment rates in physical capital, it will take a considerable amount of time for CEECs to reach the capital-output ratio existing in the EU. Whether this will be a problem depends on the dynamics of technological acquisition in these countries. Foreign direct investment (FDI) is growing but is still too small to create dramatic changes in productivity. We also examine, very briefly, the labor market conditions of CEECs. Much has been written on this issue, and our contribution here is to point out that most of the imbalances noted by commentators are endemic also to the labor markets of current EU members. In this sense, sweeping reforms affecting incentives and eliminating dead-weight losses should be advocated for both groups of countries. We complement our descriptive analysis by reporting a simple growth accounting exercise. Consistent with studies of this type, we find that, from the viewpoint of growth accounting, productivity gains, as measured by the growth rate of total factor productivity (TFP), constitute the most important engine of long-term growth. We examine possible sources of TFP growth in the CEECs: FDI, shrinkage of the public sector or the agricultural sector, and institutional changes. All appear to be important, but it is impossible to find a single cause of TFP growth. Finally, we examine the sectoral composition of employment and value added (VA) across CEECs and relative to the EU. In CEECs, more people are employed and more VA comes from agriculture and low-productivity sectors than in the EU. However, when we compare the CEEC10 with the poorer Mediterranean countries of the EU, many similarities emerge, in terms of both snapshot conditions in 2000 and dynamic evolution over the transition. Given current conditions, convergence, if any, should therefore be expected to occur toward these countries and not toward the EU average.

In the next section—Initial Conditions, Former Newcomers, New Steady States—we ask how CEEC regional/national disparities compare with those currently existing within the EU and, more crucially, with those that existed in the mid-1980s within the EU. Economic disparities between the EU15 and the CEEC10 are not different from those the EU learned to manage during previous enlargement episodes. Regional inequalities within the CEEC10 are also comparable with, if not lower than, those in the EU15. There are historical differences between the enlargement process of the 1980s and that of today, but they seem to be playing out in favor of CEECs, not against them. We perform a simple econometric exercise trying to quantify the most likely effects of accession on the growth rates of the CEECs. With some important qualifications, we estimate the changes to be relatively small. We conclude that the new enlargement is not substantially different from previous ones and that, as in those cases, holding internal policies constant, the economic gains from accession will be positive but not dramatically large—accession (and the arrival of EU funds) will not magically eliminate economic backwardness. National policies could dramatically alter these conclusions, and we detail at the end of this chapter a set of recommendations that, in our opinion, could make a difference.

In the next section—Old, Useful Lessons—we look at other studies of economic convergence in Europe to gather some lessons about policies that may increase the growth rate of the CEEC10 relative to that of the EU. Our provisional conclusions are that (a) barring particularly dramatic circumstances or changes in institutional settings, economic divergence is not a likely outcome of trade liberalization; (b) countries belonging to common trade areas with a reasonable degree of factor mobility seem to grow at a fairly common rate in the long run, and some degree of catching up should be expected in the intermediate period; (c) policies of extensive privatization, reduction in the fiscal burden, openness to FDI, and product/labor market liberalization seem to be the main engines behind the "robust" growth experiences observed so far; (d) technologically and economically backward countries that enter into a free trade arrangement with more advanced ones undergo a fairly rapid and dramatic process of structural change that leads to the destruction of employment in the agricultural sector and other backward sectors. Such a transition process, already under way in the CEEC10 since the early 1990s, is the key threat to long-term prosperity. This is because the induced regional patterns of long-term unemployment may persist over time. Elimination of structural unemployment requires strong and clearly targeted mobility and training policies. Such policies have seldom been implemented because, in the face of growing unemployment, political pressure for the adoption of grossly inefficient transfer policies is usually victorious. The likelihood of such mistaken policy choices is enhanced by the availability of external aid. Economic theory aside, historical evidence shows that subsidies and transfer policies make regional imbalances more, not less, persistent. We discuss several historical episodes within the EU15. We look in particular at Greece, Ireland, Portugal, and Spain and relate their different performances to national and EU policies. We also look at the regions of the Italian Mezzogiorno, which have been the objects of almost 50 years of national and European structural policies. Finally, we compare the *länder* of the former German Democratic Republic with some of the most dynamic CEECs. While they shared almost 50 years of communist rule, the German Democratic Republic and the dynamic CEECs have been exposed to very different policies since the transition started. The former German Democratic Republic, which had an advantage as far as initial conditions were concerned, has been the privileged target of a large amount of external funding and support, coming both from the EU Structural Fund programs and from the German government. Hungary, Poland, and other CEECs have received practically no external aid and have been exposed to a fast transition from socialism to the free markets.

The next section, Assessment of Regional Policies in the Enlargement Process, looks directly at the effects of Structural Funds. We are interested in ascertaining whether and how the allocation and use of Structural Funds is likely to affect the growth path of the EU accession economies and regions. Our analysis here proceeds in two stages. In the first, we argue why economic theory and empirical evidence suggest that Structural Funds (and the Common Agricultural Policy [CAP]) should be terminated, because they amount to nothing more than pork barrel spending favoring one lobby after another. As net transfers add up roughly to zero for most countries, all one is left with is the dead-weight loss of taxation, and the cost of maintaining an expensive and unproductive bureaucracy both in Brussels and at the national and regional levels. In the second step we recognize that, political games being what they are, structural policies are unlikely to be terminated anytime soon. It is therefore worth asking how those funds could be spent more efficiently. First, there is the need to redefine the convergence objective at a territorial level less inappropriate than the NUTS 2 regions. Second, external transfers seem to yield their highest payoff in extremely poor regions, when appropriate national policies are also in place to take advantage of such external funding. This suggests that structural funding should be concentrated only in regions that are below 50 percent of the EU average, and that conditionality should be made stronger than it currently is. Third, the focus of the support should be shifted away from funding hundreds of small investment projects in the most disparate areas. While theory is quite ambiguous on this point, historical experience suggests that investments in transport and communication infrastructures, public utilities, and productive human capital are almost invariably among the preconditions of episodes of extraordinary economic growth. The chapter by Frank Barry in this volume, detailing some important aspects of the Irish miracle, further supports this claim. We recommend, therefore, that Structural Funds be concentrated in only these areas and that the objectives of European structural policies be redefined accordingly.

The last section contains a summary of our findings and a list of policy recommendations.

Initial Conditions in the Enlargement Countries

The purpose of this section is to describe the current macroeconomic conditions of CEECs, to assess the extent of their backwardness with respect to the EU15, to highlight the heterogeneities existing both within and across candidate countries, and to evaluate the stance of those variables that theory or empirical practice found important in favoring long-term economic convergence. We concentrate discussion on those macroeconomic indicators that are more relevant from a growth perspective, leaving aside variables such as inflation, debt, and government deficit, which are outside the scope of our analysis. It should go without saying that a stable and, especially, predictable fiscal and monetary environment constitutes a key precondition for economic development. Sustained economic growth is impossible in an economy facing high and uncertain inflation and tax rates. Necessary conditions are, nevertheless, just necessary: low and stable inflation is not enough. Low and undistortionary taxation is not necessarily a consequence of a stable fiscal policy. A variety of other policies may provide the wrong set of incentives. In particular, historical experience shows that distortionary and wasteful industrial, labor market, and welfare policies may be very detrimental to long-term growth. We focus on this second set of policies.

Unless otherwise noted, data for the year 2000 are used to provide a snapshot characterization of initial conditions, while the evolution over the decade 1990–2000 is used to gauge the underlying tendencies. We divide our discussion into several subsections. The first deals with synthetic measures of the wealth of a nation: gross domestic product (GDP) per capita and labor productivity. The second addresses investment, savings, and FDI. The third discusses labor market conditions. The fourth reports the results of a growth accounting exercise and looks at the sectoral composition of output and employment. In the fifth, we look at regional disparities.

Per Capita Income and Labor Productivity

CEECs are poor according to GDP per capita, measured in purchasing power standards (PPS). Figure 3-1 graphs this indicator relative to the EU15 average for the years 1991–2000. The GDP per capita of the mean CEEC has oscillated between about 36 and 42 percent of the EU average, the oscillations reflecting, to a large extent, changing business cycle conditions. The most recent estimates put it at about 40 percent. The beginning and ending points of the time series are roughly the same, indicating that growth rates in the two economic areas have been, on average, similar. While a minor degree of catching up is noticeable in some countries in the second half of the 1990s, this is far from appearing to be an established and uniform trend.

FIGURE 3-1 GDP PER CAPITA AND LABOR PRODUCTIVITY

(share to EU average; EU average = 1)

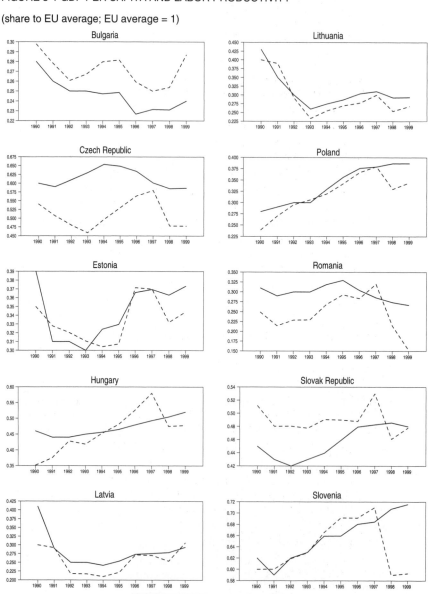

Source: Eurostat 2001c, 2002c; authors' calculations.

Focusing the discussion on averages is somewhat misleading since the past 10 years have witnessed substantial cross-country differences in the growth performances of CEECs, and, from this point of view, the heterogeneities are stronger than those among current EU members. For example, while over the decade the income per capita of Romania and Bulgaria has fallen from 28 and 31 percent to 24 and 26 percent of the EU average, respectively, during the same period the per capita income of Slovenia and Poland relative to the EU increased by about 1 percentage point per year. As of 2000, Slovenia is the richest of the group, with income per capita above 70 percent of the EU average, higher than Greece and approximately at the level of Portugal; the Czech Republic, Hungary, and the Slovak Republic all have per capita income in excess of 50 percent of the EU15 average; Poland and Estonia lag behind at about 40 percent but appear to be growing faster than average; and for the rest (Bulgaria, Latvia, Lithuania, and Romania) it is around or below 30 percent.

There are at least two reasons why GDP per capita may not be a good indicator of the wealth of the CEECs. First, underground and unrecorded activities may be large relative to total market production: recent estimates obtained using electricity consumption (see *IMF Staff Papers* 2001, p. 75) put this number at around 40 to 45 percent of current GDP. Consumption of electricity may be a distorted measure of economic activity because of different subsidies to electricity prices in different countries. Still, a reasonable estimate is that official GDP values are downwardly biased by about 20 percent. Second, because of the transition process, many nontradable activities are likely to be mismeasured. Although it is hard to quantify, this source of mismeasurement could add up to 10 percent of current estimates.

An alternative indicator is labor productivity, here measured by gross value added (GVA) per employed person, in thousands of PPS. We report the time series for labor productivity in the CEEC10 relative to the EU also in figure 3-1. Roughly speaking, there is little difference between relative labor productivity and relative GDP per capita. For example, the level of labor productivity of the average CEEC oscillates between 36 and 41 percent of the EU average and, despite some differential growth in labor productivity in favor of CEECs during the first five years, the average value has not changed much over the decade. In fact, factoring out the cyclical tendencies and excluding the first two years of the transition, when labor productivity gains were obtained through massive labor shedding, the EU/CEEC labor productivity differential in 2000 is approximately the same as it was in 1992–93. Hungary, Poland, Slovenia, and Latvia stand out relative to the others. The first three display a clear upward trend up to 1998, which was apparently reversed in the past two years, and are responsible for most of the regions' productivity gains in the late 1990s. Latvia's relative labor productivity has doubled in the past five years, but its level is still among the lowest in the group.

A word of warning about reading too much into the productivity measures is also necessary because of some aspects that characterize all transition periods. CEECs experienced huge job losses in the industrial (state) sector during the past decade, which have not yet been completely compensated by the growth of new jobs in the service and advanced industrial (private) sectors. The expulsion of workers from inefficient sectors generates mass unemployment and labor productivity gains, somewhat independently of the speed at which the rest of the economy modernizes. This is because most of the people expelled from traditional state-managed activities are unemployable in the new ones. Demography, then, plays a role in the adjustment process, with older workers entering long-term unemployment, which is terminated only by retirement. To give a concrete example, because of significantly different employment rates and demographics, Greece appears to be richer than Portugal when labor productivity is considered (more than 15 percent so, relative to the EU average), while in terms of GDP per capita the picture is reversed, with Portugal overtaking Greece by more than 10 percentage points.

In any case, since both the absolute levels and the relative ranking obtained with the two measures coincide, we may want to attribute a certain degree of reliability to our findings. This leads to the conclusion that, on average, CEECs are at about 40 percent of EU15 in per capita income, with Poland and Slovenia displaying above-average growth performances while the rest grow at more or less the same rate as the EU.

Saving and Investment Rates

High investment rates have been, by and large, a critical ingredient of the most successful growth experiences in the past 40 years. China, Hong Kong, Korea, Singapore, and a number of other "miracle" economies have had investment rates well above the developed world average (rates as high as 35 percent are not unusual) either right before or during their growth boom. At the opposite end, countries that have either stagnated or displayed negative long-term growth feature very low levels of investment (and saving) rates (for example, most Latin American countries). Over the last 40 years, the empirical literature on economic growth has consistently reported strong correlations between the rate of investment (in equipment and machinery in particular), the growth rates of labor and TFP and subsequent growth in per capita income (Miles and Scott 2002 is a recent reference). While the theoretical reasons for this correlation are far from obvious, and abundant evidence shows that capital accumulation per se is not the main cause of high labor productivity, it is important to recognize that a high investment rate provides a reliable signal of both short- and long-term potentials for growth.

Capital comes in two forms: human and physical. The first is much harder to measure than the second, so economists are usually satisfied with some weighted measure of the number of years of formal schooling accumulated by the average member of the labor force. This is, obviously, a very imprecise measure, as not all school systems are identical from the point of view of productive human capital. This may easily be the case in the CEECs, where the school system had historically been used as an instrument of ideological control. We are insisting on these caveats because, when one looks at a pure measure of the average number of years of school attended, the CEEC10, with 9.8 years of schooling on average, comes out ahead of the EU15 mean, which was only 9.5 in 1999 (OECD 2000). Controlling for content and for quality of schooling, the average CEEC may be somewhat below the EU15 average human capital stock, but this adjustment is unlikely to make a major difference. This is an important aspect: the quality of the labor force of the CEECs is already comparable to that of the EU—it is highly educated and potentially capable of adapting to new economic circumstances. Frank Barry's chapter stresses the key role played by the high-quality Irish human capital in that country's successful growth. Hence, this positive initial condition should be properly taken into consideration when evaluating policies: a highly educated work force could prove a huge asset if the proper kind of high-tech investment were attracted.

The picture is less rosy when one looks at machines, equipment, plants, infrastructures, and so forth. There are two problems in this respect: bad initial conditions (obsolete factories and infrastructures) and relatively low investment rates since the transition started. In the EU over the past 10 years, the investment rate has been 17.6 percent on average, with little variation around that level. The four cohesion countries all had investment rates in excess of 20 percent during the 1990s. Assuming similar depreciation rates of about 10 percent a year, a steady-state EU capital/output ratio of 1.7, and an initial capital/output ratio of 1.3 for the cohesion countries, it will take them approximately another 10 years to match the EU capital/output ratio.

A similar calculation can be performed for the CEEC10. Figure 3-2 plots saving and investment rates for the CEECs over the past decade. The average rate of gross capital formation was 24.5 percent in 2000, and above 20 percent for most of the last decade, but there are remarkable differences across countries and time periods. For example, the Czech Republic and the Slovak Republic have investment rates exceeding 30 percent on average, while the Bulgaria, Latvia, and Romania average is only 14 percent. Furthermore, the volatility of investment is high in all countries. More important, the countries that show or have shown the strongest potential for catching up (Hungary, Slovenia, and, to a lesser extent, Poland) are those with an investment rate that is trending more consistently upward. This fits with the received wisdom: it is not high investment per se that causes growth. Instead, when policy determines conditions that are appropriate for growth, investment flows become significant.

It is important to stress that for the CEEC10 even an investment rate of 30 percent is not especially high once we take into account that depreciation and obsolescence of old capital is significantly higher in the CEEC10 than in EU countries. As we will see, the estimated depreciation rate of capital over the decade is very high, and about half of gross investment is used to replace depreciated capacity. Clearly, these numbers overestimate the depreciation rate we should expect in the

FIGURE 3-2 SAVING AND INVESTMENT RATES

(share to EU average; EU average = 1)

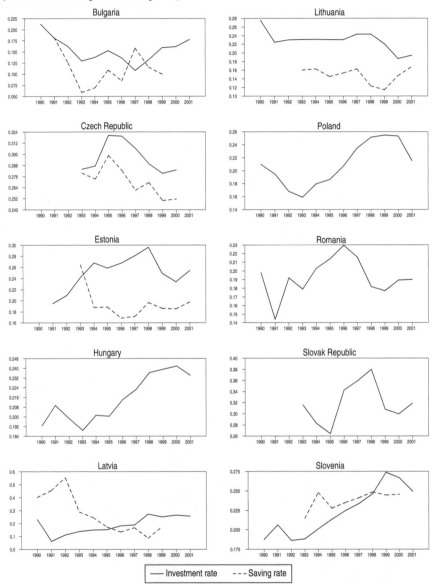

Source: Eurostat 2001a; authors' calculations.

future, but a more optimistic view of what is to come does not eliminate the fact that net investment rates in CEECs are currently too low to guarantee a fast convergence to the EU capital/output and capital/labor ratios. Under the reasonable assumption that the current capital/output ratio of CEECs is about half that of the EU, and taking a depreciation rate twice as high as that in the EU, we estimate that it will take more than 20 years for the thriftiest CEEC to reach the 1.7 level—the steady-state level consistent with the current investment and depreciation rate in the EU. Politically, 20 years may not be too long to attain convergence (Greece, Portugal, and Spain have been in the EU for 16 or more years and are still below the average), and depreciation rates may drop substantially in the near future. Nevertheless, this simple calculation indicates that hopes of miraculous convergence should not be harbored.

High investment rates can be financed by local or foreign savings. The openness of capital markets and the security of the legal system play an important role in determining the extent to which investment is financed by foreign savings. In all countries, domestic savings are the major source of funds for investment, and in only the Czech Republic does a sustained flow of foreign saving allow investment rates to exceed domestic savings by about 3 to 4 percent in every year of the sample. In fact, direct portfolio investments have been relatively small in the CEECs, and their magnitude is completely dwarfed by FDI (see Eurostat 2002d).

The role of FDI in bringing backward countries' capital stock and labor productivity in line with those of the developed world is well understood, and it is confirmed by a number of positive growth experiences in Europe and elsewhere (see Barry in this volume and Martin and others 2001). However, we do not feel comfortable taking a stand on the direction of causality and, in particular, whether technological spillovers from FDI are high or low, relative to the productivity gains internalized by firms.

The proportion of FDI in the total investment of CEECs has been increasing, in particular since 1995–96. The ratio of FDI to GDP is, on average, more than twice as large as the corresponding number for the EU (5 percent versus 2 percent). For some CEECs the net FDI inflow as a percentage of GDP has reached fairly high levels (11 percent in Slovakia, 8 in the Czech Republic, 8 in Estonia). For others, it is still around 2 or 3 percent of GDP. A 5 percent average, however, is substantially better than the one recorded in, for example, Russia, where in the 1990s the FDI rate was below 1.0 percent. It is also about 10 times better than the rate recorded by Greece, Portugal, and Spain in the early 1980s. Over two-thirds of the FDI in CEECs comes from the EU; Austria, Germany, and the Netherlands are providing the largest amounts, while the Czech Republic, Hungary, and Poland are the largest recipients, taking about 70 percent of the total flow to the region (see Eurostat 2000a, 2002c). Except in the Baltic states, FDI is concentrated in the private manufacturing sector (between 36 and 50 percent of the total), while the service sectors (trade, repairs, and financial intermediation) account for 23 to 40 percent of the total.

A distinct possibility is that, although an increase in the capital/labor ratio per se (driven by either domestic direct investment or FDI) is insufficient to ensure fast convergence of labor productivity, FDI helps to boost the TFP of CEECs by bringing in new technologies, expertise, and methods of production. Later, we provide a detailed discussion of the role of TFP in the convergence process. Here we note only that FDI rates positively correlate with TFP in many countries (figure 3-3). This seems to be particularly evident in Hungary and Poland, two of the three largest recipients of FDI, while the surprising counterexample is the Czech Republic. This, however, is consistent with the results of our growth accounting exercise: in the Czech Republic capital accumulation, and not TFP changes, accounts for most of the growth in per capita GDP.

Labor Market Conditions

Labor markets in CEECs displayed complex trends in the past decade. Activity rates in the 15 to 64 age group oscillated without a precise trend and are currently comparable to EU15 averages (slightly below 70 percent), with Hungary and Bulgaria being, from a historical perspective, the worst (at about 60 percent) and Romania the best (at about 75 percent). Employment rates in the same age group are not worse than those registered, on average, in the EU15 (about 64 percent). In comparison with the EU15 laggards (Greece, Italy, and Spain, all hovering around a 55 percent employment rate), only Bulgaria (51 percent) scores lower, while Romania, with a 69 percent employment rate, still stands out at the top. These snapshot figures have to be contrasted with differing tendencies during the decade. In figure 3-4, we plot unemployment rates together with the participation rate (defined as the number of employed and unemployed divided by the total population) in each country. Two clear trends emerge. First, the unemployment rate has dramatically increased in most countries, except perhaps Hungary and Slovenia, with long-term unemployment rates being the reason for the strong upward trend. As of 2000, in fact, the long-term unemployed account for about 10 to 15 percent of the active labor force. The exception is Poland, where about one-third of the unemployed are long term. A large and fairly rapid increase in long-term (and short-term) unemployment is a well-known consequence of transition processes. Similar trends appeared in Portugal and Spain after their transition began. Labor shedding from inefficient sectors generates mass unemployment, both because new sectors are unable to grow at the rate needed to absorb those who are displaced and because workers expelled from decaying sectors have skills that are not usable in the new sectors. This phenomenon has important social implications for the transition generations and requires appropriate welfare and labor market policies to keep it within politically acceptable bounds, an issue to which we will return later.

Second, even if now equal to those in the EU15, participation rates have declined substantially over the decade and are currently about 5 percent lower than in 1991. The largest decline was experienced by Bulgaria, whereas the best performer is

FIGURE 3-3 FOREIGN DIRECT INVESTMENT (FDI) RATES AND TOTAL FACTOR PRODUCTIVITY (TFP)

(FDI and TFP divided by GDP)

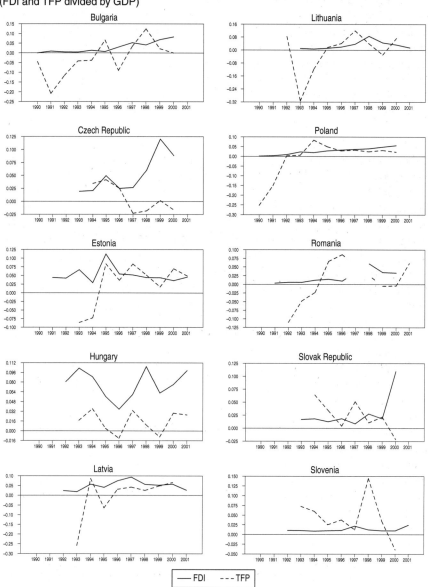

Source: Eurostat 2000a, 2002d; authors' calculations.

FIGURE 3-4 UNIT LABOR COSTS

(real wages divided by productivity; base year = 1)

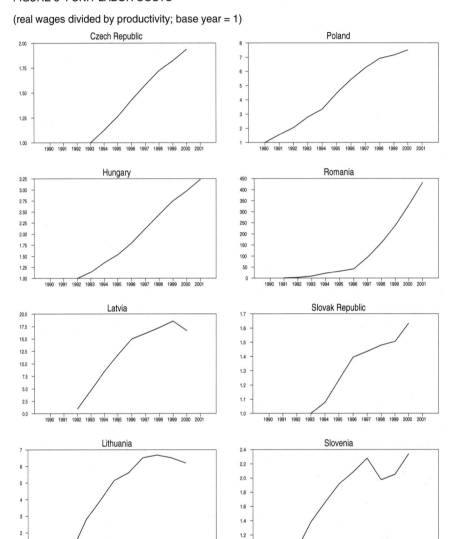

Source: Eurostat 2002a; authors' calculations.

probably the Czech Republic. In general, the decline in participation rates in the CEEC10 is the product of two phenomena. The first, common to the EU15, is the aging of the population, accompanied by a tendency to early retirement for older workers displaced by industrial restructuring. Significantly, the country with the largest decline in the labor force participation rate, Bulgaria, is also the one in which population aging is most pronounced. A second factor, also present in some EU countries but exacerbated in the CEEC10 by the transition process, is the exit of many workers from the legal labor markets and toward underground activities. Overall, the dynamics of labor market indicators in the CEEC10 and EU15 are similar. This is true for averages, degrees of variability, and overall trends.

The large increase in unemployment and the fall in participation rates contrast dramatically with the dynamics of unit labor costs (defined as real wages divided by productivity). We plot unit labor cost indexes for eight of the CEEC10 in figure 3-5, where we normalize them to one in 1995 for all countries: the growth rate of average compensation greatly surpassed the growth rate of labor productivity over the whole period. This is an alarming signal for these countries and an important source of difference from the EU15 (see Eurostat 2002d). According to the unit labor costs metric only, Slovenia and, to a lesser extent, the Slovak Republic have managed to keep the growth rate of real wages roughly in line with labor productivity gains. At the opposite extreme is Romania, where, because of the long stagnation in labor productivity, unit labor costs have more than doubled over the period. One should stress, though, that as of 2000 unit labor costs are still 50 percent lower in the average CEEC than in the EU (see Eurostat 2001c). To the extent that the quality of the human capital is about the same, this difference should make the CEECs attractive for EU FDI, especially after the enlargement is completed.

Although along this dimension the CEECs are not so different from their EU15 counterparts, one may wonder why wage growth has exceeded labor productivity growth so much in the presence of high and rising unemployment rates. Slowly, probably too slowly, the noncompetitive features of national labor markets are being dismantled. In general, we share the view of the specialized literature, according to which, while some noncompetitive aspects still remain in the CEEC labor markets, high unemployment compensation and the high level of labor income (or payroll) taxation are the main culprits in the current situation, making the switch from unemployment to employment unattractive for certain types of workers (see, for example, World Bank 2001a and 2001b). The level and the duration of unemployment compensation in transition countries with high unemployment rates clearly reflect political and social pressures, and do not require further discussion here (detailed examination of these issues appears in World Bank 2001a and 2001b, and in Vaitilingam 2002). From our growth perspective, we stress that payroll taxes in CEECs are very high, even relative to EU or Organisation for Economic Co-operation and Development (OECD) standards, which are already high compared with those of the United States. For example, EU payroll taxes are 23.5 percent, and only Italy exceeds 30 percent; in Anglo-Saxon countries the

FIGURE 3-5 UNEMPLOYMENT AND PARTICIPATION RATES

(percent of labor force)

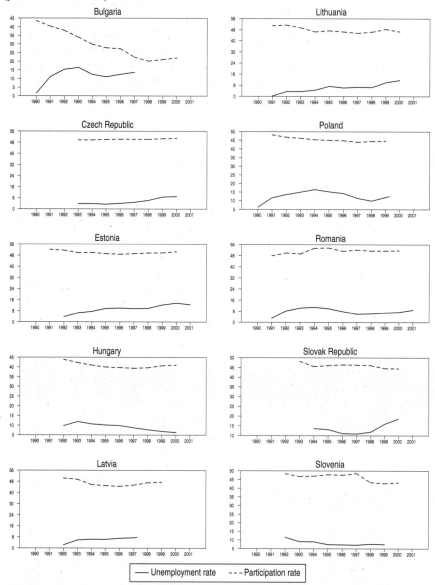

Source: Eurostat 2002b, 2001e; authors' calculations.

taxes vary between 15 and 20 percent. In the CEECs, however, the taxes exceed 40 percent, except in Estonia (33 percent) and Slovenia (38 percent). One may want to examine the rationale for keeping such high tax rates in labor markets facing tough transition problems: increasing unemployment forced governments to continuously increase spending on labor insurance policies. The recession of the mid-1990s exacerbated this tendency, since other sources of revenue declined and governments relied heavily on payroll (and inflation) taxes to finance current expenditure. Payroll taxes are slowly decreasing in some countries—for example, Hungary—but this is far from being a generalized process. Furthermore, the tax burden on labor exceeds the amount of payroll taxes as consumption, and income taxes also take away important parts of the worker's compensation. Garibaldi and others (2001) estimate that, on average in CEECs, the total tax rate on labor is around 74.7 percent, about 50 percent higher than in the EU (53 percent), with Poland (80 percent) and the Slovak Republic (81 percent) being the extreme.

Since 1999 the unemployment level has slowly begun to decrease in most of the CEECs, Bulgaria being again the most serious exception to this trend. This also appears to follow a tendency common to the EU15, even if there are no examples of employment miracles that could be compared with, for example, the Netherlands or Ireland. But then again, there are no examples among the CEECs of courageous labor market reforms either. Therefore, the appropriate comparison to be made is with those EU economies in which unemployment is still high and labor markets are still heavily regulated, such as France, Germany, Italy, and Spain. When this comparison is made, recent movements in labor markets in the CEECs very much resemble those in the EU countries.

Growth Accounting, Once Again

A growth accounting exercise requires several assumptions, most of which are somewhat heroic when applied to CEECs. Nevertheless, we believe that the exercise sheds useful light upon three questions: (a) whether the same factors account for growth across CEECs; (b) whether those factors are the same as those fueling economic growth in more developed countries; and (c) whether there is any evidence that FDI and technological spillovers have so far contributed to economic growth in the CEECs. We make the following set of assumptions:

- The share of labor in national income is 70 percent. This roughly corresponds to the estimate obtained using data for the Czech Republic, Hungary, and Poland.

- Capital stock increments are computed summing up investment over the period and subtracting yearly depreciation. Data for depreciation are available for only the three Baltic states, in which the depreciation rate is estimated to be 40, 47, and 52 percent of the gross investment rate. These estimates seem to be on the high end of the distribution; hence, we use a value of 40 percent for the remaining countries.

- Since no information about part-time versus full-time labor is available, the increments of the labor input are computed using bodies. Data for Hungary indicate that the accounting discrepancy between using bodies and hours is small. We expect the same to hold for the remaining nine countries.

- The increment in the domestic stock of capital is calculated as a residual, subtracting FDI increments from total increments. The same depreciation rate is applied to domestic capital and FDI. Since the technological content of FDI is higher and its depreciation is probably lower, this procedure biases FDI's contribution downward.

- Since reliable data on FDI flows are available for only a subset of the 10 years we consider, we make the assumption that FDI was zero in all the non-available years. Again, this assumption biases downward the estimated contribution of FDI to growth.

- We calculate the effect on growth of the shrinking of the agricultural sector by multiplying the average labor share by the decrement in the population employed in agriculture.

Table 3-1 reports the results of our exercise. Since the years of the sample period differ across countries, the first column reports the range of years for each country. Average growth rates of GDP vary substantially, from −4.0 percent per year in Bulgaria to 7.7 percent per year in Latvia. Apart from Latvia, success stories appear to be Slovenia, with an average growth rate of 5.0 percent, and Lithuania, at 4.9 percent. After Bulgaria, the worst performers are Romania (−0.4), Estonia (2.0), and the Czech Republic (2.0).

The relative contributions of labor and capital follow analogous patterns across countries: the capital stock has a small influence while the contribution of labor to growth is negative. To be precise, the contribution of capital to aggregate growth is fairly constant and centered at around 1.4 percent on average. Exceptions are Bulgaria (0.6) and Latvia (0.8) on the negative side, and the Slovak (2.2) and Czech (2.0) Republics on the positive side. In the latter two countries, growth in capital accounts almost entirely for the growth in aggregate output, with variations in the labor inputs or TFP playing a secondary role. As already mentioned, labor dismissals were intense during the 1990s. This is reflected in the uniformly negative contribution of the labor input, which averages about 1.1 percent. The drop is extremely large for Bulgaria (−4.0 percent) and quite small for Romania (−0.001 percent), with all the other countries falling in between.

Qualitatively speaking, these patterns are not dissimilar from those observed in Spain and Portugal after 1975 (see Marimon 1996). Quantitatively, the difference is one of speed and magnitude, both of which appear to be higher in the CEECs, mak-

TABLE 3-1 GROWTH ACCOUNTING

Country	Time period	$\Delta y/y$	$\Delta k/k$	$\Delta n/n$	ΔTFP	$\Delta FDI/$ FDI	$AGR \Delta$ n/n
Bulgaria	1991–2001	−0.040	0.006	−0.040	−0.006	0.001	−0.0008
Czech Republic	1993–2000	0.020	0.020	−0.002	0.002	0.003	−0.0006
Estonia	1992–2001	0.020	0.015	−0.015	0.020	0.004	−0.0055
Hungary	1992–2001	0.023	0.014	−0.004	0.013	0.003	−0.0008
Latvia	1991–2000	0.077	0.008	−0.013	0.082	0.002	−0.0027
Lithuania	1991–2000	0.049	0.018	−0.014	0.044	0.002	−0.0026
Poland	1991–2001	0.032	0.012	−0.006	0.040	0.001	0.0002
Romania	1991–2001	−0.004	0.010	−0.000	−0.015	0.001	0.0000
Slovak Republic	1993–2000	0.030	0.022	−0.010	0.017	0.003	−0.0017
Slovenia	1992–2000	0.050	0.017	−0.010	0.042	0.001	−0.0016
CEEC average	n.a.	0.025	0.014	−0.011	0.022	0.002	−0.0016

n.a. = not applicable; $\Delta y/y$ = output growth; $\Delta k/k$ = capital growth; $\Delta n/n$ = growth; ΔTFP = TFP change; ΔFDI = FDI growth; AGR $\Delta n/n$ = the contribution of agricultural employment.

Note: The increments in capital stock are computed by summing up investment over the period and subtracting yearly depreciation. Data for depreciation are available for only the three Baltic states: the depreciation rate is estimated to be around 40 to 50 percent of the investment rate. We apply a value of 45 percent to the other seven countries. The increments on the labor input are computed using bodies and not hours, which are not available in many countries. Data for Hungary indicate that the difference is small. The domestic increment in the capital stock is calculated as residual. The same depreciation rate is applied to domestic capital and FDI, therefore biasing downward the contribution of FDI to growth. The contribution of agriculture to growth is calculated by multiplying $\delta n/n$ by the decrement in the population employed in agriculture.

Source: IMF's international finance statistics; authors' calculations.

ing their transition process even more remarkable when compared with the one that took place in the Iberian Peninsula. On average, the seriously downward phase of the transition process lasted about seven years in the CEECs: this is about half the time it took for Spain and Portugal to start growing faster than the EU average after their transition began. The relative size of the sectors affected by the transition is also much larger in CEECs. The Spanish and Portuguese economies were heavily protected from foreign competition and had a strong state presence in all sectors but nevertheless were market economies. State-controlled firms never accounted for more than 20 or 25 percent of GVA in the tradable sector. In contrast, private enterprises never came to control more than 20 percent of tradable economic activity in the CEECs, excluding perhaps Hungary, before the socialist system collapsed.

An alternative measure of the relative size of the two transitions can be gathered by looking at the drop in total employment during the first decade. From 1975 to 1985, Spain, which suffered more than Portugal, shed 2 million workers out of an initial labor force of 12 million—that is, the size of the force dropped by about 17 percent. Among CEECs, the one with the smallest percentage drop in employment from 1990 to 2000 is Poland (−11 percent), followed by Latvia (−14.5 percent), the Czech

Republic (−15), and the Slovak Republic (−16). All others have larger percentage drops, with Bulgaria the most affected (−33 percent loss in total employment).

We move next to the contribution of TFP. Averaging over the whole CEEC10, TFP changes have contributed to growth of about 2.2 percent per year out of a total of 2.5 percent per year (88 percent). This result is not unusual. With few exceptions, TFP accounts for most of the growth in per capita output. However, this average masks substantial differences among countries. For example, in Latvia, Lithuania, Poland, and Slovenia, TFP growth would have implied GDP growth in excess of 4.0 percent, had the two production inputs remained constant, while in Bulgaria, the Czech Republic, and Romania the contribution of TFP changes to growth has been either negative or negligible. For Hungary and Poland, two of the largest recipients of FDI in the group, the TFP contribution is positive but not large. While this heterogeneous behavior may require further country-by-country investigation, what we learn from this exercise is that the CEEC10 transition process has not diverged from the growth accounting rule: GDP increases because TFP does, whatever the cause of the latter may be.

As mentioned, a natural candidate behind the (positive) change in TFP is FDI. One would expect this to be especially true for countries that had been sealed from the rest of the world for almost 50 years and that, at the start of the transition, were using obsolete and highly inefficient production techniques. In particular, we would expect the FDI contribution to growth to be highly correlated, across countries, with the TFP contribution. It turns out that, for the sample under consideration, this is not much the case. The overall contribution of FDI to growth has been small, approximately 0.2 to 0.3 percentage points per year. Furthermore, its cross-country correlation with TFP growth is not significantly different from zero. As pointed out already, some of the assumptions may have biased the estimated FDI contribution downward. Still, even if we double the estimate, the contribution of FDI remains quite small. It is more so when compared with the values estimated in fast-growing countries, such as Ireland or China.

Maybe we should not be surprised by this negative result. After all, the CEEC10 have *not* been growing very fast during the past decade, not even during the last half of it. Some of them may be starting to display fast growth patterns, but it is far too soon to know for sure. CEECs have come close to completing the transition, shutting down inefficient factories and farms, displacing a large fraction of labor force members from their former occupations, and starting to adopt advanced and efficient production techniques. This is clearly reflected in our growth accounting results. FDI has started to come in, but not yet at a very high rate. Apart from Estonia, CEECs have not yet established conditions as favorable to FDI as those found, for example, in Ireland. Hence, it would have been surprising to find that FDI's contribution to growth in the CEEC10 was comparable to that in Ireland.

One last possibility is that the shedding of labor in the inefficient sectors is the key force driving TFP changes. This conjecture seems to receive mixed support from our estimates. On the one hand, it seems to be rejected by the aggregate employment data: positive changes in TFP are uncorrelated, across countries, with the magnitude of the decrease in total employment. On the other hand, the correlation between TFP changes and the magnitude of the drop in agricultural employment appears to be statistically significant. Given the nature of agricultural production in the CEECs, treating the drop in employment in that sector as a proxy for the amount of labor displacement out of inefficient sectors does not seem unreasonable. Lacking better data on labor reallocation from protected to market-oriented activities, we must satisfy ourselves with this weak evidence.

In an attempt to find some evidence on the sources of cross-country variability in TFP changes, we look at where the CEEC10 stand as far as trade liberalization, capital flows, privatization of firms, and banking and legal system reforms in relation to the EU. Table 3-2 summarizes the relevant information. We report three indexes: a capital flow restriction index, an index of structural reforms, and an index of legal proxies. The capital flow index refers to data for 1997 and ranges from −0.2 to 6, with 6 indicating the most restrictive institutions and negative numbers indicating the presence of positive incentives to capital (in)flows. The reform index refers to 1999 and weights price liberalization and competition policies (0.3), trade and exchange rate liberalization (0.3), and privatization and banking reform (0.4). A value of 1 corresponds to a market economy. The index of legal proxies refers to 1997 and equally weights the predictability of law and policies, the political stability and the security of properties, government/business interface, red tape, and the efficien-

TABLE 3-2 INSTITUTIONAL INDEXES

Country	Capital flow restriction	Structural reforms	Legal proxies
Bulgaria	1.01	0.79	n.a.
Czech Republic	0.05	0.90	3.40
Estonia	0.00	0.93	3.33
Hungary	0.62	0.93	3.30
Latvia	0.50	0.86	3.77
Lithuania	1.40	0.82	3.76
Poland	1.03	0.86	3.66
Romania	1.90	0.82	n.a.
Slovak Republic	0.75	0.90	3.78
Slovenia	1.35	n.a.	n.a.
CEEC average	n.a.	n.a.	3.66
EU	n.a.	1.00	n.a.

n.a. = not applicable.

Note: The capital flow index varies from −0.2 to 6 (6 is most restrictive) (Garibaldi and others 2001). The reform index weights price liberalization and competition policies (0.3), trade and exchange rate liberalization (0.3), and privatization and banking reform (0.4). A value of 1 is a market economy (Aslund, Boone, and Johnson 2001). The index of legal proxies weights predictability of law and policies, political stability and security of properties, government/business interface, red tape, and efficiency of government infrastructure. The scale goes from 0 to 6, with 6 being the worst performer (Garibaldi and others 2001).

Source: Garibaldi and others 2001.

cies of government infrastructures. The index ranges from 0 to 6, with 6 being the worst performer.

In general, there appear to be limited differences along institutional lines. For example, the legal proxies index varies from 3.30 (Hungary) to 3.78 (Slovak Republic), while the average is 3.66. By comparison, Russia and the other Commonwealth of Independent States (CIS) countries are at about the 4.0 level. The index of structural reforms also indicates that all 10 countries are close to the EU, except Bulgaria (0.79), Romania (0.82), and Lithuania (0.82). Top performers in this category are Estonia and Hungary (both 0.93). Capital flows restrictions are now relatively low in all countries: the least restrictive is Estonia—which actually provides incentives to FDI—with the Czech Republic a close second (0.05). The most restrictive are Romania (1.90), Lithuania (1.40), and Slovenia (1.35). Once again, by way of comparison, Russia scored 1.81 in this scale and the other CIS countries 1.33.

Changes in the quality of institutions may affect TFP growth. Theory tells us that more efficient and more open countries may boost their wealth by pushing their production possibility frontier forward. Empirically, and apart from a few anecdotal cases, the relevance of institutional factors largely remains to be proved. In the last column of figure 3-3, we confirm this fact by plotting the time series of the reform index. The relationship between the trend in the index and the trend in TFP is weak: most of the changes in the index across countries took place in the early 1990s, while TFP moves over time and displays trends, if any, in only the past five years.

The size and efficiency of the financial system may constitute an important bottleneck for future growth in the area. Financial and banking systems are still somewhat underdeveloped: for example, the combined size of CEEC stock markets is about the size of the Irish stock market, and the turnover per year in the most developed CEEC (Poland) is about equal to the turnover of two regular days of trading in Frankfurt. Similarly, the size of the total banking system in all the CEECs together is equal to one large EU bank, and many banks are too small to enjoy any positive scale effect. These features of the banking system are not, however, different from those existing at the time of accession in the most backward regions of the EU.[1] Compared with 10 years ago, capital markets are different in terms of efficiency and functioning. Nevertheless, the development of an appropriate financial system is the area where CEECs may benefit most from accession to the EU.

In sum, the liberalization indexes indicate that most of the CEECs are already similar to current EU members. Since the data are slightly outdated, we expect the divergences to have been further reduced in the last few years. Although institutional reforms may still be sought in the future, the need for reform does not appear to constitute a fundamental stumbling block in harmonizing EU and CEEC economies.

Economic theory and previous transition processes suggest that the sectoral composition of VA and employment play a role in determining the impact of the trade-opening shock and that they are useful indicators of a country's stage of economic development. Differences between the EU and CEECs in the sectoral composition of VA may provide information useful to predict the shape of things to come.

Table 3-3 presents this information. Three important features of the table deserve comment. First, the agricultural sector in the CEECs is much more important than in the EU. On average, it contributes 2.6 percent of total VA and employs 4.8 percent of the active EU15 labor force, while in the CEECs agriculture represents 10.6 percent of the total VA and employs 29.3 percent of the active labor force. Such percentages also suggest that the agricultural sector of the CEEC10 is about 50 percent less productive (relative to average productivity) than the (already inefficient) agri-

TABLE 3-3 GVA AND EMPLOYMENT BY BRANCH, PERCENTAGE SHARE

Country	Agriculture	M and M	Utilities	Construction	Services, private	Services, public
GVA						
Bulgaria	14.5	19.1	5.0	3.6	42.9	13.1
Czech Republic	3.9	27.8	4.0	7.4	41.1	12.7
Estonia	6.1	19.0	3.3	5.8	46.6	14.3
Hungary	4.1	25.5	3.8	4.6	42.6	16.5
Latvia	4.1	14.6	3.9	6.8	50.8	15.0
Lithuania	7.5	22.1	4.1	6.1	39.7	17.3
Poland	3.9	23.7	3.4	8.8	42.7	13.4
Romania	15.8	27.4	2.9	5.5	36.9	9.1
Slovak Republic	4.0	25.0	4.1	5.2	45.9	n.a.
Slovenia	3.2	28.2	3.2	6.0	38.5	17.0
CEEC average	10.6	26.5	3.5	6.7	37.5	15.1
EU	2.6	23.8	5.0	5.4	41.0	21.1
Employment						
Bulgaria	27.6	21.1	2.0	4.1	27.4	15.4
Czech Republic	5.0	28.6	1.6	9.3	31.9	17.6
Estonia	6.9	23.9	2.6	7.0	35.5	18.8
Hungary	7.5	28.0	2.0	6.2	28.8	27.7
Latvia	14.7	17.9	1.7	6.3	34.6	20.6
Lithuania	19.6	16.4	2.4	6.1	27.0	21.7
Poland	25.7	20.7	1.7	6.0	28.0	15.4
Romania	41.4	21.2	2.0	4.1	19.0	10.8
Slovak Republic	8.3	30.1	1.9	9.3	25.8	24.6
Slovenia	10.2	28.7	1.3	7.5	31.4	17.1
CEEC average	29.3	22.9	2.0	6.0	20.0	16.9
EU	4.8	20.3	3.0	5.4	38.1	27.0

M and M = manufacturing and mining; n.a. = not applicable.
Note: Shares are computed using data for 2000, except for employment in Hungary and the Slovak Republic, where data for 1998 are used.
Source: Eurostat 2001c, 2002c.

cultural sector of the EU15. This is important in light of EU agricultural policies. In spite of its relatively minor weight in total VA, the agricultural sector is a political giant in CEECs *because* of its low productivity: many unproductive people are tied to the agricultural sector as the only source of income in the near future. Second, the service sector is much more developed in the EU than in CEECs. Private and public services produce about 62 percent of total VA and employ about 65 percent of the active population in the EU15, while in the CEEC10 the share of VA produced by the service sector is about 53 percent and only 37 percent of the active population is employed there. Again, these numbers also suggest that the average service sector is fairly efficient in the CEEC10. Third, the sectoral distribution of VA looks very similar to that of the most backward countries in Europe, but the distribution of employment is still skewed toward agriculture and the industrial sector.

Within the CEECs, several important facts need discussing. First, the service sector is already the largest contributor to GVA in all countries. Percentages vary from a low 48 percent for Romania to a surprisingly high 66 percent for Latvia. Agriculture is still an important source of GVA in the poor countries of the region— Bulgaria and Romania score around 15 percent—while in other countries the share of GVA produced by agriculture is around 4 to 8 percent. The share of manufacturing and mining is roughly constant across countries and on the order of 22 to 25 percent; construction is important primarily in the Czech Republic and Poland, while the utility sector is everywhere a small contributor to GVA.

Second, the growth rates of sectoral GVA have differed substantially across countries. For example, over the period 1995–2000, growth of GVA in agriculture has been significantly positive in the Czech Republic (around 4.0 percent a year) and Lithuania (around 2.4 percent a year) and negative in Bulgaria (−2.0 percent a year) and Romania (−3.0 percent a year). In manufacturing and mining, Lithuania experienced the largest growth rate in VA (an astonishing 15 percent a year), while Romania and the Czech Republic had the smallest growth rates. The utility sector has not shown much GVA growth, except in Bulgaria, and the construction sector displayed significant VA growth in Estonia, Latvia, Poland, and Slovenia (between 7 and 10 percent per year). Finally, VA in services has grown at a significantly positive rate in all countries except Romania and the Czech Republic. Such large variations in the growth rate of VA, and especially labor productivity, across sectors point to different institutional and political constraints across countries and sectors. The data are too limited to establish an explicit correlation, but economic theory suggests that the largest productivity (and VA) gains should take place in those sectors in which competition is allowed. It would be worthwhile to look carefully into the industrial organization aspects of such large differentials to uncover the linkage between labor market and competition policies on the one hand and sectoral growth and labor productivity performances on the other. Given the regional concentration of some sectors, particularly those in small countries, looking at which policies help or hamper the development of a specific sector in one country may be extremely useful to designers of growth-oriented regional policies.

Third, the sectoral pattern of employment also varies across countries. Agriculture is the main reason for cross-country differences. There are two polar extremes—the Czech Republic (5 percent) and Romania (41 percent)—while in Bulgaria, Poland, and Lithuania employment in agriculture is still around 20 percent. Employment in manufacturing and mining varies between 16 and 29 percent, while construction employs between 4 and 9 percent of the active population. Finally, the service sector employs 50 percent or more of the population in all but Bulgaria, Poland, Romania, Lithuania, and Slovenia.

Fourth, employment growth in the past five years displays the typical pattern of transition countries: employment growth in agriculture was negative in all countries but Romania; employment in manufacturing and mining declined on average by 15 to 20 percent; and job creation has been most intense in the construction and services sectors. Employment in construction increased in two of the three Baltic states and in Slovenia (3 to 4 percent a year), and the growth in the service sector was significant in every country except Romania and Bulgaria, with Poland's being the highest (3 percent a year).

It is important to look at the relationship between labor productivity and wage by sector both in relationship to the EU and within each country to identify the sectors for which employment growth is more probable. Table 3-4 presents this information. On average, labor productivity and wages in the CEECs are around 41 to 42 percent of the EU level. However, sectoral heterogeneities are important. For example, wages in agriculture are more than twice the productivity level, while the opposite is true in all other sectors, with construction being the sector where unit labor costs are the lowest. In substance, the agricultural sector is a highly subsidized sector. Productivity is

TABLE 3-4 SECTORAL PRODUCTIVITY AND WAGES BY BRANCH, RELATIVE TO EU

Country	Agriculture	M and M	Construction	Services, private	Total economy
Bulgaria	37/36	20/21	29/27	48/29	25/24
Czech Republic	88/81	53/46	72/74	59/82	58/60
Estonia	46/47	26/26	41/32	49/45	37/33
Hungary	77/75	49/41	54/43	83/75	58/50
Latvia	12/36	29/26	39/30	36/33	27/27
Lithuania	26/32	30/24	45/39	46/33	30/28
Poland	13/64	38/38	68/47	52/46	38/44
Romania	24/n.a.	31/n.a.	53/n.a.	68/n.a.	32/n.a.
Slovak Republic	54/56	42/32	51/40	90/69	53/40
Slovenia	94/121	58/56	72/61	81/74	71/70
CEEC average	28/63	41/34	58/41	68/53	41/42

M and M = manufacturing and mining; n.a. = not available.
Note: Productivity and wages are computed using data for 1998.
Source: Eurostat 2001c, 2002c; authors' calculations.

highest in the private service sector—primarily because international competition is most effective in this sector—and lowest, as expected, in agriculture. If one excludes agriculture, the VA produced by each employed worker exceeds gross labor income by about 20 percent.

Within each sector, enormous differences exist between countries: for example, in Slovenia, productivity and wages in agriculture are at the EU level, while in Latvia productivity is 12 percent of EU level and wages 36 percent. Similar disparities exist in the construction sector (compare, for example, Bulgaria with the Czech Republic). The private service sector also shows differences, but on average it is the one whose features are most similar to those of the EU. For example, in Hungary, the Slovak Republic, and Slovenia, labor productivity and remuneration in the private service sector are slightly above 75 percent of the EU average.

In sum, on the one hand the sectoral composition of employment and VA in the CEEC10 is substantially different from that of the EU15 and resembles that of the most backward EU countries. On the other hand, its dynamics are those that always characterize the development process of backward countries. Within the group, similarities and differences coexist. In all countries, the service sector contributes most to GVA creation, followed by manufacturing and agriculture. Growth patterns reflect national idiosyncrasies, but, to a large extent, growth in VA is driven by growth in the service sector. Around 50 percent of the population in every country is already employed in the service sector, and this share is increasing over time. Manufacturing and mining, and especially agriculture, are shrinking as a result of the scrapping of old enterprises. The speed at which this sectoral adjustment takes place is different across countries because of both comparative advantages and policy choices. Most important, employment in agriculture is still very high in 5 (Latvia, Lithuania, Poland, Romania, and Bulgaria) of the 10 states. The evolution of the agricultural sector presents some worrying features from the viewpoint of enlargement and economic growth. The generalized presence of a large wedge between labor productivity and labor income is important in the light of current EU15 policies. This is both cause and effect of the slow expulsion rate from agriculture and the parallel slow productivity gains. Unless local and EU support programs perpetuate this anomaly, in the years to come a substantial amount of the labor force should be expelled from farming. The construction sector has been an important (temporary) source of job creation in some countries, and its low unit labor costs indicate that it may also be able to absorb redundant agricultural employees in the near future. This sectoral shift is, however, unlikely to boost average labor productivity, given the low productivity of this sector. The Czech Republic, Hungary, and Slovenia appear to be the countries where increments in service employment are more likely to occur in the future. Since these are also the countries in which the private service sector is more productive, we should expect sectoral reallocation of labor to be more conducive to labor productivity convergence in these countries than in the rest of the CEECs.

Regional Inequalities in the CEECs

Regional inequalities are not very large in the CEEC10; to some extent, they are smaller than or at most comparable to those already present in the EU15. There are two reasons for this: most CEECs are small, in size and population, and this fact limits heterogeneity among reasonably sized internal territorial units; the high level of inequality between countries (one to three in per capita GDP) dwarfs the within-country differences. This is a crucial fact to keep in mind when thinking about economic growth and convergence in the CEECs: regional and national economic convergence are, to a first approximation, the same problem.

The basis for our statement is simple: eight of the CEEC10 can be treated in the same way as moderately large NUTS 2 units of the EU. For example, Lithuania, which is the median among these eight, is only 65,300 square kilometers, and the population is less than 4 million people, smaller than Catalonia (Spain) and roughly equal to Veneto (Italy). The largest of these eight is the Czech Republic, which is equal in population (10 million) to Bayern (Germany) or the Regione Lombardia (Italy) and much smaller than Nordrhein-Westfalen (Germany). Obviously, one can try to find large differences within these countries by looking at smaller territorial units. There is no doubt that, with enough effort, one may succeed. Nevertheless, one needs to try hard to find differences larger than those characterizing Italian and Spanish provinces, for which both unemployment and per capita GDP ratios between highest and lowest reach levels of 6 or even 7. In Hungary and the Czech Republic, for example, the ratio between the maximum and minimum unemployment rate at the regional level is about 4. Igor Strmšnik's chapter confirms this fact for the case of Slovenia, another CEEC comparable to an average NUTS 2 region. Slovenia is divided into three areas; the ratio in per capita income between the first and the second is 1.38, while that between the second and the third is 1.10. No matter how one twists it, these are small differences, especially if one takes into account that the largest share of the population lives in the richest area around Ljubljana.

The remaining two countries, Poland and Romania, are fairly large. In Poland, 38.5 million people live on a piece of land that is approximately the size of Italy. Romania is less densely populated, with only 22 million people, but the country is roughly the size of the United Kingdom. For these countries, comparison with NUTS 2 units is inappropriate and care should be exercised in interpreting the relative numbers. Nevertheless, while regional disparities exist in these two countries, they are small relative to those in several of the EU countries. For example, the unemployment rates in Poland average 16 percent (using 2001 data), ranging from a maximum of 25 percent in Warmińsko-Mazurskie to a minimum of 12 percent in the metropolitan Warsaw area of Mazowieckie. Internal labor migration is low, but it is already substantially higher than that within EU countries with similar or greater employment and income per capita differences.

Hence, the extent to which regional disparities are a problem for the CEECs is smaller than that for some of the EU15. Furthermore, regional disparities are relevant only in countries (such as Poland and Romania) that are large enough for regional comparisons to make sense. For the rest, concentrating on regional income inequalities would be tantamount to asking whether provincial or intercity inequalities in, say, Lombardia or Andalucia are important for aggregate economic growth and require intervention via some specific structural policies. For example, the city-region of Prague, in the Czech Republic, has a population of about 1.5 million people (about 15 percent of the country's total) and enjoys an income per capita of 122 percent of EU average and an unemployment rate of 3.4 percent. The other eight Czech regions host the remaining 8.9 million people, have 49 to 56 percent of the EU average in terms of income, and have unemployment rates between 5 and 15 percent. These are significant variations, although not much different from those existing between any capital city in the EU and its countryside. Should this inequality be a cause of major concern for growth-oriented policymakers? If so, then every EU15 country, with the exception perhaps of Luxembourg and the Netherlands, is a problem.

Summary

We would like to highlight a few summary points of this general overview. First, despite extremely different initial conditions, we do not observe dramatically different growth rates in GDP per capita or labor productivity between CEECs and the EU. This is particularly true for the past five years, after the end of the first transition period and in the face of an already very high degree of openness to trade with the EU (as documented in the next section). Barring dramatic changes in fiscal and labor market policies, it is hard to forecast a very rapid convergence toward the EU average levels of per capita income and labor productivity. Second, the CEECs are not homogeneous. Vastly different current levels and potentials can be observed. Treating the 10 countries as if they were one single unit is likely to produce tensions as well as contradictory policy prescriptions. Third, investment rates in the CEECs are not especially high, which may prevent a rapid convergence of the capital/output ratio of these countries to the EU average. FDI does not appear to have played a big role in this respect, at least so far. Nevertheless, its upward trends during the past five years may lead to pleasant surprises should enlargement proceed along its course. Fourth, labor market incentives are grossly distorted, probably as a consequence of the harsh transition period. Still, the labor markets in CEECs are not much worse than those of many EU countries. Fifth, TFP growth seems to be the main driving force behind output growth, with the exception of the Czech Republic and the Slovak Republic. Sources of TFP growth are always mysterious. The data show a weak relation to FDI flows and to the rate of employment reduction in agriculture, but not to recent changes in institutions, a factor often considered to be important. The amount of time since such changes took place and the dubious quantitative nature of some indexes may be the reason for this irrelevance. Sixth, the sectoral composition of VA and employment in the CEEC10 resembles that of the backward countries in the EU and is still far from the average. This is not surprising. More attention should be paid to other distinctive features of the CEEC10. The important role of agriculture in 4 of the 10 countries, its relative inefficiency, and the inability of more advanced sectors to employ the excess labor expelled by agriculture appear to be key features, at least from a social point of view. Substantial heterogeneity, both within and between CEECs, in sectoral productivity suggests that a fairly large process of intersectoral and international adjustment, following comparative advantage lines, still needs to take place. In this and many other respects, CEECs are not different from the poor regions in southern Greece, Italy, and Spain, and a number of common insights apply to both. Seventh, regional income disparities exist, but their relevance should be played down relative to the differences between countries, which appear to be much more substantial. Furthermore, and with the sole exceptions of Poland and Romania, one should look at the CEECs as territorial and economic units altogether equivalent to the current NUTS 2 units of the EU15. Finally, nominal and Maastricht indicators are already in line with those of the EU, but, except in extreme and remote (it is hoped) cases, we do not expect such factors to play a major role in determining the path of future income inequality between the EU and CEECs.

Initial Conditions, Former Newcomers, New Steady States

The EU has experienced several enlargements since its creation. During 1981–86, three countries, all poorer than the EU average, were admitted: Greece in 1980–81, and Portugal and Spain in 1985–86. We use this experience to examine two issues: (a) how the CEECs compare, in relation to EU averages, with the three earlier entrants; and (b) whether the experience of Greece, Portugal, and Spain can teach us something about the future of the CEEC10 in the EU. The punch line is, although the historical circumstances are different, macroeconomic conditions in CEECs resemble very much those of Greece, Portugal, and Spain at the time of accession. On the ground of similar initial conditions and accession to the same free trade area, and under the assumption of similar national and supranational policies, we find that the differential effect of joining the EU will be small (in terms of both levels and growth rates), so that current inequalities are likely to persist for a few decades.

Basic Statistics
Our claim is that the economic systems of the CEEC10, and in particular those of the first accession group, are comparable to those of Greece, Portugal, and Spain at the time of their accession to the EU. One major difference is the number of people involved: fewer than 60 million in the 1980s, and more than 100 million this time. A second difference is the number of countries involved, 10 versus 3, and the CEECs' much smaller average size, which generates procedural and administrative complexities probably not encountered before. Similarities, on the other hand, abound. Like

the earlier three, the CEEC10 have been part of "cultural Europe" since at least the eighteenth century and are currently emerging from a long period of political repression, autarchy, and state control of the economy. Also, in both cases (with Greece as an exception), about a decade had elapsed since the previous regime collapsed, and a fair number of changes have already been implemented in the accession countries.

Structural and socioeconomic features are also very similar, as is widely documented (see, for example, Martin and others 2002, World Bank 2001c, 2002, for public expenditure and its composition, education, demographic evolution, road and transportation systems, public pension expenditure, research and development investment, size of the information technology sector). We will therefore concentrate on a restricted number of aggregate statistics, which can provide a parsimonious measure of the "distance" between CEECs and Greece, Portugal, and Spain at the time of accession. Ideally, we would like to come up with a single number. Because we do not have a rationale for choosing particular weights, we have decided to present the various components of our index separately in table 3-5. The factors we use to measure similarities and differences are the openness of the economy (measured by exports plus imports over GDP), the share of employment in agriculture, GDP per capita relative to the EU average, and labor productivity relative to the EU average. For CEECs we take 2000 as our benchmark, for Spain and Portugal we average the conditions existing in 1985 and 1986, and for Greece we average the conditions existing in 1980 and 1981. One could consider many other indicators, but we believe these four provide a reasonably good synthesis of the kind of information we seek. Furthermore, they are highly consistent with the information in the quoted studies, as well as that reported earlier, in the Initial Conditions in the Enlargement Countries section.

A few aspects of the table need to be commented upon. First, the share of employment in agriculture (our preferred measure of backwardness) is comparable between the two groups of countries. Portugal and Spain had shares of 22 and 15 percent, respectively, while the average of CEECs (excluding Romania) is about 20 percent.[2] Similar results would have been obtained had we used other sectoral indexes of the two groups of economies—for example, the share of manufacturing in total VA of Greece, Portugal, and Spain was 15, 29, and 26 percent, respectively, and in CEECs it averages 26.5 currently.

Second, the range of GDP per capita values is also very similar: Spain was at a level similar to Slovenia at the time of accession, while Portugal and Greece were approximately at the current level of Hungary and the Czech Republic. Latvia, Lithuania, Romania, Bulgaria, Estonia, and Poland fall below the range of relative per capita GDP determined by the last three entrants. Again, the picture would have not changed if, instead of levels, we had been using growth rates of per capita GDP in our comparison. The growth rate of GDP was a meager 0.1 percent in Greece at the time of admission, while Portugal and Spain displayed healthier values at 4.1 and 3.2 percent, respectively. The range for the annualized average growth rate of GDP in the CEEC10 over the period 1996–2000 was –1.5 (Romania) to 5.1 (Estonia), with

TABLE 3-5 INDEXES OF SIMILARITY

Country	Openness	Employment in agriculture	GDP per capita	LP
Greece 1980–81	0.42	n.a.	0.55	0.52
Portugal 1985–86	0.56	0.22	0.49	0.44
Spain 1985–86	0.29	0.15	0.62	0.95
Bulgaria	1.28	0.27	0.25	0.28
Czech Republic	1.44	0.05	0.59	0.47
Estonia	0.87	0.07	0.41	0.34
Hungary	1.23	0.07	0.53	0.47
Latvia	1.02	0.14	0.30	0.30
Lithuania	1.06	0.19	0.30	0.26
Poland	0.63	0.25	0.41	0.34
Romania	0.75	0.41	0.27	0.15
Slovak Republic	1.60	0.08	0.49	0.47
Slovenia	1.20	0.10	0.73	0.50

n.a. = not applicable; LP = labor productivity.

Note: Openness is measured by exports plus imports over GDP. For Greece, Portugal, and Spain we averaged over the two years. For CEECs the values refer to 2000. The employment share and labor productivity for Greece, Portugal, and Spain are computed using the OECD Structural Statistics for Industry and Services database and the OECD Structural Analysis Database for Industrial Analysis. Values for the CEECs come from previous tables. GDP per capita is computed using the Eurostat Regio data set.

7 countries out of 10 growing at 3.4 percent or more per year. Furthermore, the absolute values of GDP per capita at PPS also match. For example, in 2000 all CEECs, except Bulgaria and Romania, were richer than Greece, Portugal, and Spain at the time of their admission; Bulgaria and Romania matched Greece and Portugal and were no more than 10 percent below Spain.

Third, except for Spain, relative labor productivity is also comparable. To explain the Spanish outlier, it is useful to remember that at the time of accession, the unemployment rate had reached 23 percent, with falling participation rates, and that Spain's labor productivity index decreased, relative to the EU average, after accession. As a further element to evaluate relative labor productivity potentials, it may be worth pointing out that schooling rates are uniformly higher in the CEECs than they were in Greece, Portugal, and Spain in the early 1980s.

The two sets of countries differ very much in terms of openness, but the difference is all in favor of the CEEC group. CEECs are much more open than previous poor newcomers. The average index of openness is two to three times as large in the CEECs as it was in Greece, Portugal, and Spain when they joined. For small economies (the Czech Republic and the Slovak Republic), the numbers are larger. In fact, even when we compare the *current* degree of trade openness of Greece, Portugal, and Spain with that of the CEECs, the latter come out ahead on average. More important, between 40 and 70 percent of CEEC trade takes place with the EU already; all these percentages have been growing steadily over the past five years. Capital flows are also larger than those for Greece, Portugal, and Spain at the time of accession, even adjusting for the fact that gross flows are much larger today. As we have seen, on average FDI to CEECs has been above 4.0 percent of GDP during the last few years. FDI as a percentage of GDP in Greece, Portugal, and Spain in 1986 was at 1.2, 0.7, and 1.3, respectively (Martin, Velazquez, and Funck 2001).

The post-1990 labor market dynamics in the CEEC10 strongly resemble those of Spain and Portugal after their transitions began. Rapid expulsion of workers from agriculture and from traditional industrial sectors (total employment in Spain dropped from 12.6 million to 10.6 million between 1975 and 1985), equally fast increase in unemployment (from 6 to over 20 percent in Spain, to around 16 percent in Portugal), reduction in the labor force participation rates (especially among young and old individuals), and creation of a substantial and lasting stock of long-term unemployed people at around 40 to 50 percent of total unemployment are important common features of the first 10 years of both transition processes. Similarly, productivity per employed person increased while income per capita decreased initially, to rebound only after 1986. In fact, relative to the EU average, it took until 1991–92 for Spanish per capita GDP to go back to where it was before 1975. It has taken less time for the best-performing CEECs to achieve the same result.

These facts, together with those illustrated in the second section of this chapter, strongly suggest that initial CEEC conditions are similar to those of previous entrants and that the costs of and gains from joining the EU will probably be comparable to those experienced by the previous three newcomers.

Different Historical Circumstances

History matters. Having stressed the similarities between the socioeconomic conditions of the CEECs and those of earlier entrants into the EU, we should elaborate further on the differences briefly mentioned above. As our goal is to evaluate the extent to which the performances of earlier entrants can predict those of the new candidates, we should limit ourselves to those factors that may influence, in one direction or another, the process of economic integration of the CEEC10 into the EU. Overall, the CEEC10 will have some advantages that the former newcomers did not. Paradoxically, while these advantages may ease adaptation to EU market conditions, they may also reduce the size of the gains the CEECs should expect from accession.

The first important difference is that the CEECs will enter a larger and richer market than the early entrants did. This should facilitate the accession process, at least in the presence of a reasonable degree of flexibility on the part of CEEC firms.

The second crucial difference is that the current level of economic integration within the EU is much higher than it was in the 1980s. A startling measure of such difference is the amount of European FDI already flowing to the CEEC10, as a percentage of their GDP, in comparison with the amount of EU-originated FDI entering, say, Spain before 1986. For the latter it was, at most, half a percentage point a year, while for the best CEECs it exceeds 5 percentage points. Total capital or trade flows follow a similar pattern. This feature should benefit CEECs and should facilitate their integration into the EU. On the other hand, unless accession brings dramatic policy changes, this fact should also make the postaccession jump in FDI smaller than the one observed after previous enlargements.

A similar argument applies to trade: trade openness of CEECs is remarkably higher than that of earlier entrants. Therefore, comparatively speaking, CEECs have less to gain from the general tariff and barrier reduction that comes with accession. However, many tariff and trade restrictions are still in place. Given the CEECs' sectoral heterogeneity, one could expect certain sectoral gains to be comparable to those of earlier entrants even if the aggregate effect may be smaller.

Finally, exchange rate risk is now gone, at least within the EU15 area. If CEECs manage to satisfy the Maastricht criteria, they would join the EU and (possibly) adopt the euro. Given that the share of EU trade within total CEEC trade oscillates between 45 (Bulgaria and Lithuania) and 68 percent (Estonia, Hungary), the absence of exchange rate risk gives the CEEC10 a huge advantage relative to earlier entrants.

Relative Steady States: Old and New

Since initial conditions in the CEECs are approximately the same as those of the former newcomers, and since, given current policies, we find it likely that joining the EU will have the same effect on these countries that it had on Greece, Portugal, and Spain, we can estimate where CEECs will be in their postaccession steady state relative to the EU average. Like all reduced-form econometric exercises, this has obvious limitations. First and foremost is the assumption of policy and behavioral invariance postadmission. What this means is that we assume that no CEEC will be able to replicate, for example, the policies that Ireland has adopted in the past 16 years. Rather, we assume that CEECs will behave, more or less, like Greece, Portugal, and Spain did during the last 16 years; that the EU structural policies toward poorer regions will remain more or less unaltered; and that the overall degree of trade liberalization within the EU and between the EU and the rest of the world will not change. But there are no guarantees. Spain and Portugal have progressively modernized and liberalized their own internal product and labor markets; slightly reduced labor taxation; improved capital mobility; and implemented a fairly large, albeit not overwhelming, privatization process. Furthermore, inflation rates have declined, budget deficits have been brought under control, public debt has been restrained, and the euro has been adopted. Making a ceteris paribus assumption implies that the CEEC10 will accomplish something similar, at least in relative terms, in the next 10 to 15 years. While feasible, this achievement will require keeping up the pace of market-oriented reforms.

With these caveats in mind, we now illustrate our econometric procedure. We plan to draw from the information we have available to infer something about the (asymptotic) distribution of growth rates for CEECs postaccession. We construct three scenarios. The first, the *no-change scenario,* assumes that the current histori-cal conditions (including current cross-country heterogeneities) will be perpetuated indefinitely. This scenario implicitly assumes that the gains from free trade and inte-gration have already been absorbed over the past 10 years and that entering the EU will not change the underlying trend behavior of the CEEC10. Rather than taking this assumption literally, we consider it a benchmark against which to evaluate the long-term gains that these countries may enjoy once they are in the EU. For this scenario, we estimate a simple autoregressive (1) model for relative (to EU average) income per capita/labor productivity for each country and, given parameter estimates, we pro-ject past behavior far into the future. Since the data set is short, estimates of the steady states are biased. Therefore, these numbers should be taken as indicating more qual-itative than quantitative tendencies.[3]

In the second scenario, the *level-effect scenario,* we assume that after joining the EU, CEECs will settle into a steady-state position that is similar (in terms of the parameters regulating the asymptotic distribution of relative growth rates) to that of Greece, Portugal, and Spain since they entered the EU. Theoretically, one can justify this scenario by using either endogenous or exogenous growth models in which coun-tries that are similar in terms of economic fundamentals face the same distribution of long-term growth rates. Notice that, because of the normalization by the unknown EU growth rate, this reduced-form statistical model makes absolutely no assumption as to the source of growth. It is consistent with old, new, and even postmodern growth theoretical models as long as they satisfy a probabilistic version of the *tertium non datur* assumption: countries that are identical at the beginning will draw their final outcomes from the same probability distribution. EU accession would therefore mean, for the CEEC10, a transition to the same distribution of growth rates faced, since 1986, by the three earlier entrants.

To implement this idea, we estimate steady states for NUTS 2 regions of Greece, Portugal, and Spain using data after their EU accession. We then use this information as a prior for the AR model we estimate for the CEEC10. The prior takes a simple form: we assume that, postaccession, the distribution of balanced growth rates of the CEEC10 (scaled by the EU average) will have the same mean and variance as the dis-tribution of poor EU territorial units after they joined the EU. Clearly, we do not pre-vent miracles (or busts) from happening; we simply require similarities in the support of the two distributions. This scenario does imply, though, that CEEC miracles will not be larger or more frequent than those experienced by poor EU regions, and simi-larly for busts. We examined whether taking Greece, Portugal, and Spain as a whole or (to have exactly comparable GDP per capita) the poorest 22 regions in these coun-tries[4] makes a difference for our calculations. We also examined whether the choice of the short sample made a difference—by concentrating totally on data for Greece, for which almost 20 years of data exist. Neither of these two variations made a sizable difference. The mean steady states we obtain oscillate, depending on the assumptions made, between 60 and 75 percent of the EU average, and the dispersion of the regional steady state ranges from 45 to about 90 percent. We capture these tendencies by assuming a normal distribution centered at 65 percent of the EU average with a standard error equal to 15 percent.

In the third scenario, the *growth-effect scenario,* we assume that joining the EU will proportionally boost the growth rate of CEECs by the same factor it boosted the growth rates of Greece, Portugal, and Spain after their accession. This scenario assumes a linear production function in which the asymptotic growth rate is country specific.[5] The scenario assumes that when two countries are exposed to the same change in their fundamentals, a common proportionality factor affects country-specific growth rates. As a trivial example, think of an A_iK model in which $A_1 \neq A_2$ are the production function parameters for the two countries. Joining the trade area implies that a common proportionality factor, say $\beta > 0$, multiplies the A_i, so that $\beta A_i K$ is the aggregate production function for country i after accession. Obviously, this is just an example; a more complicated model in which the parameter A_i is endogenized by means of external effects, public capital, agglomeration effects, rate of technological innovation, and so on would also be consistent with our statistical procedure. For the case at hand, joining the EU will make the country-specific growth rates in the CEEC10 jump, so that for a given initial condition, output will grow at a permanently higher (or lower if $\beta < 1$) rate. To implement the idea behind this scenario, we estimate average and dispersion of growth rates using regional data for Greece, Portugal, and Spain before and after accession. We use these two distributions to estimate the common proportionality factors β_μ (for the mean) and β_σ (for the standard deviation). As before, we use this information as a prior for the AR model we estimate using CEEC10 data. Since we have very few data points before accession, estimates of the jump are very imprecise. The mean effect is, however, very small (1.009), probably because most of the growth gains in Greece, Portugal, and Spain predated EU accession. We take into account the uncertainty present in the data by letting the dispersion of the potential jump be relatively large (the maximum range we allow is [1.0, 1.03]).

Table 3-6 provides a summary of the results. For each scenario, the first column refers to relative GDP per capita and the second to relative labor productivity. We would like to emphasize two results. First, in the absence of any structural change (no-change scenario), we should not observe significant variations either in the ranking or in the level of GDP per capita of the CEEC10 relative to the one observed in 2000. In other words, CEECs are already close to their steady state. The only two countries that, at the steady state, seem able to reduce significantly their distance from the EU are Poland (currently at 41 percent) and Slovenia (currently at 73 percent).

Second, adding the information about the behavior of the poor EU countries after accession does not radically alter the estimates of the relative steady states. The distribution of relative steady states in the level- and growth-effect scenarios is only marginally different from the one estimated for the no-change scenario. This follows from the fact that the growth patterns experienced by CEECs during the 1990s were not so different from the growth patterns experienced by Mediterranean countries

TABLE 3-6 ESTIMATED STEADY STATES

Country	No-change scenario		Level-effect scenario		Growth-effect scenario	
	GDP	LP	GDP	LP	GDP	LP
Bulgaria	0.23	0.26	0.34	0.35	0.37	0.37
Czech Republic	0.61	0.50	0.50	0.56	0.51	0.53
Estonia	0.33	0.33	0.39	0.38	0.40	0.39
Hungary	0.48	0.46	0.45	0.49	0.45	0.45
Latvia	0.26	0.25	0.35	0.36	0.37	0.36
Lithuania	0.28	0.26	0.37	0.35	0.36	0.37
Poland	0.48	0.34	0.46	0.39	0.47	0.37
Romania	0.27	0.23	0.42	0.31	0.38	0.33
Slovak Republic	0.49	0.48	0.45	0.49	0.46	0.48
Slovenia	0.80	0.61	0.76	0.68	0.74	0.60
CEEC average	0.38	0.38	0.41	0.45	0.42	0.41

Note: Estimates obtained in the columns "Level-effect scenario" and "Growth-effect scenario" are computed using a Bayesian procedure that weights information contained in domestic data and information in the time series of poor EU regions after they joined the EU. In the first case, it is assumed that the distribution of steady states to which the CEECs will belong is the same as the one of poor EU units. In the second, it is assumed that joining the EU has a level effect on the growth pattern that is the same for CEECs as it was for poor Spanish and Portuguese regions. *Source:* Authors' calculations.

after they joined the EU. Our estimated gain for the average CEEC is about 3 to 4 percent (GDP per capita would go from 38, to 41 or 42 percent of the EU average), but this is not statistically different from zero. There are some sizable gains for the poorest of the CEEC10; for example, the steady-state levels for Bulgaria and Romania will be about 50 percent higher if they join the EU, and they are predicted to do slightly better in the growth scenario. Conversely, the richest among the CEEC10 are predicted to do worse after accession than they would do otherwise; see, for example, Slovenia. The reason behind this reversal of fortunes should be kept in mind when discussing policy implications. Greece, Portugal, and Spain have performed well but far from spectacularly after accession and only marginally better than they had in earlier decades. The strongest among the CEEC10 have done well in the last half of the 1990s; in fact, they have done better than the earlier entrants did, on average, after accession. The opposite is true for the weakest five among the CEEC10. Hence, applying to the CEECs the distribution of growth rates experienced by Greece, Portugal, and Spain induces a "reversion to the mean" effect in which the currently fast growers grow more slowly and the laggards' growth accelerates. Closeness to the steady state, lack of measurable effects from joining the EU, and, absent changes in national policies, relatively similar "engines of growth" lead us to predict that the EU and CEECs will grow at fairly similar rates in the next couple of decades. Similar steady-state growth implies constant ranking in the distribution of GDP per capita and persistence of current inequalities. Integration and extension of the current EU regional policies to CEECs will not sweep away income inequalities. National policies, if anything, must do the job.

Why compare CEECs with Mediterranean countries and not Ireland? We have shown that there are similarities in the historical circumstances of the two experiences that make the exercises meaningful. One could, however, argue that Ireland in 1976 was as backward and as closed as Mediterranean countries but has experienced extraordinary growth over the past 10 years. Clearly, we would have had a much rosier picture had we assumed that the growth experience of CEECs after accession would resemble that of Ireland in the 1990s. However, Irish growth did not come in a vacuum: as Barry tells us, national policies make a difference. If CEECs are willing to adopt the policies that Ireland implemented in the last decade, our current estimates are on the pessimistic side. Accession, however, does not guarantee good national policies: bad governments exist both within and outside the EU. Since history and social norms matter, we find it unlikely that the CEECs will enact the kinds of sweeping changes in labor, financial, and capital market conditions that would justify the alternative scenario.

This sobering fact should not take our attention away from the fact that there are differences in the dynamics of per capita GDP within CEECs and that these differences may be relevant in projecting current conditions far ahead. For example, the regions of Prague, in the Czech Republic, and Bratislava, in the Slovak Republic, have enjoyed sustained growth during the past five years, which pushed their regional GDP per capita respectively to 122 percent and 99 percent of the EU average. Nevertheless, if we exclude some dynamic region, typically centered around the capitals (Prague, Bratislava, Ljubljana, and Budapest), growing at a reasonable pace relative to the average of the EU, the majority of the CEEC inhabitants are expected to live in the future with an income per capita that is about 55 or 65 percent of the EU average.

Finally, since the dynamics of labor productivity in CEECs are comparable to the GDP per capita, steady-state calculations are unaffected if we substitute one for the other. Projecting current labor productivity into the future implies that the Czech Republic, Poland, and Slovenia look more dynamic in terms of GDP per capita than in terms of labor productivity, but the uncertainty in the estimates does not permit us to make statistical statements. Bringing in information from the previous newcomers in the EU does not change the pattern we have described. If anything, the higher relative productivity level recorded for Spain at the time of accession implies a distribution of steady states that is more spread out than the one of GDP per capita in the second scenario.

Old, Useful Lessons

Probably the most important lesson from previous studies of economic growth in trade-integrated areas is that the predictions of "new growth" or "new trade" theory models are comfortably rejected by the data. These kinds of models almost unanimously predict that trade openness combined with increasing returns and a variety of external effects will produce agglomeration phenomena, poverty traps, economic divergence, and increased inequality. Hence, when two differently endowed countries start trading with each other, the richer or more advanced one "wins" while the other "loses." Victory takes the form of a higher rate of income growth (because of faster capital accumulation or faster rate of innovation), a concentration of productive factors, or both. Agglomeration theories, which seem to be particularly popular among policymakers and technocrats involved with regional and structural policies, predict that capital and labor move toward where their complementary factor of production is more abundant, leading to a concentration of economic activity in a few privileged areas and leaving the rest far behind. Hence the need for active public intervention to prevent factors (especially labor) from moving around too much and for subsidizing economic activity in poorer areas where it would not otherwise take place.

We are not aware of any historical experience of trade integration supporting this kind of prediction. In fact, all recorded episodes of increased trade openness, at the national or international level, have generated the opposite outcome: poorer areas have either strictly gained (in both absolute and relative terms) on the leader or kept distances roughly constant. What we have in mind here are the increasing trade and factor mobility among the 50 U.S. states since the end of the Civil War; the increasing trade and economic integration among the initial 6 members of the European Economic Community (EC) since the 1950s and then, since the end of the 1980s, among the current 15; the recent successful integration of Canada, the United States, and Mexico in the North American Free Trade Agreement; and the almost 50 years of progressive and still increasing trade integration of Japan and Southeast Asian countries among themselves and with Europe and the United States. One is hard-pressed to find a single "loser" in any of these episodes. It is quite important to stress that, in all but one case (the post-1980s EU), trade integration and increased factor mobility took place without any kind of regional, structural, or transfer policy meant to compensate the poor countries or areas for the losses of trade integration with the richer ones. While the extent to which trade openness and integration have generated convergence varies greatly from one situation to the next, divergence has *never* been observed at any reasonable level of spatial disaggregation. The latter is not a minor point. The European Community integrated trade first among six and then among a higher number of countries for about 20 years, practicing very few "compensatory" or "structural" policies (aside from the infamous CAP, the consequences of which are well known), and income differences sharply decreased both across and within the EC countries. During the past 20 years the EU has increased dramatically the amount of funds invested in structural and regional policies, without any visible impact on the rate of economic convergence within countries. Empirical estimates suggest, in fact, that regional convergence has come close to a halt just at the time structural and cohesion policies have been introduced (see Boldrin and Canova 2001). East Asian countries have practiced almost no compensation or structural policies. Still, their convergence to the average income of their trading partners (that is, Europe, the United States, Canada, and Japan) seems certain. The list could be continued indefinitely, but it would become redundant. The message is clear: opening up trade among regions that are economically heterogeneous does not lead to divergence, not spontaneously at least.

Unfortunately, when looking at convergence data we have a strong tendency to see what our personal prejudices would like them to show. It is for this reason, we believe, that in spite of all the evidence to the contrary, the "agglomeration" hypothesis seems to be more popular than ever. Research produced at or around the European Commission, especially the Directorate for Regional Policies, is an excellent example of this phenomenon. NUTS 2 and even NUTS 3 regions are often used to measure inequality. At a fine enough level one can certainly find fairly large inequalities in per capita income or other measures of economic well-being. Less obvious is the conclusion that public policy aimed at eliminating economic differences at such a fine territorial level should be carried out centrally by the EU (violating the most elementary interpretation of subsidiarity) and that income transfers and subsidies are the appropriate instruments to make the poor regions grow faster than average.

The second lesson we have learned is that trade integration facilitates economic growth but is far from guaranteeing it, especially if appropriate internal economic policies are not adopted. Large amounts of regional aid may temporarily increase the income of recipient regions and in this sense postpone the need for serious structural reforms, but there is no evidence that they generate higher growth rates in the long run. Empirical evidence has consistently shown that when reasonably large territorial units are chosen for the analysis, opening up trade and allowing internal markets to work lead to a certain degree of convergence (see, for example, Ben David 1994). How fast this "spontaneous" or "automatic" convergence takes place is still a topic of debate. In fact, on average and across very many political systems and fiscal and monetary policies, the most likely result seems to be that convergence takes place in growth rates but not in levels: countries that start ahead tend to stay ahead, even if distances are somewhat reduced. Somehow, a combination of initial conditions, factor endowments, and, most important, national policies seems to determine country-specific steady states (or balanced growth paths) to which individual countries converge. Such steady states are different across countries and are affected by trade policies, but trade integration *alone* improves the relative performances of the poorer countries by only a handful of percentage points relative to the richer ones. In certain circumstances, convergence in levels does seem to take place, but such circumstances are rare. For example, Western European countries and Japan came very close to the per capita income levels of the United States in a period of roughly 30 years between the end of World War II and the oil crisis of the 1970s. However, convergence was not, and still is not, complete; in fact, since about the mid-1970s, the three parties (the EU, Japan, and the United States) have kept their relative positions approximately unchanged. For the "miracles" of Southeast Asia a large amount of convergence toward the U.S. level has taken place, but one has the impression that these countries converge to some relative steady-state position that is strongly determined by national characteristics. Portugal, Spain, and, to a much lesser extent, Greece have somewhat reduced their distances from the EU average income level since 1986, while Ireland has managed to overtake the EU average income level in a period of less than 20 years.

One may legitimately wonder whether structural and regional policies are behind the miracles or, at least, the growth convergence we observed. We doubt that this is the case for several reasons. First, as mentioned above, no regional policies were ever implemented among Southeast Asian countries, and divergence was not observed. Second, one may think of the Marshall Plan—the historical analogy to the current European transfer policies—as key to the European convergence to the United States. However, both the financial size and the duration of the Marshall Plan are orders of magnitude smaller than those of the European structural policies or, at the national level, of the German transfers to the East German *länder* and the Italian transfers to the southern regions. If what it takes for convergence is a Marshall Plan, then Sicily and Calabria have received approximately 20 of them since the 1950s. Furthermore, in Boldrin and Canova (2001), we have shown econometrically that, at least in the EU15, the conjecture that regional transfer policies are behind the partial convergence episodes is not supported by the data. Regional policies, at least in the form implemented by the EU since the mid-1980s, made little difference on long-run growth at the regional level.

It should be self-evident that this does not mean that the transfers involved with the structural policies made no difference for the countries and regions on the receiving end. They certainly did and still do: receiving a nice yearly check for an amount between 2 and 5 percent of national income is valuable. The net of transfers, health and social insurance payments, and public expenditure in the EU is never above 25 percent of GDP. European transfers increase the funds for public expenditure available by 10 and 20 percentage points and by much more when we look only at public investments. When used appropriately, these funds can help to ease social tensions, especially in transition situations. When used inappropriately, they enrich unscrupulous politicians and those backing them. No wonder that transfers are most welcome by receiving countries, and members of the EU, old and new, are no exception to this rule. But to claim that transfers have made a difference for growth is an entirely different matter.

The valuable contribution by Angel de la Fuente to this volume should be interpreted in the light of these observations. He shows that the Structural Funds flowing to Spain were mostly used for productive investments and that such investments have indeed been productive. That is, they contribute to gross national product, proportionally to their estimated share in the aggregate production function. This is certainly correct: transfer of funds from the EU to Spain has helped the accumulation of productive infrastructures in that country. It would be really dramatic if it were otherwise. But the crucial claim is not that Structural Funds are wasted. The crucial claim is that they do not alter the long-term growth rate of the recipient regions in any significant way. In our statistical work we looked in many different ways for such an effect but could not find it. Pedro Arevalo (2002) has carried out a painstaking and meticulous investigation of Spanish regional development since the late 1950s, using a high-quality data set of both provincial and regional human, public, and private capital stocks, and sectoral VA. He shows that TFP growth accounts for the lion's share of economic growth and convergence across Spanish regions, with little left for public and private capital and a somewhat larger share for human capital. More important, he shows once again that, even at this very detailed and disaggregated level, there is no sign of a positive impact of Structural Funds on provincial and regional TFP growth rates. While speaking against current EU regional policy is a political taboo, other people have also started looking at the question. A recent paper by Ederveen, de Groot, and Nahuis (2002) is a prime example. It is relevant here also because, in our view, de la Fuente quotes it erroneously as a piece of statistical evidence contradicting our earlier analysis. It does not do so; in fact, it reinforces it. The authors use a statistical methodology that is quite different from the one we used in Boldrin and Canova (2001) but reach the same conclusions: Structural Funds by themselves are ineffective. Their estimates show a statistically significant *negative* effect of Structural Funds on regional growth rates and convergence. They find a small positive effect of Structural Funds only for countries with the "right policies." Placing this "right policies" condition does not work in Ederveen and others either: low inflation, low budget deficit, and a cohesive social policy do not make Structural Funds effective. Only high institutional quality and low corruption do. More interesting is Ederveen and others' country-by-country breakdown of this conditional effect (table 4-2): in *all cohesion countries but Ireland* the impact of Structural Funds is strongly negative even when one accounts for the variables measuring corruption and institutional quality. In fact, the impact is also negative in Italy and, in two cases out of three, France. The authors apply their methodology to the EU accession countries and show that, also in these countries and even after conditioning for institutional variables, the likely impact of Structural Funds on convergence is negative. Only openness, not surprising in the light of our earlier discussion, may help make the impact somewhat positive for some of the accession countries. Hence, contrary to de la Fuente's assertion, Ederveen and others (2002) reach conclusions quite supportive of our analysis.[6] In summary, neither de la Fuente nor any other serious study we know of shows that the growth rate of TFP is significantly affected by structural policies. Overwhelming evidence shows that long-term growth is the product of increasing TFP, not just of capital accumulation. TFP growth is, indeed, a fairly mysterious object. Nevertheless, no data show that regional TFP growth has been affected by Structural Funds.

A second point should be made. Structural Funds are transfers supported by distorting taxation, which implies a dead-weight loss. The dead-weight loss could be justified on public policy grounds if the social rate of return from the investments financed via Structural Funds were large enough to compensate both for this dead-weight loss and for the opportunity cost of the funds. The latter, after all, could have been used by private agents in other productive activities. Deciding what a reasonable social rate of return on public investment would be is hard, and we are not going to try to quantify it here. The Congressional Budget Office of the U.S. Congress, for example, recommends a 10 percent real annual return as an absolute minimum for any public investment project. Has such a minimum rate of return been obtained by the investments financed by the EU Structural Funds? Even without capitalization, the accumulated investment financed by Structural and Cohesion Funds in Spain amounts to at least 40 percent of Spanish GDP. This is a benevolent choice, first because we are not capitalizing and second because the number would have been 70 percent for Portugal and more than 100 percent for Greece. Have Structural Funds increased the Spanish GDP by at least 4 percentage points each year? If sound empirical analyses can show numbers anywhere comparable to this figure, we will be willing to step back and revise our position on the effectiveness of Structural Funds. Until that is the case, we will keep our current position.

Sometimes *some* poorer countries grow faster than richer ones. The debate is still open as to the magical mix of policy and circumstances that makes miracles happen. We do not have an answer to such a question, but we can come up with an incomplete list of factors that help, that hurt, and that are more or less irrelevant. To illustrate the point, look again at the four cohesion countries of the EU—Greece, Ireland, Portugal, and Spain—and at the Italian southern regions of Basilicata, Calabria, Campania, Molise, Puglia, Sardegna, and Sicilia (that is, the Mezzogiorno). We can break the group into two, based on initial conditions. Back in 1960, Ireland and Spain were both at about 60 percent of the EU average in terms of per capita GDP, while Greece, the Mezzogiorno, and Portugal stood at 50 percent.

During the 1960s and until 1974 Spain liberalized trade unilaterally and adopted internal policies that, relative to earlier policies, were market oriented. By 1974 its income per capita stood at almost 80 percent of the European average, which is where it still stands now, after 25 years of oscillations in both growth rates and internal policies. Irish relative per capita income stagnated for more than 20 years, without apparent effect from either the 1973 EU accession or the receipt of EU Structural Funds: by the mid-1980s its income per capita was around 65 percent of the EU average. Since then the government has fully embraced free trade, low taxes, low public spending,[7] and well-known competition-oriented policies. Its income per capita now exceeds 110 percent of the EU average. Look next at Greece, the Mezzogiorno, and Portugal. Greece stands now at about 65 percent of the EU average. This is exactly where it was 21 years ago, when it first joined the EU and began receiving transfers: all the catching up that Greece managed to do since 1960 took place before it started to receive Structural Funds. It is also a fact that, since accession, Greece has been the EU country least likely to indulge in market-friendly internal policies, reduction of public expenditure and taxes, and privatization and liberalization of its markets. Portugal seems to have done almost the opposite: it followed its neighbor Spain in unilaterally liberalizing trade in 1960; shifted to a regime of high public spending and taxation coupled with heavy state intervention in labor and product markets right after the 1974 revolution; and resumed liberalization, privatization, and labor market reform in the late 1980s. Its per capita GDP, relative to the EU15's, followed a similar sequence: from 45 to 60 percent between 1960 and 1974, unchanged between 1974 and 1988, and from 60 to 78 percent between 1988 and 2000. The Mezzogiorno's itinerary is slightly more complex, as it has been the object of Italian and EU transfers at the same time. In any case, during the 1960s the flow of external funds to the Mezzogiorno was relatively low: the 1950s and 1960s were the decades of the labor migration to northern Italy and Northern Europe. By the time of the oil crisis in 1974, the Mezzogiorno per capita GDP was about 63 percent of the EU average. Since then, the Mezzogiorno has become one of the privileged targets of EU Structural Funds and the Italian government has stepped up its subsidy and transfer policies. Migration flows ended and official unemployment started rising. By the year 2000, the Mezzogiorno per capita income was around 68 percent of the EU average.

Historical experience and economic analysis have also taught us something important about the short-term effects of trade integration policies. Technologically and economically backward countries that enter into a free trade arrangement with more advanced ones undergo a fairly rapid and dramatic process of structural change that leads to the destruction of employment in the agricultural sector and other backward sectors. The adjustment is socially costly, and the job destruction it generates is the key threat to long-term prosperity because the unemployment wave induced by the transition tends to be persistent over time. Elimination of structural unemployment requires strong and clearly targeted mobility and training policies. Such policies have seldom been implemented because, in the face of growing unemployment, political pressure to adopt grossly inefficient transfer policies usually succeeds. The likelihood of such erroneous policy choices is enhanced by the availability of external aid funds. Economic theory aside, historical evidence shows that subsidies and transfer policies make regional imbalances more persistent.

To summarize the points, (a) while structural transfers carried out at the European level leave growth rates roughly unaffected, national policies do make a huge difference; (b) national policies that reduce distorting taxes and unproductive public spending, liberalize labor markets, foster job search and retraining, attract FDI, and minimize income support transfers seem to lead to a sustained period of above-average growth.

To lend support to our claims, we look at the recent East German experience as another emblematic case of badly conceived and highly perverse transfer policies.

The Big Brother Effect

Unlike CEECs, the German Democratic Republic enjoyed the protection of its big Western brother during its transition. From an economic point of view, this has meant that (a) a number of domestic income support policies, financed with taxation from the West, have shielded the residents of the former German Democratic Republic from the most unpleasant costs of the transition; (b) firms operating or installing themselves in the former German Democratic Republic received abundant public subsidies; and (c) the East German *länder* have been classified as Objective 1 regions, receiving Structural Funds from the EU. The total amount of transfers involved is enormous. For example, during 1991–97 the German government alone transferred to the East German *länder* a total of €571 billion corresponding to about 50 percent of their GDP over the period. During that same period, total lending and transfers from the World Bank to CEECs and Central Asian transition countries equaled approximately 3 percent of this quantity (see World Bank 2001c). Beside these windfalls, firms of the East German *länder* had immediate access to the EU15 markets and did not face the restrictions, tariffs, and other administrative obstacles that apply to products and services coming from outside the EU. Given that the initial conditions in the German Democratic Republic were substantially better than those of other CEECs when transition started and given the plenitude of public support, how did the East German *länder* economy perform relative to the less fortunate CEEC10?

It is well known that the growth performance of the former German Democratic Republic has been quite mediocre. After a spurt of rapid growth, right after unification, growth for the East German *länder* slowed down, and during the past six years they have grown more slowly than the rest of the EU. From 1995 to 2000, growth in GDP per capita averaged less than 2.0 percent, much lower than growth in every CEEC but Bulgaria and Romania. Labor productivity, which started at about one-third of the West's in 1991, grew to 65 percent in 1995 but has stagnated ever since. Over the 1995–2000 period, growth in the former German Democratic Republic's labor productivity was only 1.5 percent a year, the lowest in Europe, with manufacturing and the business service sectors performing particularly poorly.

The observed slowdown has lasted long enough to rule out any "cyclical" interpretation of this phenomenon: in spite of the enormous transfers, the economy of the former German Democratic Republic is not converging to either the EU or the German averages. While it may be a bit too early to classify the East *länder* as the Mezzogiorno of Germany, it is certainly another example of persistent backwardness, lower productivity, low labor force participation rates, higher unemployment, and high subsidies. The analogies with the Mezzogiorno go further. In particular, the "backwardness" or "poverty" of the East German *länder* is, like that of southern Italy, quite relative. After all, GDP per capita in the former German Democratic Republic has reached 76 percent of the EU average, approximately the level of Portugal and several points above the level of Greece. However, to the extent that half of this amount is financed by the Federal Republic of Germany, it is clear that in comparing the GDR's *länder* with CEECs, a much lower level, say 45 or 50 percent of the EU average, should be taken as a true value. This places the East German *länder* just below the Czech Republic, Hungary, and Slovenia in terms of both labor productivity and per capita GDP. In other words, once the large income transfers from the West are factored out, the East German *länder* are, in terms of domestic productive capacity and produced income, a few percentage points below where they were 12 years ago. Since the best performing CEECs appear to have done better and are projected to do significantly better in the near future, one should seriously ask why the extraordinary amount of resources poured into the economy of the former German Democratic Republic have provided income support but failed to deliver sustained growth incentives.

There may be several reasons why this has happened. A number of hypotheses have been analyzed in the existing literature (see, for example, Canova and Ravn 2000; Sinn 2000; Franz and Steiner 2000; and Ragnitz 2001 for some of the most insightful examples). A highly counterfactual but nevertheless popular point of view, paralleling earlier literature on the failures of state aids to the Mezzogiorno or the poor growth performances of Objective 1 regions, has reached the Panglossian conclusion that while the amount of aid transferred was large, it was evidently not enough and/or it was not well spent. This refrain, heard also at the Barcelona conference, reminds one of the old story according to which socialism had not been implemented correctly in the U.S.S.R., but it could and would produce wonders in, say, Albania.

In our opinion, the most coherent explanation has to do with the perverse effects that income support policies generate on the incentives to work, produce, and invest for citizens of eastern Germany. Since 1990 total employment in eastern Germany has fallen by 30 percent, from 9 million to 6 million, roughly the fall observed in Bulgaria, the largest fall in the CEECs. As in most transition countries, the manufacturing sector has experienced the largest decline in employment, and job creation has occurred only in the construction sector. The expansion of the latter has been particularly abnormal in eastern Germany because funds from western Germany for reconstruction have led to an oversized construction sector with poor or negative efficiency gains in the sector itself, which had low TFP and a low technological content at the beginning. Obsolete and unproductive firms have been scrapped, and despite an initial boom (1990–91) in the creation of new firms, the entrepreneurial process stopped right after the first enthusiasm for reunification waned. The registration of new enterprises in the east, which was almost twice as large as that in the west in 1991, fell to only one-tenth of the west's in 2000. Interestingly, over the period 1995–2000 German FDI flow to CEECs was larger than to eastern Germany (Eurostat 2002d). This may not be altogether surprising. In 1990 gross nominal wages in eastern Germany were 46.7 percent of western Germany's, while in 1999 they had reached 73.9 percent of western Germany's. In comparison, average labor productivity was only 31 percent of western Germany's level in 1990 (implying unit labor costs 50 percent higher in East Germany) and was 59.4 percent in 1999 (implying unit labor costs that are still 24 percent higher in eastern than in western Germany). As we have seen, unit labor costs in the CEEC10 as a whole are substantially lower than in the EU, where in turn they are lower than the unit labor costs of western Germany.

Like employment, labor force participation has dramatically declined as a consequence of generous early retirement programs and the large number of women exiting the labor market. Overall, labor force participation has shrunk by 7 to 8 percent in the past 10 years, 50 percent more than in the average CEEC. Income support to the unemployed has become substantial: one-fifth of eastern Germany's population received income support in the form of benefits or state assistance in 1999. The level of support is high in absolute (about 1,000 per capita in the first case and about 750 in the second case) and relative terms. So-called active labor market retraining programs provide extremely generous support for participants, in some cases higher than the monthly wage earned by a low-skilled worker. Not surprisingly, they have a remarkably poor record at increasing participants' employment levels. Overall, more than 60 percent of total transfers to eastern Germany are for social protection. In this situation, we should expect to see stagnating growth performance, little downward pressure on wages, rent-seeking activities by nonparticipants and the unemployed, and a strong incentive to maintain the status quo—a picture that duplicates to a large extent the experience of southern Italy and of a number of provinces of southern Spain. Subsidized income support has become a modus vivendi and has created incentives for its perpetuation. Ragnitz (2001) has also suggested that the abundance of assistance programs has produced a very inefficient allocation of new capital. Funds have been used to maintain an inefficient and unproductive manufacturing sector, and new enterprises have been established mostly in sectors with low levels of competition, low levels of research and development, and low technological content.

In comparison, new investments in CEECs have been typically directed to the most productive sectors and, at least in the most successful countries (Hungary and Slovenia, and Poland to a lesser extent), direct income support has been low and indirect income support via a high minimum wage negligible enough to prevent the creation of counterproductive incentives and gross malfunctioning of labor markets. The case of Poland is, from this point of view, almost paradigmatic since the economy is large and heterogeneous and its per capita income levels were, and still are, lower than those in eastern Germany. Poland initially followed a well-established EU policy of promoting interregional labor immobility, subsidizing or giving workers incentives not to leave areas where unemployment rates were higher, ignoring their poor housing situation, and increasing minimum wages to the point of making them binding, especially in the less developed areas. Facing rising unemployment, Polish authorities have started reversing these tendencies in recent years. To the businesspeople of western Germany, Poland may seem to offer much better growth prospects than eastern Germany.

Assessment of Regional Policies in the Enlargement Process

We begin this section with a very short summary of what regional policies are, how much funding EU regional policies currently provide, and how those funds are distributed. The EU budget was, in 2000, equal to about 1.05 percent of aggregate GDP, of which 46 percent was taken by the CAP and 36.5 percent by the Structural and Cohesion Funds. Greece, Ireland, Portugal, and Spain are the big net receivers, while all the other countries are net contributors. Relative to national GDP, the Netherlands is the largest contributor. The Irish position as a large net receiver of funds (about 4 percent of GDP) still reflects the recent past, when Irish per capita GDP was below 90 percent of the EU average. From the point of view of gross flows, Germany and Italy (with 1999 30 billion each, over the 2000–06 cycle) and France and the United Kingdom (with 15 and 16 billion, respectively) should also be added to the list of great beneficiaries of regional funds. For the sake of comparison, over the same budget cycle Spain is set to receive 56 billion, Greece 25 billion, Portugal 23 billion, and Ireland 4 billion (all figures in 1999 euro).

The Structural Funds (European Agricultural Guidance and Guarantee Fund [EAGGF], European Regional Development Fund [ERDF], European Social Fund [ESF], and Financial Instrument for Fisheries Guidance [FIFG]) are supposed to finance projects pursuing at least one among six (three as of 2001) policy objectives. Each of them corresponds to a different subset of regions of the EU, even if the Commission makes a distinction between "regional objectives," which concentrate about 85 percent of the budget, and "nonregional objectives." Objective regions are designated at the NUTS 2 level.

The Structural Funds cofinance multiannual programs in the member states. In contrast with the expenditure of the CAP, where payments from the fund are largely determined by a formula, there is a substantial discretionary element in the spending of the Structural Funds. Taking full advantage of the Structural Funds is a labor-intensive exercise for member states, both because of the technocratic standards projects are expected to match and because of the extensive coordination required to satisfy the partnership principle.

The Cohesion Fund, introduced by the December 1992 European Council (Edinburgh), is the second pillar of the current EU regional policy. The Cohesion Fund aims specifically at improving European transport networks and overall environmental conditions. Interventions have not a regional but a national basis, and eligibility requires a national GDP per capita below 90 percent of the EU average. This requirement has de facto limited the Cohesion Fund in the four poorer countries (Greece, Ireland, Portugal, and Spain). Ireland, which has been effectively well above that threshold since the late 1990s, is still receiving funds during the 2000–06 budget cycle.

A European Commission communication of March 1998 titled "Reform of the Structural Funds" aims at reducing the number of regions covered by the funds. The proposals, which were not incorporated into the deliberation of the European Council of Berlin and which (as far as we know) have not yet been implemented, envision a reduction in the number of objectives from six to three and a stricter enforcement of the 75 percent threshold for the NUTS 2 regions that are covered under Objective 1.

Should the current criteria for eligibility for Structural Funds be maintained after accession of the CEEC10, current recipients would see their transfers evaporate almost entirely. For example, in the financing cycle that is supposed to start in 2007, only two Spanish regions (Andalucia and Extremadura) are likely to qualify for Objective 1 funds. In Italy, only Calabria may remain. At the same time, Spain's and Portugal's income per capita would most likely move above the 90 percent threshold for admission to Cohesion Fund transfers, so these transfers would also disappear. Other likely losers of funds are the *länder* of the former German Democratic Republic. At the same time, nearly every administrative division of the new countries (with an exception made for the cities of Prague, Bratislava, Ljubljana, and possibly Budapest) would qualify for Structural Funds support.

Preaccession aid to the CEECs, a form of Structural Funds aid, has been operating since the 1994–99 budget cycle. The Commission's suggested policy for the postaccession system, so far, implies an effective cap at 4 percent of GDP for the receipts of any country and an overall target of spending on Structural Funds equal to 0.46 percent of total EU GDP. Such limits will be effective until the end of the current budget cycle (2006), after which they will be open to modification. A crucial policy issue that is actively debated concerns the new limits (if any) for such spending.

As far as the Cohesion Fund is concerned, the issue is blurrier. Since the Cohesion Fund was created to facilitate the respect of the so-called stability pact by the poorest countries of the EU15 in the wake of the euro adoption, it is not obvious that it should be maintained now that (a) the euro has been successfully adopted, and (b) only Greece is still below the 75 percent threshold and it may not remain there if CEEC10 countries are admitted in 2004 and 2008. Taking the planned admission as a given, two options seem possible: keep the Cohesion Fund, diverting its resources almost entirely to the newcomers, or abolish it.

Our main suggestion is that European regional policies be terminated after the current budget cycle ends in 2006. This is, we believe, the best choice of policy because current regional policies are ineffective, based on incorrect or at least unsubstantiated economic theory, badly designed, poorly carried out, and a source of wrong incentives and, in some cases, corruption. The lack of direct enforcement mechanisms that evaluate the efficiency and effectiveness of fund allocation creates an environment where corruption is bred. The recent episode of misallocation of ESF and CAP funds (highly publicized in the Spanish press) indicates that these are not merely "theoretical" problems.

The presence of Structural Funds may have some indirect economic benefits for CEECs: solidify the democratic rule in the East, help implement institutional changes, create international partnerships, and reduce social tensions generated during the transition. The funds' existence, however, generates two sets of serious problems for the growth prospects of CEECs.

On the one hand, they create a clear political obstacle to the enlargement process: all current beneficiaries of the regional transfers are trying to avoid losing them, while the current contributors are trying to avoid paying for a much larger bill. Under current policies both events are very likely, especially when one adds the Structural Funds and the CAP together. Barring the courageous choice of shutting down regional policies altogether, the two opposite camps are likely to find a murky compromise, with exemptions and suspension provisions, compensatory transfers, and so on. If the accession of Finland and Sweden into the EU has led to the creation of Objective 6 to compensate the two countries for what they contributed to Brussels, the accession of the CEECs is likely to create a whole set of new objectives, special clauses, exemptions, and "temporary" compensatory transfers.

On the other hand, making the vast resources of the EU regional policy available to the CEECs may provide them with a substantial incentive to insist on the wrong policies. Practically, they may postpone the elimination of state subsidies to obsolete and inefficient enterprises. They may also create new or reinforce existing "income maintenance programs," thereby reducing labor mobility and providing incorrect incentives to entrepreneurial capital. The availability of such funds and their tendency to focus on large projects of public utility may also provide a further reason to delay adjustments in the utilities sector, with negative implications for overall efficiency. As we argue in the next section, the sequence of policy choices is not only crucial to foster growth but also a key precondition to a much-needed reduction in labor income taxation. The accumulated experience of eastern Germany, Greece, the Mezzogiorno, and southern Spain suggests that the risk of falling into the "big brother trap" when large external subsidies are available is very high. Overall, we believe that the costs greatly surpass the benefits and that the radical suggestion of eliminating them after 2006 could make a large percentage of the future EU better off.

Since our preferred option will not find many supporters in Brussels, it is worth looking at which reforms would keep Structural Funds alive but limit their damaging effects and enhance their positive impact on economic growth in the CEEC10.

The theoretical principles underlying the EU regional and structural policies are, prima facie, commendable and hard to dispute. The Commission calls for (a) concentration of funding where it is most needed, on the basis of explicit and certified (b) planning of such intervention in (c) cooperation with local and national authorities whose funding the EU transfers are supposed to (d) complement (with cofunding going from 50 to 80 percent of the value of the project). As is often the case, the reality is quite different. We have already emphasized the lack of both common and economic sense behind the choice of NUTS 2 and NUTS 3 regions as the territorial levels at which economic convergence should be measured. We will not harp further on this point, but we list it as the natural first step in a long-overdue reform of European regional policies: elect territorial units that are both homogeneous and large enough to make convergence in per capita GDP a reasonable target and coordination at the European level justifiable. Common sense suggests choosing areas with a population of about 10 million people. In the light of the CEEC accession, this would imply that convergence should be measured at a country level, with an exception made for Poland and Romania.

The choice of appropriate territorial units for measuring convergence leads to the issue of the level at which resources are funneled. Currently, various subnational administrative levels are involved, sometimes particularly small ones. Theoretically, the choice of subnational unit is meant to stimulate decentralization. However, the restrictions imposed make the approach resemble a degenerate form of fiscal federalism. First, the administrative entities involved are very unequal, and since the Commission imposes homogeneous technical requirements on planning, financing, and implementing the projects, this places a huge burden on small regions or administrative units. All but a handful of very large local administrations use the services of consulting companies located in Brussels to handle Structural Funds projects. Alternatively, they let their central governments elaborate, present, bargain for, and manage those projects on their behalf—not much decentralization or federalism. Italy, where Structural Funds for the Mezzogiorno are de facto handled, coordinated, and almost dished out by a dedicated Direzione Generale at the Italian Treasury, is the most egregious example.

Second, while EU funding is not supposed to replace local spending, it obviously does because of the aggregate budget constraint at the level at which resources are funneled. Furthermore, as central governments are active partners in the funding process and are allocating national resources to the same regional entities to which European funds go, it is at the level of central government budgeting that substitution takes place. With the exception of Germany, the administrative units involved have little or no autonomous fiscal power: their resources flow from central governments that, obviously, count Structural Funds provisions as part of total financing. Finally, the desired territorial concentration of funding is, to say the least, long gone: all EU15 countries receive some regional subsidy. Counting in a map of Europe, the number of NUTS 2 regions receiving some transfer under some Objective 1 reaches more than 90 percent of the total. In fact, as we learn from Chapter 11, at most 70 percent of the total amount of funding goes to areas with an income per capita lower than the EU average. One way or another, almost all regions of Europe need to converge to the average European income.

These arguments reinforce the need for radical reform of both criteria and methods for funding. Concentration of funding where most needed should be reestablished as a relevant criterion by setting a much lower threshold for the definition of a disadvantaged region. Cooperation and complementarity should also be ensured by funding only regions that are true federal units, with autonomous taxing/financing power, and that are able to handle their budgeting process in cooperation with the

European Commission and independent of their central governments. Where such entities are not present, one should choose between financing central governments directly (as should be the case with most CEECs) or not providing funds at all. If realpolitik implies that some side payments going from the richest to the poorest members of the EU have to be maintained as a polite form of "bribing" and political "consensus building," then such side payments should be handled at the country level with the exception of those subnational units that have achieved some form of true federal autonomy. This is similar to the views expressed by de la Fuente in this volume and, for different but complementary reasons, by Guido Tabellini, who argues, "More likely, the main goal of structural and cohesion funds was redistributive: not to increase economic efficiency, but to redistribute the benefits of integration among countries, providing side payments so as to facilitate compromise in bargaining situations. The question then is whether the same goal could have been achieved in less distorting ways. Participants at the bargaining table are countries, not regions. Side payments are thus needed among countries, not among regions or groups of individuals" (Tabellini 2002, p. 19).

We are convinced that the recognition that Structural and Cohesion Funds are just transfer payments used to facilitate political bargaining and coalition building is not forthcoming. Hence, the fiction of the "convergence goal" and of "growth and efficiency enhancing" objectives is likely to be maintained, scientific evidence to the contrary notwithstanding. In this case, two reforms should still be advocated. One is a drastic lowering of the maximum income for admission to funding. A level equal to 50 percent of the EU average would, in our view, be a good choice, allowing funds to be concentrated where they are most needed. Such a cutoff would not only exclude all current EU members from funding but, among the CEEC10, also exclude the Czech Republic, Slovenia, and possibly Hungary. Of the first entrants, only Poland (minus the metropolitan area of Warsaw) would clearly be a potential beneficiary of Structural Funds. It seems most likely that (by 2008) Bulgaria, Latvia, Lithuania, and Romania would still be below 50 percent of EU average income per capita and therefore would qualify for this target. Second, we recommend a drastic reduction of the number of objectives to be pursued (as proposed by the Commission in 1998 and being implemented currently). In our view, Objective 1, properly rephrased to focus on structural deficiencies (especially large public goods, transportation and communication infrastructures, and environmental protection), is the only one that should be retained on a permanent basis. In the light of the CEEC10 accession, it appears that Objective 2 (recovery from industrial restructuring) and Objective 5 (agriculture structural transformation) should also be maintained during the first budgeting cycle following admission (2007–13) because of the relevance of both industrial and agricultural restructuring in these countries.

From a practical point of view, the tough part consists of effectively financing large-scale projects that favor recovery from industrial crisis and agricultural restructuring. A couple of criteria are worth suggesting. First, we would, contrary to much common wisdom, deemphasize the support for small and medium enterprises. Policies of support to small and medium firms should be the task of national governments via properly designing fiscal and labor market legislation and granting small firms easier access to financial markets. It is our view that such national policies are far more effective (when properly implemented) and relevant than some general subsidies coming from Brussels that are linked to complicated business plans, the elaboration of which is often too demanding for truly small companies. Anecdotal evidence and common sense coincide in suggesting that supporting small and medium enterprises via Structural Funds equates to supporting those firms that look small, have good political connections, and have a comparative advantage in rent-seeking (rather than VA) activities. Second, we recommend insisting quite strictly on the "public good" nature of the projects to be financed. We recommend concentrating funds to provide productive infrastructures: transport, communication, power and water distribution, and educational infrastructures. This we advocate for three simple reasons. First, both theory and empirical evidence suggest that if there is anything like a poverty trap, this is determined by the shortage of the kind of productive public goods we have just listed. Second, besides a favorable fiscal and labor market environment, these are the kinds of public goods that generate the "absolute advantage" (in the sense of Jones 2000) that is crucial to attracting mobile factors of production, FDI in particular. Third, no matter how corrupt the allocational system for the production of such large public goods may be, it allows more control from the EU and engenders less damaging collusion between the private sector and the political system than the subsidization of a large number of small private enterprises.

There are also a number of actions we would discourage. One is lifting current spending limits on Structural Funds (as suggested in Vaitilingam 2002). The subtle plan behind such advice seems to be that of getting the old beneficiaries to agree to the admission of the new members without having to give up the sacred cow of the "structural policies." Such commentators have often insisted on the existence of "enormous income gaps" between current and future members. This is incorrect: the current differences between the EU15 and CEEC10 are similar to, or even smaller than, those that the EU managed to overcome quite successfully during previous enlargements.

Second, various commentators have insisted on the opportunity and necessity for enlargement countries to forge ahead with deep labor market reforms, such as relaxing minimum wage requirements and lowering labor income taxes. These recommendations are most welcome. Nevertheless, it is hard to see why one would advocate labor market reforms in these countries when labor markets in many EU countries are less flexible and when labor market policies, at both the national and supranational levels, in the EU do not meet the standards. The labor market in, say, Hungary is more open and liberalized, although maybe less efficient, than that of several of the members of the EU15. Similarly, the structure and the dynamic of the labor market structure in Slovenia are not dissimilar from those of its largest EU neighbor,

Italy, and growth rates of labor productivity and employment in Slovenia actually look significantly better in recent years.

Third, mixing good intentions with bad economics, other commentators have recommended the creation of minimum guaranteed income schemes similar to those in place in most current EU member countries as a condition for accession, and even EU coordination of the level of these minimum guaranteed income schemes. The long-term plan seems to be that of building up a pan-European social safety net as one of the pillar institutions of the EU. We find such proposals dangerous, especially for the future growth perspectives of the CEEC10 and other poorer areas. The rationale is simple: the big brother effect kills labor mobility and entrepreneurial efforts and price flexibility, all of which are key ingredients of successful growth. Furthermore, minimum guaranteed income schemes need financing, and this financing can come either from additional transfers from richer countries (increasing their fiscal burden and reinforcing the subsidization culture on the receiving side) or from labor income taxation at home. Surely, CEECs do not need an increase in their labor income taxes. Nevertheless, given that we do not expect income support to poor countries to end with accession, we would like to suggest two general principles to minimize the induced distortions. First, income support policies should target job seekers (as is done right now in the Netherlands). Second, Structural Funds directed to the creation of employment opportunities—as opposed to those directed to the creation of high productivity levels via provision of public goods—should aim at enlarging labor force participation, which plays a crucial role (as the Irish experience shows) in fostering income convergence.

This leads us to another theme, which is also stressed in the next section: labor income taxation. Theory tells us that, especially when unemployment is high and sectoral reallocation of labor an important priority, the optimal tax rate on labor should be low. When total taxation on labor is too high, two types of distortions are created: potential job seekers are discouraged, and the productive side of the population is heavily penalized to subsidize the income of those who are unproductive. These distortions may perpetuate a vicious cycle, which is particularly vicious in countries (like the CEEC10) facing major restructuring, destruction of a large number of firms, entrance of new firms from abroad, and a rapidly changing distribution of skills in the labor force. If a labor market reform is needed in the CEEC10, it consists of reducing unemployment subsidies and income maintenance programs (together with enterprise subsidies) in order to free labor income of the gigantic fiscal burden it carries.

Labor market reforms should probably be coupled with policies that favor the efficient reallocation of labor across not only sectors but also regions. "Labor migration" seems to be a well-guarded taboo among both current EU members and CEECs: right-wing politicians use the potential size of migration from the East to increase EU citizens' fears of losing jobs and current benefits. On the other side, CEECs worry that labor mobility may exacerbate the drain of high-skilled workers, thereby rendering national disparities even larger. Overall, we believe that these fears have been over-

stated and that regional misallocation of labor and persistent poverty is greatly amplified by the equity-without-efficiency approach upon which many EU policies have
been forged. This regional misallocation is going to be even larger if the existing policies are mechanically extended to CEECs: effective removal of Objectives 3 and 4 of
the Structural Funds should be sought. By creating incentives against labor mobility
across regions, these objectives perpetuate income inequalities across regions.

Furthermore, like Vaitilingam (2001), we believe that the fears of mass migration
from the CEEC10 are overstated. Most of those who wanted to and were able to
migrate from the CEEC10 to the EU15 countries have already done so since 1990.
This may sound surprising, given the current fears of migration from the CEECs to
the EU and the relatively small number of workers from those countries who have
made it inside the EU so far. Available estimates place the stock of CEEC immigrants
residing in the EU at around 800,000, 60 percent of whom are concentrated in Austria and Germany. After an initial surge, the flows from the CEECs to the EU have
subsided, with minor movements from one country or the other, all clearly associated
with cyclical fluctuations in the home country. There is no evidence that current
restrictions on labor migration from the CEECs to the EU are holding back a gigantic
mass of potential migrants. Just to cite an example, while before unification a net
300,000 people from the German Democratic Republic migrated to West Germany in
1990, in the period 1992–2000 the net flow dropped to about 50,000 a year. Because
of the natural linguistic and cultural links we think of this as an extreme case not to be
used as a reference point to forecast what will happen in the case of accession but only
as a very high upper bound. Furthermore, although nonnegligible in size, the percentage of people potentially migrating toward the EU represents only 0.2 to 0.5 percent
of the total EU labor force, an amount that a large labor market like the EU should be
able to absorb with little difficulty. This number is substantially smaller, for example,
than the annual flow of immigrants who find employment in the United States. Historical experience shows that when the migrant masses want to come in, they do.
Medium-term economic perspectives in the home country relative to those in the host
country count a lot more than absolute levels in determining the intensity of migration. To the extent that growth rates in the CEEC10 equal or exceed those of the EU,
the migration flow will be kept within very reasonable limits. Finally, to go back to
the comparison with early enlargements, the flow of immigrants from Greece, Portugal, and Spain after their admission to the EU was quantitatively irrelevant: we see no
reason to fear that the flow from Poland or Slovenia after 2004 will be much larger.

Conclusions

Overall, experience from earlier EU enlargements and current economic conditions
within the CEEC10 suggest that placing very high expectations on enlargement per
se is not useful. It will help politicians, but it will not lead to economic convergence.
Furthermore, regional transfers taking place under the structural and cohesion poli-

cies are unlikely to become the growth engines of the CEEC10. They may increase income in the receiving countries by an amount equal to the one transferred, but there is no evidence that they will have an impact on long-term growth rates. To achieve long-term growth at rates higher than average, an appropriate mix of European and national policies is needed. This includes further fostering of trade integration within the EU, restructuring of public spending, creation of supply-side incentives by proper reforms of fiscal and social insurance policies, and free movement of capital and labor, together with a competitive level of labor income taxation. Based on historical experience, two assertions appear to be particularly relevant. First, public programs for long-term income support, corporate subsidies, and other forms of income transfer have a negative effect on economic growth. We believe they should be terminated as soon as possible. Second, labor and capital mobility are good for growth and economic convergence. In particular, the adoption or continuation of various transfer and/or regulation policies aimed at eliminating labor migration from CEECs is wrong and damaging. The fear of migration has been magnified by skillful politicians: migration after past enlargements has been small. There is no reason to expect it to be large in this case. A more detailed list of findings and policy implications follows.

First, although theoretically possible under fairly special circumstances, there is no reason to believe that trade integration per se would lead economies to diverge. On the contrary, all past experiences of trade integration, especially those that have taken place in Europe since the 1950s, have led to sizable improvements in the factor endowments of the poorest partner and in the efficiency with which such factors were allocated in production. These improvements have reduced income inequalities and enhanced production possibilities across participating countries. Hence, as a principle, further trade integration should be pursued among European countries and between the EU15 and the CEEC10 in particular.

Second, pure trade integration generates a leveling effect more than a growth effect on participating countries. In particular, there is no hard evidence supporting the idea that trade integration alone may increase the long-term growth rates of participating countries. This implies that, when absolute convergence is the objective, other national policies than liberalization of international trade play an important role. The experience of various European countries shows that reduction in fiscal pressure, accompanied by parallel reduction in public spending, is among such policies. Capital and labor mobility, together with a competitive level of labor income taxation, also play a role in fostering real convergence.

Third, while a fairly stable macroeconomic environment is certainly necessary for growth, there is no evidence that, by themselves, a low inflation rate, low public deficit, and low public debt will foster economic convergence. In fact, the experience of many regions within the EU proves that, when facing the same monetary, fiscal, and exchange rate policy, poor regions need not grow faster than rich ones.

Fourth, both evidence and economic theory suggest that, given a stable macroeconomic environment, the presence or lack of supply-side incentives plays a crucial role in determining long-term regional performance. The half-century experience with southern Italy and the more than two decades of experience with southern Spain show that the availability of large and permanent income support transfer programs has a negative impact on economic efficiency and long-term growth. The relatively more recent experience of the East German *länder* leads to the same conclusion: public programs for long-term income support, corporate subsidies, and other forms of income transfer have a negative effect on economic growth. They hamper instead of foster economic convergence.

Fifth, the experiences of Ireland, Portugal, and Veneto in the EU15 and of Poland and Estonia in the CEEC10 show that sustained above-average economic growth is the consequence of an attractive environment for FDI and new small firm creation, risk-taking entrepreneurial behavior, and exploitation of local comparative advantages via enhanced labor and capital mobility. Low marginal taxes, efficient transportation and communication infrastructures, good financial facilities, and a relatively flexible supply of high-level human capital appear to be the key ingredients of a growth-friendly environment.

Sixth, labor and capital mobility are good for growth and economic convergence. Free capital movement across national borders seems to have become an obvious and accepted policy stance in the EU. Things are different with respect to labor movement. A number of researchers are recommending the adoption or continuation of various transfer and/or regulation policies aimed at reducing or even eliminating labor migration from European regions. We consider this prescription wrong and damaging. While the social and political costs of mass migration are certainly large and cannot be underestimated, a certain amount of free labor migration is necessary to a well-functioning labor market. Furthermore, labor migration from one EU country or region to another has often been temporary and has been associated with episodes of rapid economic growth and convergence. Evidence shows that movements of labor within Europe and the United States have been among the major forces behind economic convergence. Labor migration is one of the most important channels through which precious productive skills are acquired in advanced regions and brought into poorer regions to be applied. Finally, a variety of arguments and considerations suggest that the size of the postadmission migration flows from the CEECs to the EU countries will be much smaller than envisaged by catastrophe-predicting politicians and will have very little impact on the labor markets of the EU15. In essence, we find no reason to adopt direct or indirect policies to restrain free movement of labor from the CEECs to the EU. The best policy would allow free movement of labor without creating incentives or disincentives in either direction.

Seventh, experience from earlier EU enlargements and current economic conditions within the CEEC10 suggest that placing very high expectations on the economic consequences of the enlargement would be incorrect. Hopes that EU regional and structural policies will be the key to rapid economic growth and convergence are not likely to be fulfilled. Regional transfers taking place under the structural and cohesion policies are just that, transfers. To achieve long-term growth at rates higher than average, an appropriate mix of the policies described in the second, third, fifth, and sixth points above seems to be needed.

Eighth, in the light of their very secondary effect on long-term growth and of the particularly acute political tensions their availability and allocation create among current members, one should reconsider the very existence of regional Structural Funds within the enlarged EU. This also applies, with stronger force, to the funding of the CAP. Theory and evidence show that Structural Funds are pure income transfers with few positive long-term effects. The availability of such transfers generates two very negative effects. First, it leads to rent-seeking behavior on the part of poorer regions that want such funds. It also creates rent-seeking coalitions of the "half-poor" against the "even poorer" or the "very rich," giving rise to spurious coalitions whose only objective is to increase the amount of transfers accruing to one particular region or country. Both activities cloud the political discourse and, as in the case of the current enlargement, create artificial and purely redistributive obstacles to otherwise valuable and efficiency-enhancing political decisions. Second, it leads to inefficient allocation of resources within regions that are the beneficiaries of such transfers. All the microeconomic and anecdotal evidence available shows that a large share of Structural Fund resources are wasted in the lobbying and advocacy of projects. Many projects, either public or private, that would not have been financed under normal competitive conditions are financed by Structural Funds simply because the latter are tied to a certain area. This leads to a suboptimal allocation of regional labor, capital, and entrepreneurial resources and to a self-perpetuating system of expectations in which below-average income levels are almost "sought" by the regional administrations as a conduit for additional structural funding. In the long run, both of these effects lead to the misallocation of resources, corruption, underground activities, and lack of sustained growth that characterize the Mezzogiorno. This is bad for growth and most definitely does not help economic convergence. Structural Funds should be phased out over the next EU budget cycle (2006–12). The Cohesion Fund, whose objective has been achieved with the successful establishment of the euro, should be terminated at the end of the current spending cycle (2006). Short of this, the recommendations listed in the second part of the Assessment of Regional Policies in the Enlargement Process should be followed.

Appendix A—Data Sources

The majority of the data used in this study come from International Monetary Fund's International Finance Statistics. Data for investments, savings, FDI, depreciation, government deficits, employment, unemployment, population, the consumer price index, nominal wages, and nominal GDP are all taken from that database. Discrepancies and incoherencies are checked against the OECD Main Economic Indicator data bank and integrated when needed.

Data for GDP in PPS relative to the EU come from Funck and Pizzati (2002, p. 31). Regional data on GDP for CEECs is obtained from Eurostat (2000b, 2001d, 2002e).

Data for labor productivity are reconstructed by the authors using data on a labor productivity index provided in Martin, Velazquez, and Funck (2001) and labor productivity data contained in a number of Eurostat publications (2001c, 2002c).

Important information about FDI in candidate countries is obtained from Eurostat (2000a, 2002d).

Data for the EU are also obtained from a number of Eurostat publications. In particular, data on the investment rate come from Eurostat (2001a), those on employment from Eurostat (2002a), those on unemployment from Eurostat (2002b), and those on labor force participation from Eurostat (2001e).

GVA and employment by branch are constructed by the authors using the information contained in Eurostat (2001c, 2002c).

Notes

1. Spain would make a positive exception in this case. Since the beginning of the transition, and thanks mostly to the presence of four or five large private banks, the Spanish banking system has been much more advanced and its banks much larger than those of Spain's Mediterranean counterparts.

2. Romania is a clear outlier in this sector; see the chapter by Giurescu in Funck and Pizzati (2002) detailing the circumstances surrounding this phenomenon.

3. What we call "steady state" here and in what follows is, in reality, a growth path. It can be treated as a steady state, that is, as a fixed point of a stationary dynamic system, because we are normalizing everything by the (unknown) average long-term growth rate of the EU. It is relative to this unknown growth rate, whatever it may turn out to be, that the position we compute is a steady state.

4. These are all 14 Greek regions, 4 of the 5 Portuguese regions (Lisbon is excluded), and all 4 southern Spanish regions (Extremadura, Andalucia, Murcia, and Canarias).

5. We recall here that the asymptotic growth rate depends on the production function parameters, the discount factor, and the intertemporal elasticity of substitution in consumption. Hence, we are assuming that at least one of these parameters may vary across countries.

6. We refrain here from getting into the methodological, but unsubstantiated, other point advanced by de la Fuente, according to which, if one conditions by regional fixed effects, Structural Funds may turn out to have a positive impact. On the one hand, fixed-effect esti-

mates are inappropriate with heterogeneous dynamics. On the other hand, at a more technical level, assume this did happen: regional fixed effects are catchall variables that may well hide the true determinants of convergence, and no conclusion could be reached without an explicit model and measurement of such regional fixed effects.

7. Ireland's public expenditure and taxes are slightly below 30 percent of GDP, while the EU average is about 42 percent.

Bibliography

The word *processed* describes informally reproduced works that may not be commonly available through libraries.

Arevalo, P. 2002. "Crecimiento y Convergencia en España y sus Regiones: 1960–2000." Ph.D. diss. Universidad Carlos III de Madrid, Spain.

Aslund, Anders, Peter Boone, and Simon Johnson. 2001. "Escaping the Under-Reform Trap." *IMF Staff Papers* 48:88–108.

Ben David. 1994. *Quarterly Journal of Economics.*

Boldrin, Michele, and Fabio Canova. 2001. "Inequality and Convergence: Reconsidering European Regional Policies." *Economic Policy* 32 (April):205–45.

Canova, Fabio, and Morten Ravn. 2000. "The Macroeconomic Effects of German Unification: Real Adjustment and the Welfare State." *Review of Economic Dynamics* 3(3):423–60.

Ederveen, Sief, Henri L. F de Groot, and Richard Nahuis. 2002. "Fertile Soil for Structural Funds? A Panel Data Analysis of the Conditional Effectiveness of European Cohesion Policy." Netherlands Bureau for Economic Policy Analysis, Amsterdam. Processed.

EU Commission. 1998. *Reform of Structural Fund.* Brussels.

European Council. 1999. "Presidency Conclusions, European Council, 24 and 25 March 1999." Available at http://www.inforegio.cec.eu.int.

Eurostat. 2000a. Statistics in Focus, Economic and Finance, Theme 2, "European Union FDI with Candidate Countries: An Overview." 26/2000.

———. 2000b. "Statistics in Focus, General Statistics, Theme 1, Regional GDP in Candidate Countries." 2/2000.

————. 2001a. "Free Data, General Statistics, Theme 1, Business Investment." 11/5/2001.

————. 2001b. "News Release, General Statistics, Key Data on the Candidate Countries." 129/2001.

————. 2001c. "Statistics in Focus, Economic and Finance, Theme 2, Value Added, Employment, Remuneration and Labor Productivity in the Candidate Countries." 13/2001.

————. 2001d. "Statistics in Focus, General Statistics, Theme 1, Regional GDP in Candidate Countries." 4/2001.

————. 2001e. "Statistics in Focus, General Statistics, Theme 1, Regional Labor Force in the EU: Recent Patterns and Future Perspectives." 2/2001.

————. 2001f. "Statistics in Focus, General Statistics, Theme 1, Regional Population Changes in Candidate Countries." 6/2001.

————. 2002a. "Free Data, General Statistics, Theme 1, Employment Rate-Total." 12/7/2002.

————. 2002b. "Free Data, General Statistics, Theme 1, Unemployment Rate-Total." 12/7/2002.

————. 2002c. "Statistics in Focus, Economic and Finance, Theme 2, Candidate Countries' National Accounts by Industry." 17/2002.

————. 2002d. "Statistics in Focus, Economic and Finance, Theme 2, the Evolution of FDI in Candidate Countries: Data 1995–2000." 3/2002.

————. 2002e. "Statistics in Focus, General Statistics, Theme 1, Regional GDP in Candidate Countries." 2/2002.

Franz, Wolfgang, and Viktor Steiner. 2000. "Wages in the East German Transition Process: Facts and Explanations." *German Economic Review* 1:241–70.

Funck, Bernard, and Lodovic Pizzati, eds. 2002. *Labor, Employment, and Social Policies in the EU Enlargement Process.* Washington, D.C.: World Bank.

Garibaldi, Pietro, Nada Mora, Ratna Sahay, and Jeromin Zettelmeyer. 2001. "What Moves Capital in Transition Economies." *IMF Staff Papers* 48:109–45.

IMF. 2001. "Special Issue on Transition Economies: How Much Progress?" IMF Staff Papers. Washington, D.C.

Jones, Ronald W. 2000. *Globalization and the Theory of Input Trade.* Cambridge, Mass.: MIT Press.

Marimon, Ramon, ed. 1996. "La Economía Española: una visión diferente." Universidad Pompeu Fabra, Barcelona, and Ministerio de Economía y Hacienda. Barcelona: Antoni Bosch.

Martin, Carmela, Francisco J. Velazquez, and Bernard Funck. 2001. "European Integration and Income Convergence: Lessons for Central and Eastern European Countries." World Bank Technical Paper 514. Washington, D.C. Processed.

Martin, Carmela, Jose A. Herce, Simon Sosvilla-Rivero, and Francisco J. Velazquez. 2002. "La Ampliación de la Unión Europea: Efectos sobre la economía Española." Colleción Estudios Economicos de la Caixa, No. 27.

Miles, David, and Andrew Scott. 2002. *Understanding the International Economy.* London School of Business, U.K.

OECD. 2000. Main Economic Indicators. Paris.

Ragnitz, Johachim. 2001. "Lagging Productivity in East German Economy: Obstacles to Fast Convergence." Institut für Wirtschaftsforschung, Halle, Germany. Processed.

Sinn, Hans A. 2000. "Germany's Economic Unification: An Assessment after Ten Years." NBER Working Paper 7586. Boston: National Bureau of Economic Research.

Tabellini, Guido. 2002. Principles of Policymaking in the European Union: An Economic Perspective. IGIER-Universita Bocconi, June. Milan, Italy. Processed.

Vaitilingam, Romesh, ed. 2002. "Who's Afraid of the Big Enlargement?" CEPR Policy Paper 7. London: Centre for Economic Policy Research.

World Bank. 2001a. *Employment and Labor Market in the Czech Republic.* Washington, D.C.

———. 2001b. *Poland's Labor Market.* Washington, D.C.

———. 2001c. *Transition: The First Ten Years.* Washington, D.C.

———. 2002. *Expenditure Policies toward EU Accession.* Washington, D.C.

CHAPTER 4

Discussion of "Regional Policies and EU Enlargement" by Boldrin and Canova, and "Public Policies and Economic Geography" by Martin

Carole Garnier

Each of the two chapters offers ample scope for debate. They will, however, be discussed jointly. This is no easy task since they start from very different theoretical views, namely the neoclassical and the new economic geography models. There may nevertheless be some advantages in a joint discussion. It may illustrate the dilemmas faced when considering long-term growth and convergence issues with a view to policy implications.

These dilemmas are worth summarizing briefly. Different views of the world are captured by different models based on different sets of assumptions. None of these views can be ruled out with any degree of certainty, not only because there are limitations in the data and in the methodologies used by the models presently available but also because researchers tend to focus on a single theory without attempting to integrate or at least compare alternative theories. These different views are supported by limited empirical evidence, which furthermore has often no clear link with policy guidelines. When, nevertheless, strong policy statements are made—as is the case here—they may entail divergent policy recommendations.

For ease of presentation, I shall follow the structure of the Boldrin and Canova chapter. The initial conditions and growth prospects of the Central and Eastern European countries (CEECs) will first be briefly discussed. Then consideration will be given to real convergence issues and policy recommendations, starting with what the authors consider as lessons from the past before turning to their policy suggestions for the future. It is in this policy-oriented part that the work of Martin, which does not touch upon enlargement issues, will be discussed.

Initial Conditions and Growth Perspectives in the CEECs

There would be no point in discussing the purely descriptive analysis of the evolu-tion over the past decade of some main aggregate indicators. More open to debate would be an analysis of the underlying explanatory factors and of their likely impact on future performance. But this goes well beyond the scope of this chapter and may explain why, contrary to expectations, there are no obvious links between the pre-sentation of the CEECs' situation, as a whole and individually; their growth per-spectives; and the policy recommendations that are formulated later.

Of interest to a discussion are the future growth prospects of the CEECs, taking into account the effects of enlargement. This forward-looking question is answered through a backward-looking approach. Three scenarios are proposed. First, the "no-change" scenario projects the behavior observed in the period 1991–2000. This benchmark is highly debatable since it includes the recession that has followed the transition to a market economy. Starting from 1994, when most countries had man-aged to recover positive growth rates, would significantly alter the results and call into question the authors' opinion that the CEECs' position compared with that of the European Union (EU) 15 is no different than it was a decade ago. From 1994 to 2000, the CEECs have achieved a positive growth differential vis-à-vis the EU15. This does not imply that the 1994–2000 period would be an ideal benchmark. It would indeed be difficult to distinguish between the countries with high but transi-tional growth and those initiating a more sustainable growth trajectory. What needs to be pointed out is that the very specific context of transition that is downplayed in the chapter does not allow for a "trend" methodology.

Caution is also required with regard to the other two scenarios. They are based on the claim that candidate countries are similar to the three southern countries, Greece, Portugal, and Spain. The second scenario assumes convergence of the CEECs in a probabilistic sense to the same steady-state level and the third a similar boost in growth rates after accession. The second scenario is driven by the initial pre-diction of absolute convergence of the neoclassical theory, a prediction considered implausible since the mid-1990s, when the possibility of having only conditional convergence, because of differences in fundamentals between economies, gathered support. The third scenario has no articulated theoretical point of view. In both cases, applying to each of the CEECs—regardless of their initial conditions, specificities, and potential—the same constrained "level or growth effect" leads to a biased con-vergence toward the mean. The best performers do worse after accession, the worst performers better. Such an exercise adds little to the understanding of the growth potential and patterns of countries that are rightly acknowledged as being very dif-ferent. Nor does it give much insight into their potential evolution as a whole com-pared with that of the EU15.

In both scenarios, a major problem is that the assumed similarity of the three southern countries is far from warranted. This is clearly demonstrated by the so-called index of similarities itself, used to justify the approach, which is restricted to four indicators. Just looking at the first indicator—openness—as an example, the difference is striking. Even at the time of accession in 1973, Ireland's degree of openness was a lot closer to that of the CEECs, while other indicators are not more dissimilar than those of southern countries—or than their average. Assuming convergence to the Irish steady-state level would have drastically changed the results. This does not mean that all CEECs would be expected to mimic the Irish performance. It simply indicates that the similarity assumption used in the approach is not robust enough for conclusions to be inferred. Beyond the lack of evidence from the index, the underlying assumption of similar transition patterns is rather dubious. The jump in unemployment in Spain from 1975 to 1985 (from some 3 percent to 21.6 percent) that is viewed as the effect of transition on the labor market is mainly the consequence of a very long and severe economic crisis, probably amplified by structural rigidities, resulting from the oil shock and world recession. Other major structural differences can be identified, for instance, in the product markets. The 1976 nationalization in Portugal basically froze the public sector until 1989, while the so-called state corporatism in Greece implied direct and indirect government interference in the running of private industry. In addition, though the authors claim that history matters and mention some differences in historical circumstances with earlier entrants, a crucial difference is ignored. There had been convergence between some CEECs and Western Europe until divergence set in after World War II. A country like Czechoslovakia had significantly higher gross domestic product (GDP) per capita growth rates than Western Europe in 1870–1913 and 1913–50 (more than double in the latter period). Even in 1950, its GDP per capita was much higher than those of Greece, Portugal, and Spain and close to that of Germany. Regaining positions may imply different patterns of catching up than those observed in countries that have started from initially low GDP per capita.

To give a more forward-looking dimension to this econometric exercise, an additional scenario that identifies the conditions and potential for catching up and exploits the full benefits of EU membership should be considered. Impulses to a growth model such as those stemming from further scope for trade and possibly foreign direct investment, the reallocation of resources to more productive sectors, the deepening of structural reforms, or a clearly focused investment strategy would be helpful in outlining a realistic growth path, given initial conditions and policy developments. The standard Solow growth accounting model with some adaptations would be a useful starting tool that could yield interesting insights.

Policy Lessons from the Past

As mentioned before, policy issues and recommendations are not considered in the light of the conditions and prospects of the CEECs but are based on what the authors call "old, useful lessons." These lessons are basically three and concern the respective impacts on convergence of trade integration/openness, the EU cohesion policy, and national policies.

Trade Integration/Openness

The impact of trade on long-term growth and convergence deserves discussion since the evidence remains somewhat mixed. While the benefits of trade at the aggregate level are generally accepted, their distribution is more controversial.

Nevertheless, strong and contrasting views are expressed by Boldrin and Canova, on the one hand, and Martin, on the other. Boldrin and Canova claim that the predictions of new growth/trade theory on agglomeration and divergence are rejected by the data and that openness is beneficial or at least neutral to poorer areas. Martin seems to endorse Krugman's views in stating that specialization and geographical concentration, though lower than in the United States, have increased in the EU15 over the past 20 years. Since labor mobility is low in the EU, increased disparities and even divergence would not be precluded.

These are strong statements given the evidence provided by the authors and that currently available.

Boldrin and Canova do not provide any data or empirical evidence. They list some examples of trade openness at national and international levels. Observing convergence during the same period, they conclude that causality runs from trade to convergence. The sensitivity of the issue would call for a more in-depth analysis together with some empirical grounding. Account should be taken of the other factors that influence convergence, of the possibility of reverse causation (that is, trade may be endogenous to the process of growth), and of scarce analysis on the impact of trade on poorer areas.

For instance, it cannot be asserted that increasing trade has led to convergence between the U.S. states, since the data on interstate trade are too scarce to isolate the contribution of the latter from the contributions of capital and labor mobility, central government intervention, or other factors. According to Kim (1997), who investigated regional specialization and convergence in the United States from 1840 to 1987, the decrease in GDP per capita disparities between the northern and southern states is linked to the shift from industry to services.

Mention is also made of trade integration and convergence among the initial six members of the European Economic Community. This relationship has mainly been investigated by Ben David (1996). He observes that in the six countries and more generally in countries that trade extensively with one another, convergence generally occurs simultaneously with the removal of trade barriers and its speed is higher than in other countries. He also acknowledges that the income gap in six of the European Free Trade Association members did not begin falling as obstacles to trade were removed in 1961 but later, and that there had been no regime of interstate trade barriers that had to be abolished when income convergence between the U.S. states resumed. He does not investigate as such the impact of trade on poorer areas. He thus concludes that trade policy is not the most important policy from a long-run-growth perspective and that investment in education and infrastructure, preservation of property rights, and other ingredients are needed to enable a country to enjoy the fruits of openness. One should also add that contrary to the authors' statement, convergence in the European Commission (EC) took place in the context of national transfers. Implicit interregional transfers were made through budget revenues and expenditures. In addition, the German scheme of explicit interregional fiscal equalization dates back to 1949/1950—that is, to the constitutional objective to broadly equalize living conditions. Specific regional policies were also implemented in the EC, for example in the Mezzogiorno since the early 1950s and in France (*aménagement du territoire*) since 1960. There were no EU cohesion policy transfers, but their small financial size compared with national redistribution, state aids, and regional policies should be kept in mind.

Thus, the only conclusions one can reach are those that have been evidenced by previous research. First, aggregate growth—such as the exceptional one experienced by the EC during the 1950s and 1960s—is beneficial to convergence, though the mechanisms implied have not been fully explained. Second, trade policy can contribute to growth but may not be the most important factor for long-run growth and convergence. Frank Barry, John Bradley, and Aoife Hannan (2001) have pointed out that "openness has been a feature of the Irish economy ever since the 1970s if not earlier and Irish performance over most of the 1960s–1970s and 1980s exemplified failure rather than success." Indeed, success came only in the 1990s, when Ireland also benefited from significant EU cohesion transfers.

Consistent with the new trade theory that assumes increasing returns, Martin finds some evidence of increasing agglomeration and geographical concentration, at least in the EU, in the empirical work initiated by Brühlart and Torstensson to test the new economic geography theory. It should be specified that agglomeration does not necessarily lead to divergence in the long run. The most recent models of the new economic geography suggest a possible evolution of the spatial patterns of activity that can be stylized via a U-shaped relationship between trade costs and agglomeration. With the lowering of trade costs, firms will tend to exploit economies of scale by concentrating production close to larger markets and to other firms, and concentration will develop endogenously. When trade costs tend to disappear, higher wage costs in agglomeration lead industries to disperse to regions where they can benefit from labor cost advantages.

As the empirical evidence to test the validity of the new economic geography theory was scarce, rather aggregated, and strongly focused on manufacturing, two studies were carried out for the EC. They arrive at similar conclusions and give a nuanced view of spatial evolutions at the country level in the EU15. Based on production data for 14 EU member states and 36 manufacturing industries between 1970 and 1997, the study by Midelfart-Knarvik and others (2000) shows decreasing specialization during the 1970s and a slow and uneven increase from the early 1980s.

Industries have experienced some changes in their spatial concentration. A number of industries initially dispersed have become more concentrated in southern Europe. These are mainly labor-intensive industries such as textiles, clothing, and leather. Among industries initially concentrated, about half remained so (for example, aircraft, motor vehicles). A number of medium- and high-technology industries with high skill intensities (for example, office machinery, televisions and communication, professional instruments) have spread out from the central EU, to the benefit of Ireland, Finland, and southern countries. The most concentrated services—financial, insurance, real estate, and business services—have also become less concentrated over time.

EU Cohesion Policy

Boldrin and Canova claim that the EU cohesion policy has had no impact on long-term growth and convergence. This is a very strong statement since EU cofinancing assistance is granted for specific investment purposes and inserted into a complex system of monitoring, evaluation, and control, ensuring that it is spent according to targets. However, one cannot find arguments or empirical evidence to support their claims. The authors refer to some econometric work presented in a previous paper (2001). In this paper, two econometric exercises are reported. In the first, which looks for indirect evidence regarding the impact of cohesion support, β convergence-type regressions are run using data for either 101 or 185 NUTS 2 regions for the period 1980–96. The results are mixed. However, they indicate some convergence in labor productivity. Such types of regressions have numerous methodological weaknesses, which have been highlighted in the literature. Reviewing some of the numerous existing econometric studies, Ederveen and others (2002), who argue that government failures reduce the positive effect of cohesion support, stress a main criticism, the lack of data. Researchers draw different conclusions from different data, time periods, and methodologies. In addition, in this specific case, the period retained is too short to adequately encapsulate both the long-term dimension of convergence and the impact of the Structural Funds. It is only at the end of the 1980s that the latter were given an efficiency-oriented design and less negligible financial means. Furthermore, because of their targets (investments in infrastructure, education, and so forth), their impact on the supply side of the economy takes time to materialize. But even more important, no link can be established between the cohesion policy and the convergence results of the simple regression methodology used. The impact of the former can be identified only by comparison to a counterfactual situation. This implies the use of models that are at least able to capture the factors that appear constantly in the academic literature as being important in explaining the process of growth as well as the channels via which it can be affected by Structural Funds and also account for their interactions. Obviously, no structural model of growth can be presented by a single equation with two variables. For this reason, the second econometric exercise intended to directly measure the impact of cohesion policy on regional convergence does not throw more light onto the subject. The authors run a simple univariate regression attempting to explicitly link indexes of regional productivity to a portion (limited to the European Regional Development Fund) of the Structural Funds received. Since the regression is not picking up other explanatory variables and since a negative correlation is to be expected between Structural Funds amounts and low productivity growth, the former are likely to act in such a regression as an indicator for low productivity growth. Funds are flowing to predominantly rural/agrarian regions, which may show low productivity growth due to low technology spillovers compared with regions with larger industrial sectors.

The econometric exercise can give no insight into the impact of the EU cohesion policy on regional growth and convergence. More surprising is the fact that the issue of its impact on national growth and convergence is fully ignored. Data are more readily available at the national level, and more sophisticated methodologies can be used. In addition, the authors repeatedly express the view that the NUTS 2 territorial units, which reflect the member states' subnational institutional divisions (for example, *länders,* Communidades Autonomas, regions), are not suitable targets for convergence, which would be more adequately assessed at a higher territorial level. Silence on this point may be explained by general agreement on the positive contribution of the Structural Funds to national convergence. Even if one excludes the impressive performance of Ireland, the GDP per capita of the three cohesion countries (Greece, Portugal, Spain) compared with the EU15 average, which stood at 68 percent in 1988, has increased to 79 percent. The contribution of the Structural Funds assessed with the help of two models with different specifications, including an explicit supply side—Hermin and Quest—is positive and significant, as reported in the Commission's (2001) publication. In addition, and contrary to Boldrin and Canova's assertion, the EU transfers may have had a positive effect on the profile of convergence in a long-term perspective. Unlike what the neoclassical theory would predict—that is, faster growth while GDP levels are still low, and then a slowdown in convergence—the patterns of convergence in Spain and Portugal since 1960 (with GDP per capita increasing respectively from 59.2 percent and 40.6 percent of the EU average to some 82 percent and 74.3 percent in 2001)[1] seem rather linear and are even reversed for Ireland.

National Policies

One can only agree with the assertion that national policies are crucial for long-term growth and convergence. Indeed, the effectiveness of the Structural Funds is likely to be limited if they are inserted into a context that is not conducive to growth.

However, there are two points worth discussing in Boldrin and Canova. First, proactive regional policies, focused on improving knowledge and factors of production, should not be confused with implicit and unconditional interregional transfers. Out of the average DM 180 billion per year gross transfers to eastern Germany in the second half of the 1990s, only about DM 30 billion was investment. Similarly, gross capital formation has represented a limited part of the transfers to the Mezzogiorno, which took the form mainly of welfare payments and a high level of public employment. In 1988, support provided by the public sector in the form of public employees' salaries and transfers to households amounted to 49 percent of southern GDP and gross fixed capital formation to 6 percent. Because of budget consolidation, central and local government current and capital expenditures have decreased since the early 1990s.

Second, among the range of national policies that can influence convergence, macroeconomic stability should be more emphasized, as it seems to play a strong role. This can be illustrated by many examples. At the EC level, the 1960s and early 1970s were periods of exceptionally high growth and low inflation. Convergence occurred. After the two oil shocks in the 1970s, macroeconomic conditions deteriorated in terms of inflation and budgetary positions, especially in the cohesion countries, and so did convergence. At the individual country level, Ireland's GDP per capita compared with the EU average was not much different at the end of the 1980s than in 1960. High convergence set in when an economic policy combining stable public finances and a new approach to industrial relations leading to wage moderation was implemented. Conversely, after a phase of unbalanced policy mix and income divergence in the 1980s, Greece displayed a positive growth differential vis-à-vis the EU from 1996, when a stability-oriented policy was implemented to fulfill the criteria for participation in the European Monetary Union. Macroeconomic stability may not be a sufficient condition for growth and convergence, but it would seem to be a prerequisite.

Recommendations for the EU Cohesion Policy

The description of the EU cohesion policy that is provided does not allow for a clear understanding of the facts, a necessary step before formulating and discussing reform proposals. For instance, the revision of the Structural Funds in 1999 and their main features are overlooked; for example, objectives are only three since 2000; a performance reserve has been introduced; some of the Objective 1 regions have reached a GDP per capita higher than the 75 percent threshold and EU assistance is subsequently being phased out; and the geographical concentration of support has been increased. Eligibility for the Cohesion Fund has been based since its creation on *gross national product* and not *gross domestic product*. This is why Ireland is a beneficiary. In many cases, the assertions are not in line with reality. The EU assistance cannot be assimilated into income maintenance programs. EU budgetary transfers are distributive, as they are made to the less wealthy. But spending is allocative, as it is tied to specific investments. Financial and physical outputs are monitored and controlled. The principle of additionality, which entails verification, is neglected. The claim that convergence at the NUTS 3 level is an objective of the policy is unfounded. It has never been. Subsequently, no attempt to assess convergence at this territorial level has ever been made in the Commission's reports and evaluations.

Nevertheless, a few reforms are suggested. These basically touch on two main issues: the criterion and territorial level for assistance, and the forms of assistance.

Who Should Benefit?

The territorial level—national or regional—to be targeted in terms of both eligibility and long-term growth strategy is a recurrent issue, raised in the Commission's second cohesion report (2001), which launched a debate on the future of the cohesion policy post-2006. It is of special relevance to the CEECs that display stronger income disparities at the national than at the regional level.

The suggestions made by Boldrin and Canova are not fully clear and contain contradictions. While they start advocating convergence at the country level, they end up with two proposals targeted at the regional level: funding only regions that are federal units—a proposal that targets the constitutions of member states but has little relevance from an economic development perspective—and lowering the threshold in the definition of disadvantaged regions. Only the latter, reduced to 50 percent of the presumably current EU average to ensure concentration of the financial means on the very poorest, is fully clear. Since there is no empirical evidence of higher returns in the extremely poor regions, such predominance given to equity is surprising in a chapter that criticizes at length the equity-oriented policies pursued in the Mezzogiorno and eastern Germany. Efficiency considerations could point to an opposite approach, as outlined by Martin. He shows that national convergence in the EU15 has been accompanied by generally increasing regional disparities within countries and thus finds evidence of the importance of efficiency gains due to agglomeration. There is indeed some evidence that catching-up countries enjoying high national growth often see a widening of interregional disparities, as national growth tends to be driven by growth poles effects that emerge in capital cities and other major agglomerations. This has been the case in Ireland and Spain, while Greece has until the mid-1990s experienced low growth and a fall in regional dispersion.[2] Thus, in the early stages of the catching-up process there may be a potential trade-off between national and regional convergence. Efficiency would ultimately lead to focusing public investment on the regions with the highest potential rather than on the most backward ones. At the least, an appropriate balance has to be found between equity and efficiency, and this may be best ensured in catching-up countries by an approach and strategy for economic development at the national level. Any extreme policy recommendation, such as depriving the relatively less poor regions of poor countries of EU support, can be misleading, as it may not improve economic development and convergence very much.

What Should Be Financed?

While Martin expresses doubts about the effectiveness of state aids to attract and develop enterprises in less favored regions, Boldrin and Canova take a more "institutional" view of the issue. They distinguish between large-scale projects related to industrial and agricultural restructuring, which could be financed by the EU, and support to small and medium enterprises, which should be the task of national governments. It would indeed be difficult to find any empirical evidence that state aids have been instrumental in fostering regional development, as exemplified by the Mezzogiorno and eastern Germany experiences. Such aids have important dead-weight effects. However, regional state aids represent only some 14 percent of total state aids in the EU15, which means that the regional component has to be tackled in a wider context. This is why a coordinated stance committing member states to a downward trend is being implemented at the EU level. Total state aids have thus decreased by 12 percent from 1995/1997 to 1997/1999, and aids to manufacturing from 35.8 to 27.6 billion.

Boldrin and Canova recommend concentrating funds on "public goods" understood as different types of infrastructure, including transport infrastructure. However, as highlighted by de la Fuente, the productivity effects of infrastructure investment have been the subject of an economic debate that is still ongoing. Martin insists on reducing transaction costs on exchanges of "ideas" and calls for caution in supporting transport infrastructure, as it may be detrimental to less favored regions (for example, Mezzogiorno). He acknowledges, however, that public infrastructure may have very different effects depending on the region concerned. Indeed, the available empirical evidence would hardly support Martin's views. For instance, several analyses find that infrastructure has had a positive and highly significant effect on regional growth and convergence in Italy. There is some evidence that the construction of highways in some California counties and U.S. states has even been detrimental to the others. The only conclusion is that the context is important. No one could imagine that growth and catching up would take place without infrastructure. But infrastructure per se is not a panacea and may not necessarily lead to growth.

Finally, the types of intervention financed by the EU cohesion policy appear to be rather consensual. Caution may be advocated in some cases, and the weight to be given to the different components of the investment mix may differ (for instance, both Martin and Boldrin and Canova seem to put less emphasis on human capital), but except for the cofinancing of state aids to the corporate sector, no drastic change is advocated concerning the basic ingredients of the policy.

To conclude, the main lesson I would like to draw is one of modesty. It would certainly be convenient if an economic process as complex as growth could be captured by one or a few variables. Unfortunately, this is not possible. A growth policy implies a mix of ingredients ranging from national policies for macroeconomic stability and a smooth functioning of markets to improvements in factors of production and access to knowledge. The specific mix to be implemented is a function of each particular situation. Each experience of growth is unique. Overlooking such diversity or giving predominance to one factor while ignoring the others is likely to lead to misleading policy suggestions.

Notes

The views expressed are those of the author and do not necessarily reflect those of the European Commission.

1. These changes occurred despite relatively reduced convergence in Spain in the 1980s compared to the previous decade, where GDP per capita had even peaked at some 79.5 percent of the EU average in 1975 and 1976.

2. For a more complete discussion of the issue based on available data, see *The EU Economy 2000 Review* (European Commission 2000).

Bibliography

The word *processed* describes informally produced works that may not be commonly available through libraries.

Barry, Frank, John Bradley, and Aoife Hannan. 2001. "The Single Market, the Structural Funds and Ireland's Recent Economic Growth." *Journal of Common Market Studies* 39(3):537–52.

Ben David, 1996. *Technological Convergence and International Trade.* Foerder Institute for Economic Research Working Paper 4196. Tel Aviv University.

Boldrin, Michele, and Fabio Canova. 2001. "Inequality and Convergence: Reconsidering European Regional Policies." *Economic Policy* 32:205–53.

Ederveen and others. 2002. "Does European Cohesion Policy Reduce Regional Disparities? An Empirical Analysis." Netherlands Bureau for Economic Policy Analysis, The Hague. Processed.

Ederveen, Sief, Joeri Gorter, and Richard Nahuis. "The Wealth of Regions: The Impact of Structural Funds on Convergence in the EU." Netherlands Bureau for Economic Policy Analysis, The Hague. Processed.

European Commission. 2000. *The EU Economy 2000 Review.* Luxembourg: Official Publications Office.

————. 2001. *Second Report on Social and Economic Cohesion.* Luxembourg: Official Publications Office.

Kim, Sukkoo. 1997. *Economic Integration and Convergence: U.S. Regions, 1840–1987.* NBER Working Paper 6335. Boston, Mass.: National Bureau of Economic Research.

Midelfart-Knarvik, K. H., H. Overman, S. Reading, and A. Venables. 2000. *The Location of European Industry.* Economic Papers 142. Luxembourg: European Commission.

CHAPTER 5

Issues and Constraints of Regional Convergence

Alfred Steinherr

I really like de la Fuente's work, but I cannot believe the results in his chapter despite his very reasonable and extremely good points. I am not convinced by his argument that regional policies produce a dramatic increase in investment and, therefore, employment has very high returns, up to 40 percent.

We saw already in previous chapters that in a way economics stacks the cards against that result simply because, as we have seen, there are missed externalities and scale economies for investments outside of the established centers. In poorer areas one cannot expect to achieve social rates of return of 40 percent. Second, statistics is also a bit of a problem because the way regions are defined is problematic and gives a very unclear picture.

Let us think about what regional policy based on transfers could achieve. What are the effects a study may wish to capture? First there could be a financial constraint for the entire economy so that national savings are not sufficient and there could be limited access to foreign borrowing. I do not think that any member of the European Union (EU), given that we now have a very large and relatively efficient EU capital market, faces such an overall macroeconomic constraint. Let us therefore put that argument aside. Second there could be a microeconomic constraint. There may be projects that do not find financing. While I can think of many projects that are so unattractive that they will not find any financing, I have difficulty identifying projects that are economically sound but cannot find the resources in Europe for financing.

I think we need to comb through projects in poorer regions and identify those that would not have been executed without transfer payments from the European regional aid program.

Of course, regional funds add to the money a country has at its disposal. They may have induced effects, which Antoni Castells' and Marta Espasa's chapter takes into account. For instance, if a good project would not have needed the subsidy, the rate of profit is increased and the recipient institution may increase its overall investment—but not necessarily in the poor region concerned. So there could be an induced effect in the form of more investment, but this may result in overinvestment. More is not always a good thing. I think there is an optimum that is determined by the standard marginal conditions.

That approach is therefore, in a way, misleading. What is not shown is which projects would have been crowded out had these funds not been available. There is no support for contentions that good projects in Europe sometimes cannot be carried out because financing is lacking.

Now I want to discuss the statistical problems that arise in the application of European regional policy.

In order to make regional policy operational, the Commission has made an attempt to classify regions. Its general geostatistical plan is known as the Nomenclature des Unités Territoriales Statistiques (NUTS) classification, and there are different levels of refinement. The NUTS level that is mostly used for European regional policy—NUTS 2—refers to the provincial or county level, such as the French Régions or the German Regierungsberzirke.

Map 5-1—which I borrowed from the sixth periodic report on the regions—shows the variation in the standard of living among these regions. The darker the region, the wealthier it is. Clearly, there are five large problematic zones:

1. Virtually all the regions in Greece

2. The Mezzogiorno in Italy

3. Most of the regions in Portugal and southern Spain

4. The most northern regions of Europe

5. Regions in East Germany.

The geographical distribution of unemployment very much reinforces this pattern.

The Commission has prioritized the affected regions and labeled them Objective 1 areas. From a technical point of view, Objective 1 concerns in general those NUTS 2 regions with a per capita income lower than 75 percent of the EU average (there are, admittedly, a few exceptions to this rule). In map 5-2 they are the dark

MAP 5-1 GDP PER HEAD BY REGION (PPS), 1996

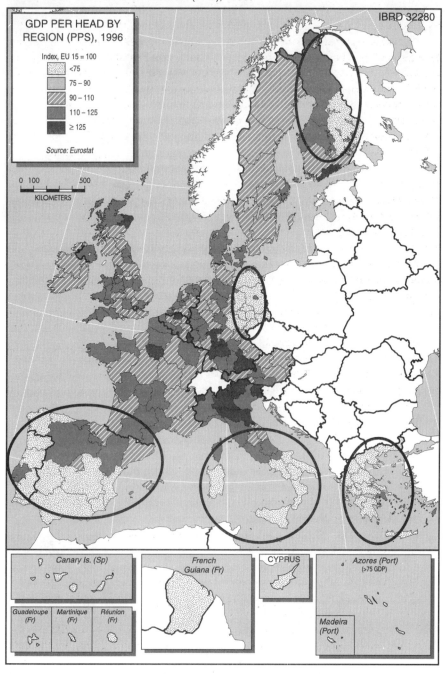

GDP PER HEAD BY
REGION (PPS), 1996

Index, EU 15 = 100

- <75
- 75 – 90
- 90 – 110
- 110 – 125
- ≥ 125

Source: Eurostat

IBRD 32280

0   100   500
KILOMETERS

Canary Is. (Sp)

French
Guiana (Fr)

CYPRUS

Azores (Port)
(>75 GDP)

Guadeloupe
(Fr)

Martinique
(Fr)

Réunion
(Fr)

Madeira
(Port)

MAP 5-2 OBJECTIVE 1 AREAS

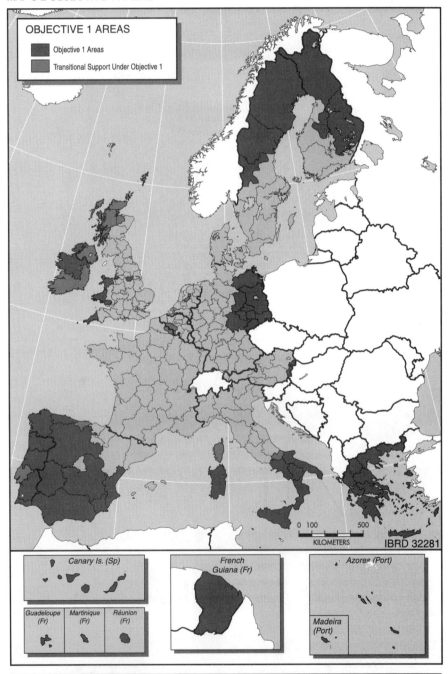

OBJECTIVE 1 AREAS

Objective 1 Areas

Transitional Support Under Objective 1

Canary Is. (Sp)

French Guiana (Fr)

Azores (Port)

Guadeloupe (Fr)   Martinique (Fr)   Réunion (Fr)

Madeira (Port)

IBRD 32281

0   100   500
KILOMETERS

zones; they coincide very well with the peripheral areas from map 5.1. It is precisely these areas that are eligible for the major share of regional development aid.

The core part of the EU also shows substantial differences in the degree of economic development. Just compare, for instance, the per capita income:

- Of Île de France versus the north of France

- Of Inner London versus the northern United Kingdom

- Of Flanders versus Wallonia in Belgium.

Perhaps it is useful to reflect for a moment on what level of inequality we are willing to accept. Indeed, the size of regional imbalances has to be put into perspective. Table 5-1 presents the level of disparities *between* the NUTS 2 levels in countries. The United Kingdom has the widest spread between its average per capita incomes among the NUTS 2 regions, Sweden the least. In the right-hand part of the table I have computed the same measure for the dispersion *within* the NUTS 2 areas. From this perspective, France has experienced the highest level of imbalances (in the region

TABLE 5-1 MAXIMUM PER CAPITA INCOME/MINIMUM PER CAPITA INCOME
(purchasing power parity)

	Between		*Within*		
	NUTS 2		*NUTS 2*		
			Most unequal		*Least unequal*
Country			*NUTS 2 regions*		*NUTS 2 regions*
United Kingdom	3.16	3.62	Inner London	1.08	Cumbria
Germany	3.11	5.23	Reinhessen-Pf.	1.25	Gießen
Austria	2.33	2.24	Oberösterreich	1.16	Voralberg
Spain	1.82	1.58	Castilla-la-M.	1.07	Canarias
Netherlands	1.79	2.57	Gröningen	1.11	Gelderland
Finland	1.75	1.44	Uusimaa	1.04	Pohjois-Suomi
Greece	1.72	2.76	Dytiki Ellada	1.11	Sterea Ellada
Belgium	1.70	2.14	Antwerpen	1.20	Vl. Brabant
Portugal	1.46	2.89	Norte	1.91	Alentejo
France	1.35	6.53	Ile de Fr.	1.04	Alsace
Sweden	1.33	1.17	Östra Mellansv.	1.01	Sydsveirge

Source: Eurostat. 2003. "Regional Gross Domestic Product in the European Union 2000." Luxembourg.

surrounding Paris—Île de France), followed by Germany (the Reinhessen-Pfalz area) and the United Kingdom (Inner London). In fact, what this table suggests is that the level of imbalances in the standard of living are much higher—*yet far more accepted*—in large urban regions that include a major city than the inequalities that are found between larger geographical units.

It can hardly be said that little effort has been made to assist affected areas. For instance, every year, the Structural Funds spend approximately a third of the EU budget in these zones, and the European Investment Bank gives a similar amount of money in the form of loans and guarantees. The resources we are talking about represent more than half of what is produced within the entire Portuguese economy! At the same time, member states provide complementary fiscal resources for regional development. Unfortunately, it is difficult to give exact figures—regional policy is not an explicit item in the national accounts—but the few figures I have seen seem to indicate that these expenditures are roughly 0.5 percent of gross domestic product (GDP). This would bring the annual total for regional policies to well above the Irish GDP (some 75 billion in 1998) (see figure 5-1), and this does not even take into account the many indirect efforts, such as tax advantages. Thus, regional development aid alone would be sufficient to guarantee that inhabitants of a small country would have a decent standard of living without ever having to work. But are these resources efficiently spent? After all, as I showed earlier, disparities are still substantial.

FIGURE 5-1 STRUCTURAL FUNDS
(percentage of EU budget)

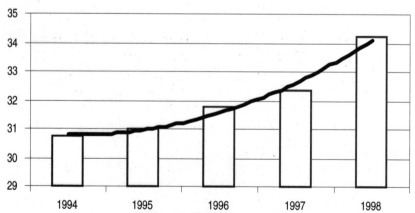

Note: EU budget is 1.12 percent of EU15 GDP, and as of 1998 Structural Funds reached 34.23 percent of EU budget. In addition, another 35.18 percent of EU budget (€25.5 bil) is allocated to EIB loans, of which 56.17 percent is for regional development.

Of course, the illustrations I started off with are nothing but static records and may hide the impact of regional policy. Let us, therefore, investigate the *evolution* of the dispersion.

Let us look at the distribution of relative regional GDP per capita in 1988 and 1996 (see figure 5-2). Clearly, the shape of the distribution has remained almost the same, and the small increase in the standard deviation can be attributed mainly to German unification. The aggregate picture thus seems to suggest that not much convergence has taken place among NUTS 2 regions.

FIGURE 5-2 DISTRIBUTION OF THE DEVIATION OF REGIONAL PER CAPITA INCOMES FROM THE EU AVERAGE

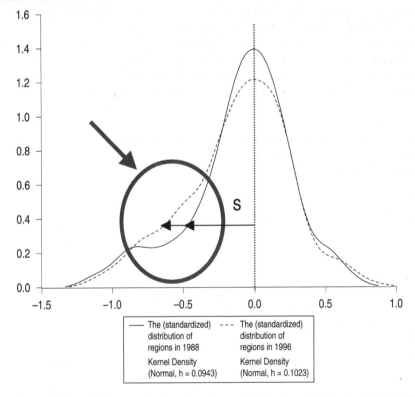

| —— The (standardized) distribution of regions in 1988 Kernel Density (Normal, h = 0.0943) | – – – The (standardized) distribution of regions in 1996 Kernel Density (Normal, h = 0.1023) |

Note: The y-axis indicates distribution, that is, the number of regions that fall under each deviation from the average GDP. The x-axis indicates the deviation of per capita GDP from the average. For example, 0.5 means it is 50 percent above average and –0.5 means it is 50 percent below average. S, circle, and arrows indicate the standard deviation.
Source: Author's calculations.

FIGURE 5-3 IMPORTANT "WITHIN" MOVEMENTS

Average yearly GDP growth rate, 1982–96

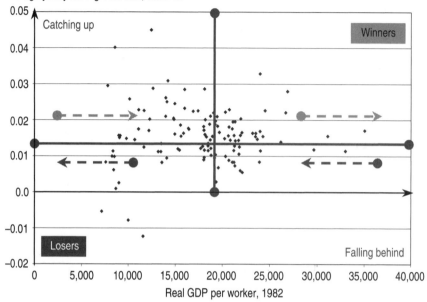

Real GDP per worker, 1982

Source: Author's calculations.

Yet to believe that productivity gaps are immutable is a mistake. Important "within movements" take place in the distributions, which I shall illustrate again with a graph (figure 5-3), showing a plot of the average annual growth performance against the initial income per capita in 1982. The horizontal and vertical lines in the middle represent the EU averages. It is easy to distinguish four zones. Convergence toward the EU average took place in the regions situated in the northwestern and southeastern parts of the chart. Regions that have been lagging further behind are in the lower right-hand portion. Some of these "within movements" may offset one another, which may explain the quite constant overall distribution.

But, in spite of this partial convergence, the pattern in the tails of the distribution has been remarkably stable. For instance, the 25 regions with the lowest unemployment rates have hardly changed over the past decade, with rates steady at around 4 percent. In the worst affected regions, by contrast, rates have climbed from as much as 20 percent to nearly 24 percent and—in some cases—are continuing to increase. So why are the goals not being met?

I do not think it would be fair to say that the EU does not try hard enough to address the problem, but two factors may prevent policies from achieving the desired result:

1. Market failures

2. Rigidities in the labor market.

Let us discuss market failures first. Imagine an economic paradise—a system in which economic agents behave rationally and production factors are freely mobile. To be more precise, capital and labor go to this paradise because returns there are the highest.

In such a perfect world, there are three factors that impair the working of the market in such a way that persistent economic imbalances may still prevail. I will clarify them briefly.

First, the market outcome is less than optimal when there are *substantial technological externalities.* By this I mean that firms learn from one another how to do things better through observation, casual conversations, and so forth. As a result, firms tend to locate in zones where there is already economic activity and a well-developed market, because in that way they benefit from investments by other agents without having to pay for the gains. Of course, companies will try to account for this externality in their location decisions, reasoning along the following lines: "If I move to that region and invest, I might give a competitive advantage to others, for which I cannot ask for remuneration. Perhaps it is better to stay put." Therefore, the market results in an outcome that further disfavors the lagging regions.

This brings me to the second market failure—*pecuniary externalities,* another academic term that requires explanation. As a result of the productivity differences among regions, both skilled workers and capital will tend to flow into the well-developed areas. However, firms and workers do not take into account the impact of their relocation on the well-being of those who stay put or those who live in the destination region. For instance, migration will put a downward pressure on the wage level in the destination region, while demand, and hence prices, will be boosted. The market may, in this case, lead to excessive imbalances.

The last market failure is a *coordination problem.* In some cases a region does not take off because a minimum threshold of economic activity has not been reached. No one knows how a business would perform in such an area, because too little price information is available. Lack of adequate information then prevents the development of a network of services and intermediate goods suppliers, so there is a vicious circle of persistent underdevelopment.

With these flaws operating, it may not be very straightforward to develop an effective regional policy, not least because it may not be very clear what the dominant market failure is. The least one can say is that an efficient regional program should be sufficiently tailored to the region-specific problem. By consequence, *not every region needs the same type of infrastructure* to get its growth engine going, and I think it is worth underlining this point. Moreover, the infrastructure—and regional policy in general—should help regions to develop their comparative advantages.

Thus, a regional policymaker must understand the externalities at play, and the policy should be *a function of the local comparative advantage.*

In fact, too loose a regional approach—one that is not sufficiently fine-tuned—might lead to perverse effects. I will illustrate this with an example. Suppose that a new highway is built between a relatively lagging region and an industrial region. Lower transportation costs will be an incentive for firms and skilled workers to move to the industrial region. In that way, their businesses can benefit from technological externalities, while the competitive price advantage associated with local production in the prehighway period is still maintainable because of the lower transport costs. Thus, the lagging region may become a net importer of goods. Of course, this does not necessarily mean that the living standard will go down. But, in the longer run, it may imply that unemployment rates will rise, especially if the relatively immobile unskilled workers become a dominant group in the local labor force and if—for whatever reason—they are unable to retrain themselves. Yet higher unemployment is the opposite of what the policymakers had in mind.

Discussing a low degree of labor mobility and skill differences leads me naturally to the second problem I mentioned earlier—rigidities in the labor market. As many people know, Europeans still have a tendency to stick to their geographical origins, despite substantial regional differences in the standard of living. Studies indicate that the degree of interregional labor mobility, for instance, is roughly only one-third of that in the United States (see table 5-2). Important reasons behind this phenomenon are an inflexible market for housing—that is, substantial costs for selling and buying due to high registration taxes and the like—and a lack of information on jobs elsewhere. Moreover, in a broader European context, language barriers contribute in an important way to the labor immobility.

TABLE 5-2 EUROPEAN VERSUS U.S. MOBILITY

Years	United States	Germany	Italy	United Kingdom
Percent of the regional population				
1970–79	1.20	0.27	0.37	0.47
1980–89	0.84	0.34	0.33	0.26
1990–95	0.87	0.31	0.40	0.20
Average net international migration				
Average	100	32	38	32

Source: Obstfeld and Pine, www.nber.org.

Now, limited labor mobility would not be too much of a concern if the unemployed were able to price themselves back into the labor market. However, wages in many European countries are often influenced by factors decided at the national level, such as wage bargaining between unions and employers, wage indexation, unemployment packages, or social security taxes. Such a system does not necessarily yield wages that are in line with the degree of labor productivity in every region. The result is that workers in poor regions—mainly relatively unskilled workers—are priced out of the market. In my view, this factor has played a tremendous role in the persistent unemployment rates in eastern Germany and the Mezzogiorno.

This story would not be complete without the buzzword "new economy." Will subsidizing "new technologies" lead to fewer regional imbalances? Even though such technologies are tremendously useful, their implementation may have undesired effects from a cohesion point of view given the current European setting. Let me explain this point.

The "new economy" may eliminate workplaces, especially among those less skilled, but it may at the same time create well-paid jobs for people with high human capital and information technology skills. Add to this the European tendency toward downwardly rigid wages and labor immobility. The new economy would then hold the potential to increase both unemployment and wage inequalities. In this respect, the recommendations of the Portugal summit may thus work against greater social cohesion.

But there is good news, too. I understand that new technologies also have the potential to reduce the need for regional migration. People will be able to work from home while being paid the salaries that prevail at headquarters. Given the three market failures mentioned above, this force might reduce the impact of pecuniary externalities. New technologies may thus reduce the level of imbalances.

It remains an open question whether new technologies can offset the annoying problem of failure of coordination, too. Some people argue that it does not matter where your main server is located if you are running an e-commerce business. I do not agree. If a region has no local network of services for equipment repair, legal and accounting services, food stores, and the like, and no flexible labor market for workers with the required skills, I would not be inclined to start my business in that region, not even in this "new economy" century.

CHAPTER 6

European Integration, Regional Policy, and the Nonintervention "Hands-off" Approach: Some Comments on the Boldrin and Canova Study

Jiří Blažek

The Boldrin and Canova study, "Regional Policies and EU Enlargement," covers a wide range of issues, provides a lot of empirical analysis, offers a wealth of opinions, and has several policy implications. My comments will be structured into three sections:

1. General comments on the fundamental assumptions of the authors' approach

2. Discussion of a few specific statements or policy recommendations

3. An attempt to provide some experience on regional development and regional policy in the Czech Republic in the European context.

General Comments on Fundamental Assumptions

The authors clearly adopt a neoclassical nonintervention approach and suggest contracting the public sector and removing the European Union (EU) regional policy because it is a costly, bureaucratic, and ineffective intervention.

I am not going to say that the neoclassical nonintervention model of management of economy is wrong and the competing model of social market economy[1]—now quite widespread in the EU countries—is right. The principal difference between the two is in their solution of a basic dilemma—the dilemma between the principle of solidarity and principle of meritocracy.

Neoclassical/neoconservative approaches (represented, for example, by F. Hayek or M. Friedman) stress individual responsibility and the principle of meritocracy, while the leftist or social democratic orientation (for example, J. M. Keynes, W. Molle, M. Castells, and D. Harvey) accent the role of the state and the principle of solidarity.

My personal belief is that there is a need to search for a proper balance between these principles and that any one-sided approach can do a lot of harm. (Consider, for example, the economic and moral crisis caused by the nonintervention approach of the conservative Czech government in the first half of the 1990s or the reasons leading to the resignation of M. Thatcher.) An important point is that in the economy and society there is frequently a trade-off between short-term and long-term efficiency and prosperity. Therefore, what might seem very efficient (or inefficient) in the short term might be highly inefficient (or efficient) over the long term. In addition, a one-sided stress on efficiency arguments might lead to monopolization of the economy and—due to loss of competitive pressure—to its gradual degeneration (see Hampl and others 1999).

The rationale for cohesion policies is based on both economic and social motives. The list of these arguments is quite extensive and ranges from improving efficiency by removing barriers to development and better utilizing resources to moderating inflation pressures by decentralizing economic activities from congested urban areas. As to social motives, Molle (1997) stresses that a huge inequality is morally unacceptable for large population groups.

However, in the postcommunist countries, there is at least one additional motive for cohesion policy. An insensitive approach to social and regional problems might lead to frustration in a sizable part of the population with limited opportunities and thus discredit not only the market economy but even the system of parliamentary democracy itself. This situation would have profound long-term consequences for the future development of these countries (as illustrated by the contrasts in public opinion on the acceptance of the former communist regime in Russia versus the countries of Central and Eastern Europe and the consequent differences in their political stability and their development trajectories). Moreover, in the case of regional policy implemented on the European level there are also other arguments in its favor, some of which are clearly of an economic nature (see also Molle 1997). So, why is there a regional policy on the level of the EU? The main arguments can be summarized as follows:

1. The oldest argument for EU regional policy was directly connected with the formation of a larger market with more intensive competition. The first aim was to facilitate and coordinate the restructuring of old industries under conditions of stronger competition in a larger market.

2. A second goal was to eliminate the distortion of free competition by an equal approach toward the provision of subsidies to private firms in all member countries.

3. The weakest regions are located in the weakest states with the smallest potential to support these regions sufficiently.

4. Finally, and most important, creation of the EMU (European Monetary Union) requires that member states have a similar level of socioeconomic development and similar macroeconomic characteristics, as adaptive mechanisms in some countries or regions are very weak. This concerns especially the limited potential of adaptation via international migration within the EU and the negligible volume of the EU fiscal policy in relation to volumes allocated to national fiscal policies. The discrepancy between strong and unified monetary policy and weak EU fiscal policy is one of the principal threats to proper functioning of the EMU. (In addition, national fiscal policies are nearly uncoordinated—for example, there are different tax systems.) From this point of view, the EU regional/cohesion policy stipulates at least on a very limited scale the stabilization role of fiscal policy. In this context, however, one has to stress again that the overall volume allocated to cohesion policy (0.47 percent of EU gross domestic product [GDP]) is very small, especially when compared with the share allocated to redistributive policies within national fiscal policies or to the volume of international trade, which in some countries exceeds the GDP.

Boldrin and Canova's main conclusion is that the EU regional policy did not make any significant contribution toward growth and convergence. The problem with conclusions derived from these types of empirical analyses is that they do not compare the present situation with a situation in which regional policy had not been implemented at all. Only such a comparison—however difficult—would allow for drawing such conclusions.

In addition, there is a parallel with social policy. For example, one might say that social inequality has increased dramatically over the last decade in all transitional economies, so the social policy was ineffective—and therefore suggest abolishing it completely.

Moreover, regional policy can be and should be considered an intervention that helps prevent social problems (and hence saves expenditures on both active and passive labor market policy). In other words, regional policy, by stressing the enhancement of firms' competitive position operating in assisted regions (via elimination of infrastructure deficits, support for a productive environment, and human resource development) aims at eradication or at least moderation of the roots of the problems, not just at mitigation of their consequences.

Practical examples of this relation between regional and social policy are the structurally affected regions in transitional economies that were suddenly exposed to intensive competition in the European and global markets. Without national support policies, including regional policy and also preaccession support programs, especially Poland Hungary Aid for Restructuring the Economy (PHARE), a considerably higher number of people made redundant by radical restructuring of heavy industries—together with their families—would fall into poverty, with related implications for social marginalization. The experience from cities in both Western Europe and the United States shows what a tremendous challenge it is to fight urban problems when a vicious circle of social deprivation has been in operation for decades or even for generations. Intervening in the early stages of formation of this negative cumulative process is much more effective and efficient.

Finally, in the case of implementation of cohesion policy there are also important benefits of a "nonfinancial" nature, such as inducing institutional changes, demonstrating new support mechanisms, and creating partnerships among relevant subjects of local and regional development.

Discussion of Specific Statements and Policy Recommendations

The authors argue that a combination of initial conditions, factors endowments, and most important, national policies seems to determine country-specific steady states or growth paths to which individual countries converge. Therefore, they do admit the importance of the state's role. The EU is much more than a free trade area and is (or until recently was) moving in the direction of a federal state, despite the fact that this word had to be erased from the Maastricht treaty. Consequently, if one accepts that the EU is "half" state, then there is a role for its policies.

I agree with the authors that there is a danger of creating a "dependency mentality" in countries or regions receiving support from the Cohesion Fund (CF) and the Structural Funds (SFs). But I would challenge their support for deemphasizing small and medium enterprises (SMEs) and attracting foreign direct investment (FDI). Attracting FDI usually means creating another type of dependency—dependency on someone else's know-how and decisions. Support of SMEs might mobilize countries' own initiatives.

In the sphere of policy implications, the authors put forward a number of less radical proposals along with abolishing EU regional policy completely. I agree with several of them.

I think everyone would agree with the need to simplify and debureaucratize EU cohesion policy, but in practice it is quite difficult to achieve consensus on such changes. For example, the increasing stress on evaluation of efficiency and effectiveness of EU cohesion policy as well as on promotion of public awareness of EU-funded projects is in fact increasing administrative burden. However, I can personally imagine, for example, that there could be only the Cohesion Fund and the number of SFs could be reduced to one, instead of four of them, each with different regulations. Or at least, if there are just two objectives of the EU cohesion policy beginning with the next budget cycle in 2007, the number of SFs could be cut to two.

Similarly, one can agree with larger territorial concentration of regional policy to the neediest regions (Objective 1), even though it is quite likely that some of the future members (Slovenia, Czech Republic) would soon completely or partially lose eligibility for Objective 1.

Several criticisms raised by the authors might be mitigated by an increase of volume of the Cohesion Fund and a corresponding cut of SFs, as the procedures for the CF are more straightforward; place more stress on large-scale projects with measurable effects; and place responsibility on central governments, which usually offer a better guarantee of efficient use of resources than do weak and in some countries newly established regional bodies. (This was already partially done for new members for the period 2004–06.)

I also agree with the authors that there is a danger of over-expectation that structural policies will solve the problems and lead to growth and convergence. At the very best, they can contribute to such goals by eliminating some deficits, demonstrating new approaches, and inducing some institutional changes, but each state must find its own way from a low-road to a high-road competitive strategy.

Recent Trends of Regional Development in the Czech Republic and Outlook for the Future

On the basis of an extensive analytical effort (for example, Bachtler, Downes, and Gorzelak 2000; Blažek 1999; Hampl 1999; Illner 2001), it can be concluded that the basis of regional development during the transition is vertical geographical position (that is, a qualitative hierarchy of regional centers). The role of vertical geographic position of cities and regions can be expected to continue as a dominant factor of regional development after the accession.

While a qualitative hierarchy of regional centers will most likely continue to be the basis of regional development in the future, a second significant factor can be identified: more profound differentiation on microregional and local levels (Blažek 1999). This will be a consequence of the formation of new spatial forms of regional development such as development axes, clusters, or even "nonspatial" networks. The creation of these new forms of spatial organization of production will depend especially on the local initiative of both the private and public sectors but also will be influenced by differences in the external conditions of particular regions and localities.

Therefore, the variation in local initiative—in combination with different starting conditions—will operate as a multiplier, stimulating more profound differentiation on the microregional level. Embryonic versions of these new spatial forms can be identified in the Czech Republic. The spatial agglomeration of some of the suppliers for Škoda Auto in and near Mladá Boleslav is an example of such a cluster. An example of a nonspatial network might be the association of eight Czech historical cities called "Czech Inspiration," which cooperate in the sphere of culture and attract tourism.

The significance of these new forms will increase in the future, especially within the framework of the integration process, by the widespread use of modern communication technologies and by people's growing geographic mobility, facilitated by the construction of new infrastructure. All these changes will enhance the opportunities for cooperation. The ability of local subjects to form or join these new organizational structures will significantly influence their future development. While development axes or clusters will be based locally, they will be more and more connected to (or even integrated into) international structures (Blažek 2002).

From the policy perspective, it should be stressed that a vital asset in the formation of these new spatial forms will be the quality of human resources, including the ability to cooperate and the formation of an atmosphere of commitment, professionalism, and optimism (see Hirschman 1958; Krugman 1991). These assets are in principle nonmobile and are almost exclusively dependent on bottom-up approaches (see also Malmberg 1997). Thus new space opens up for local and regional development strategies, which until now have been one-sidedly oriented on the construction of technical infrastructure in the Czech Republic.

Policy Implications

The main driving force in the sphere of Czech regional policy is preparation for the EU policy of economic and social cohesion (Blažek and Boeckhout 2000). The following paragraphs provide a critical assessment of the current state of the art in the key spheres of preparation for EU cohesion policy.

In the sphere of regional policy, the Czech Republic has recently made several important steps. In the institutional sphere, the coordination and implementation structures were strengthened, for example, by establishing 14 self-governing regions, forming management and monitoring structures on the level of cohesion regions (NUTS 2). The first generation of programming documents has been drafted and approved or acknowledged by the government, a new legislative framework for regional policy has been developed (Regional Development Act No. 248/2000), and the volume of financial resources has increased due to state-support regional development programs for the two most affected regions (Northwest Bohemia and Ostravsko NUTS 2 regions). Moreover, these new regional programs are more integrated than most other support programs.

However, despite these positive changes, Czech regional policy is still highly fragmented into an array of small programs and still departs significantly from the EU cohesion policy. Table 6-1 compares the main differences between the Czech and the EU regional policies.

TABLE 6-1 THE MAIN DIFFERENCES BETWEEN THE CZECH REGIONAL POLICY AND THE EU COHESION POLICY

Sphere	Czech regional policy	EU cohesion policy	Remarks on Czech policy
Programming	Czech Republic until recently without programming documents, now "over-programming" (two sets of programming documents—one for Czech regional policy; the other for EU cohesion policy), standard programs, low invention, top-down motivation for drafting programming documents	Already the third generation of programming documents	Excessive emphasis on analytical part, weak strategic part, no consideration of alternatives
Implementation structure	Prevailing sectoral approach	Different systems	
Integrity of approach	Narrow concept of regional policy and insufficient coordination with other policies	Integrated multi-sectoral approach	Progress recently, especially "regionalization" of sectoral policies and implementation of more integrated state support programs for affected regions
Incentives of regional policy	Limited spectrum of incentives	Wide spectrum of incentives	Regional Development Act is consistent with the EU principles
Size of projects	Prevailing small projects	Prevailing large projects	
Selection of projects	Problems with transparency	Clear separation of management, monitoring, and control functions	
Evaluation of efficiency and effectiveness	Weak tradition, performed infrequently and ad hoc	Systematic attention and pressure for further enhancement	Chance posed by preparation of the monitoring system for Structural Funds
Partnership	Weak tradition, especially in the case of projects on supramunicipal level	Different practice	
Involvement of private sector	Low participation of private sector in preparation for and limited awareness about cohesion policy	Strong role, often significant initiative	

(continued)

TABLE 6-1 THE MAIN DIFFERENCES BETWEEN THE CZECH REGIONAL POLICY
AND THE EU COHESION POLICY (*continued*)

Sphere	Czech regional policy	EU cohesion policy	Remarks on Czech policy
Public administration	Huge instability (14 new regions, planned dissolution of districts and creation of smaller districts in 2003, large horizontal fragmentation of local government and unprecedented instability of their financing systems)	Different systems	Serious disadvantage given large expected role of regions, towns, and municipalities
Volume of financial resources	Small but increasing	Many times higher	

Source: Blažek 2002.

The Future

The forthcoming accession has several immediate implications for reorientation of the Czech regional policy. Specifically, by the time of accession into the EU the very relevance of the existing Czech regional policy would be in question. The primary task of national regional policy should be to eliminate the leverage effect of support from the SFs in the form of matching grants, as subjects from poorer regions would not be able to provide sufficient financial resources for cofinancing of eligible projects. Therefore, the Czech regional policy might provide, for example, an additional 15 percent cofinancing of projects implemented in the neediest regions so that local subjects would be able to obtain support from SFs.

The reorientation of national regional policy toward the EU cohesion policy would also require a change in its time horizon, from the current annual programs to a multiyear approach. The Czech Republic is also missing an evaluation culture to guarantee effective and efficient use of public resources, not only in the sphere of regional policy but also in the public sector in general. In addition to these mostly technical changes of national regional policy, conceptual questions must be addressed.

One of the big challenges facing future EU members is a gradual switch from a low-road to a high-road strategy of competitiveness (see also Porter 1999). The current advantage of low costs does not offer a sound basis for catching up with the West. Therefore, for example, the current emphasis of state policy for internal investors should be refocused from traditional investment incentives, first to aftercare programs aimed at maximizing the positive effects of existing foreign investments and second to improving the structure of incoming FDIs toward the industrial branches with higher added value and more sophisticated production requiring high-quality human capital. The immediate goal should not necessarily be high-tech industries, but medium-tech would be a good start (including service or customer software centers and audit or consultancy firms operating on a global scale). Second, from a regional point of view, it would be desirable to promote more even spatial distribution of FDIs. Along with hard measures like the provision of adequate infrastructure, this promotion could take the form of soft measures, such as an application of the concepts of complex territorial marketing.

These changes would help the Czech Republic to switch from a low-road to a high-road competitiveness strategy and thus facilitate its real integration into the European economy.

Notes

1. The model of *social market economy* "seeks to combine a system of economic organization based on market forces, freedom of opportunity and enterprise with a commitment to the values of internal solidarity and mutual support which ensures open access for all members of society to services of general benefit and protection" (European Commission 1996, p. 13).

W. Molle (1997) defines *cohesion* as "the degree to which disparities in social and economic welfare between different regions or groups within the Community are politically and socially tolerable" (p. 429).

Bibliography

Bachtler, John, Ruth Downes, and Grzegorz Gorzelak, eds. 2000. *Transition, Cohesion and Regional Policy in Central and Eastern Europe.* London: Ashgate.

Blažek, Jiri. 1999. "Regional Development and Regional Policy in Central East European Countries in the Perspective of EU Enlargement." In M. Hampl, ed., *Geography of Societal Transformation in the Czech Republic.* Prague: Charles University, Faculty of Science.

———. 2002. "Regional Impacts of the Czech Accession into the EU: An Attempt of Qualitative Analysis." In M. Hampl, ed., *Regional Development: Specifics of the Czech Transformation, European Integration and a General Theory* (in Czech). Prague: Charles University, Faculty of Science.

Blažek, Jiri, and Sjaak Boeckhout. 2000. "Regional Policy in the Czech Republic and the EU Accession." In John Bachtler, Ruth Downes, and Grzegorz Gorzelak, eds. *Transition, Cohesion and Regional Policy in Central and Eastern Europe.* London: Ashgate.

European Commission. 1996. "The First Report on Economic and Social Cohesion." Brussels.

Hampl, M., ed. 1999. *Geography of Societal Transformation in the Czech Republic.* Prague: Charles University, Faculty of Science.

Hirschman, Albert. 1958. *The Strategy of Economic Development.* New Haven, Conn.: Yale University Press.

Illner, M. 2001. "Czech Regions Facing European Integration." In Grzegorz Gorzelak, E. Ehlrich, L. Faltan, and M. Illner, eds., *Central Europe in Transition, Towards EU Membership.* Warsaw: Regional Studies Association, Polish Section, Wydawnictwo Naukove.

Krugman, Paul. 1991. *Geography and Trade.* Cambridge, Mass.: MIT Press.

Malmberg, Anders. 1997. "Industrial Geography: Location and Learning." *Progress in Human Geography* 21(4):573–82.

Molle, Willem. 1997. *The Economics of European Integration: Theory, Practice, Policy,* 3rd ed. Aldershot, U.K.: Ashgate.

Porter, Michael. 1999. *The Competitive Advantage of Nations.* New York: The Free Press.

CHAPTER 7

Regional Policy Experience in Southern Italy

Fabrizio Barca

We should stop discussing European Union (EU) regional policy or Structural Funds, and, as a matter of fact, national regional policies, as separate from state intervention at large.

Let us consider two very different types of state services: the provision of public goods, like safety, roads, communications, and training (type A services); and state transfers to firms and households (type B services). If we raised hands around this table, there would probably be a great deal of support for type A services, though we might have differences of opinion about how much should be provided. There would probably be little support for type B services. But, whatever our views are, I find it extremely difficult to take part in discussions where we talk about the regional policy of Europe or regional policy at the national level as separate from type A and type B services.

Whenever a state provides those services, whether the services are labeled "regional" or not, it is influencing and changing the attractiveness of the sites where those services are provided. So regional policy is inherent in any public action.

Most regional policy is implemented by state departments or regional departments or municipalities, and the tariff levels of municipalities also influence the attractiveness of metropolitan towns. That is regional policy. But it is not labeled "regional."

So then, what is "regional policy" about? It is about putting a label on public action that has territorial effects. Regional policy is about targeting some regions (backward regions, regions with undercapacity, or politically sensitive regions) and devising and implementing policies aimed at those regions.

This is also the case with EU regional policy.

What then is the specific purpose of EU regional policy? There is first one very clear purpose, a political one. It is the same purpose that explains why, in a different field—that of short-term countercyclical policy—the U.S. federal government compensates for differences in cycle among U.S. states. Federal funds in the United States represent one of the major sources of adjustment of the economic cycle, together with labor movement and with rents coming from portfolio holdings in other states; federal funds perform the role of increasing the political support for the federal government. In the area of structural adjustment, EU Structural Funds—however small their amount—serve primarily the same political purpose: to increase consensus regarding the EU, in Slovenia as well as Hungary's eastern areas, in southern Italy, in the hills of France, and so on.

But there is also another reason for regional policy to be enacted at the EU level. This is the part of the story that interests me most.

I will not refer to type B service policies—to policies delivering subsidies and incentives. I will refer only to the provision of public goods to areas with under-capacity, and I will argue that EU Structural Funds can improve the effectiveness of type A service policies—training, infrastructure, roads, water, electricity, or the maintenance of archaeological sites.

Does Brussels add something to countries providing public goods to territories that are lagging behind and show clear underutilization of resources? This is the question. In order to provide an answer I will consider the Italian case.

Figure 7-1 shows the growth of Mezzogiorno (which has about one-third of Italy's population and accounts for about one-quarter of Italy's gross domestic product [GDP]) since 1989 and the rising contribution of Structural Funds.

Structural Funds do not seem to have helped growth much. But at some point, apparently independently of policies, something happened in the southern economy; this change is easier to see on figures 7-2 and 7-3.

Halfway through the 1990s, Mezzogiorno was still an area with 13.5 percent of employment in the agricultural sector. In 2002 the share is only 8.6 percent. Around 1995 the employment in the service and industry sectors started picking up, together with a very strong rise of net initiation rate of firms and a continuous rise in export and tourism.

The shift (which is described in Barca 2001a and 2001b) seems to be linked to a change in policy, or more appropriately to the end of a bad policy. In 1992–93, thanks to an agreement with Brussels, *Cassa del Mezzogiorno,* a centralized state agency managing both subsidies and infrastructures, was brought to an end, while transfers to state-owned corporations in the south were interrupted drastically. To the southern people, these events indicated that their incomes might drop. Suddenly, their saving propensity increased, their propensity to work in the public sector dropped, and their propensity to become self-employed and start new enterprises jumped.

So the problem for policy was very clear. The first goal was not to make mistakes: not to bring back poor incentives for the youth of Mezzogiorno. But was "doing nothing" the answer? Unfortunately, the south has an extremely low provision of public goods. The infrastructure is terrible. The quality of training is appalling. Security and

FIGURE 7-1 GDP GROWTH AND STRUCTURAL FUNDS

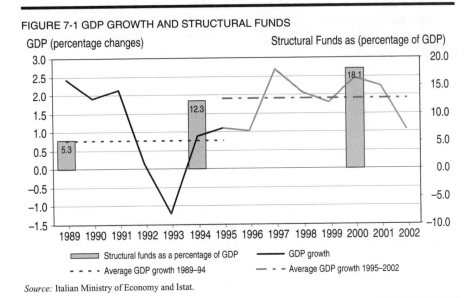

GDP (percentage changes)   Structural Funds as (percentage of GDP)

Structural funds as a percentage of GDP   GDP growth
- - - - Average GDP growth 1989–94   — - — Average GDP growth 1995–2002

Source: Italian Ministry of Economy and Istat.

FIGURE 7-2 NONFARM EMPLOYMENT

(1995 = 100; seasonally adjusted quarterly data)

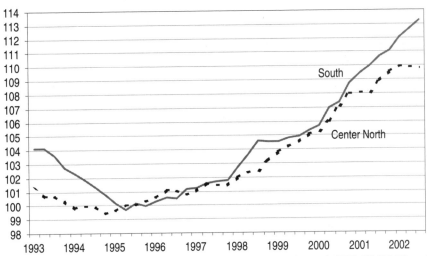

Note: Unit of measure on the y-axis is thousands of employees. So if nonfarm employment in 1995 is 100,000, 110 equals 110,000 employees.
Source: Istat.

FIGURE 7-3 EMPLOYMENT

(1995 = 100; seasonally adjusted quarterly data)

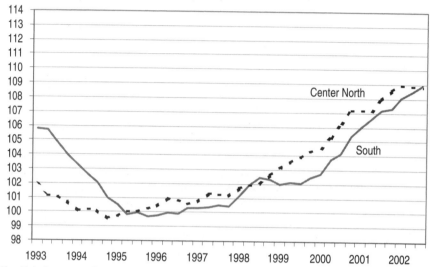

Note: Unit of measure on the y-axis is thousands of employees. So if nonfarm employment in 1995 is 100,000, 110 equals 110,000 employees.
Source: Istat.

safety, for both citizens and firms, is inadequate. Many extraordinary natural and cultural sites are inaccessible. This situation keeps profit expectations low. State provision of public goods is therefore indispensable for a breakthrough to take place.

The question then was—and is—how to bring about a change, how to have the state coming back into the picture without making major mistakes and actually producing public services, public local goods, and not making transfers to firms, or restarting the old game, or leaving everybody feeling safer at home? Which level of government should provide these public goods? What information should be used to decide what to do?

The information is obviously very local, especially in a country like Italy, which—it should be kept in mind—is not like Ireland. There are not many green fields. Both urban and rural areas are thickly inhabited, and many cultural, natural, and human resources are waiting to be used to their full capacity.

The local agents know what to do, but they cannot do it. They do not have the institutions to do it, or a system through which they can evaluate which project should be done, which road should be built, how Pompeii should be turned into a great source of development.

The way to approach the issue is rather straightforward. If the knowledge is local, then the local municipalities, not Rome, need to be given the means and the incentives to bring about the projects and the power to select the projects. But there is a problem: regions are terribly inefficient.

The further and final question then becomes how to create the right incentives for the political leadership of regions to drastically modernize their public administrations and to liberalize the markets for the provision of local public services (water, transportation, and so forth) so as to allow regions to properly select and implement local projects?

The idea came about to use as an incentive tough and credible rules set by an enlightened central administration, which happens to be the one I head at the Italian Ministry of Economy and Finance. We were going to give regions a list of 20 institutional changes to enact before they would be given additional authority: "If you—region—don't have employment services, e-government, or evaluation units, you can't evaluate projects. You need institutional reforms that change completely the working of public administration. You can neither provide water nor privatize the water system if you don't have an administration that is able to write a tender offer or a programming document, to negotiate well with the private sector."

The institutional changes were going to be turned into 20 targets to which 10 percent of all funds were going to be linked, to be distributed in 2004.

Here is where Europe finally comes into the picture. My administration would not have had the strength to set this mechanism in place, nor the credibility to carry it to the end—as we eventually did, with remarkable results, about which I will elaborate elsewhere—had we not had the rules sealed in a contract with Brussels. And that is true for many other institutional adjustments that I will not have space to mention here.

As Joseph Stiglitz would say, the EU regional policy gave us the credibility we lacked. And so it happened in many other states and regions all over our old (EU15) Europe; and so it is happening now all over our new (EU25) Europe.

The EU method, which results from the coordination and "institutional melting pot" of many European countries, gave us and many other administrations not only credibility but ideas and principles that are becoming part of a shared vision of economic policy. Many bureaucratic mistakes and misconceptions came, too, but we can address them—and indeed urgently remove them in the reform of EU regional policy—once we have made clear that EU regional policy is indeed an indispensable tool of our Union.

Bibliography

Barca, Fabrizio. 2001a. "The European Challenge." *Italy: Resilient and Vulnerable.* Vol. I (Spring/Summer).

———. 2001b. "Rethinking Partnership in Development Policies: Lessons from a European Policy Experiment." In Mark Drabenstott and Katharine H. Sheaff, eds., *Exploring Policy Options for a New Rural America—A Conference Summary.* Kansas City, Mo.: Federal Reserve Bank of Kansas City.

CHAPTER 8

European Union Regional Aid
and Irish Economic Development

Frank Barry

Regional aid does not guarantee a real convergence of living standards in the recipient region. This is obvious from the experience of the Italian Mezzogiorno, to a lesser extent from the experience of Greece, and perhaps to some extent from the experience of Spain. Regional aid is likely to be of greatest benefit when the other requirements for real convergence are satisfied.

From this point of view the Irish and Portuguese experiences are of particular interest. These countries have followed very different industrial strategies. Ireland's has been based substantially on a policy of attracting inward foreign direct investment (FDI) in high-tech manufacturing sectors, while Portugal has experienced substantial real convergence on average European Union (EU) incomes with a manufacturing sector that remains dominated by indigenous low-tech industry (figure 8-1). (Finland represents another interesting case of a geographically peripheral though not historically poor country that has prospered through indigenous high-tech industry.)

I will have something to say later about why I think the Portuguese and Spanish experiences differ. Mostly, however, I will be concerned with the Irish experience.

The period of substantially increased EU regional aid overlapped with the Irish boom, which saw unemployment fall from a high of 17 percent in the late 1980s to around 4 percent today; numbers at work increase spectacularly (by more than 50 percent); and average incomes rise from less than 65 percent of the EU average, a level around which they had hovered since 1960, to reach parity by the decade's end.[1]

FIGURE 8-1 THE CONVERGENCE EXPERIENCES OF GREECE, IRELAND, PORTUGAL, AND SPAIN

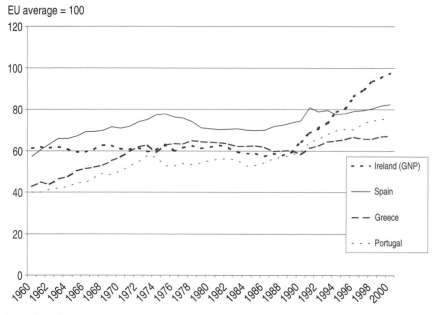

Source: Eurostat.

To some extent the boom can be seen as an episode of "delayed convergence," simply making up ground that had been lost during decades of poor economic management. The failure of the 1950s resulted from eschewing free trade as the rest of Western Europe shed its protectionist policies. The underperformance of the 1960s and 1970s was a consequence of the failure to increase student numbers in line with the rest of Western Europe. The 1980s were lost as the country struggled with problems bequeathed by a period of undisciplined fiscal policy.

What explains the timing and rapidity of the boom, however? Both were undoubtedly influenced by the country's strong FDI orientation. The amount of FDI from both within Europe and outside Europe exploded in the late 1980s because of the Single Market and the extent of investment funds made available by the long U.S. boom. Ireland's share of these flows also increased considerably. At the same time, in the late 1980s, the country's fiscal crisis, with which it had struggled for almost a decade, was finally resolved. And then of course there was the substantial increase in EU Structural Funds (SFs), following reform and reorganization in 1988; SF receipts per annum over the course of the 1990s were more than double the levels prevailing in the latter half of the 1980s.[2]

Indeed, SF expenditures have been substantial throughout the EU periphery. Community support in the 1994–99 period accounted for almost 15 percent of total investment in Greece, 14 percent in Portugal, 10 percent in Ireland, and 6 percent in Spain.

Analysis undertaken so far (by the present author and others) suggests, however, that the *direct effects* of these EU regional aid programs were modest. In the Irish case it is estimated that they contributed a maximum of about 0.5 percent per annum to the gross domestic product growth rate of the 1990s, whereas the boom saw Irish average real growth exceeding that of the EU15 by around 6 percent per annum.[3]

Notice my use of the term *direct effects*. By these I mean the increased demand associated with EU transfers *plus* the supply-side effects associated with an improved stock of human capital and physical infrastructure, evaluated on the assumption that the response of Irish output is in line with estimates emerging from the international empirical literature.

In this chapter I want to focus on something different—that is, on what we might call the *indirect effects* that can arise via interactions between SF expenditures and other concurrent developments in the economy. I begin by asking what the SFs were needed for and what they were spent on. Then I discuss their interaction with three other developments that were taking place: the resolution of the fiscal crisis, the emergence of a greater degree of labor market flexibility, and the coming to fruition of the FDI-oriented development strategy. Finally, I will comment on the implications for the candidate countries of Central and Eastern Europe.

Strategic Target Areas for SF Spending

Unfavorable Initial Conditions in the Cohesion Economies

Ireland had a number of characteristics that made it attractive as an export platform for foreign (primarily U.S.) multinational companies. EU membership, of course, was crucial.[4] The country also was an English-language environment, which may have been particularly important for U.S. companies. Of major importance was the fact that Ireland has long had the lowest rate of corporation tax of any EU member state.

Ireland shared with the other EU cohesion states a number of unfavorable characteristics, however. They included relatively low levels of human capital, relatively poor physical infrastructure, and a poor record in research and development (R&D). I now briefly discuss these unfavorable characteristics.

Educational Attainment

Table 8-1 provides some illustrative statistics in regard to the educational attainment of the population, showing that, overall, the cohesion countries remain behind the Organisation for Economic Co-operation and Development (OECD) average in this respect.

TABLE 8-1 EDUCATIONAL ATTAINMENT OF THE POPULATION AGED 25–64, 1998
(Country percentages are expressed as a fraction of the OECD mean)

Country	Percentage that has attained at least upper secondary	Percentage that has attained at least tertiary B (diploma level)	Percentage that has attained at least tertiary A (degree level)
Ireland/OECD	0.84	1.00	0.79
Greece/OECD	0.72	0.76	0.79
Spain/OECD	0.54	0.95	1.00
Portugal/OECD	0.33	0.43	0.50

Note: "At least tertiary B" includes "at least tertiary A."
Source: OECD 2000.

Physical Infrastructure and Peripherality

The cohesion economies also lagged behind in terms of physical infrastructure. Indeed, the European Commission report *One Market, One Money* (1990) stated that firms in peripheral regions identified infrastructural deficiencies in the areas of education and training, transport and communications, and the supply and cost of energy as more important impediments to their development than geographical aspects of peripherality such as the proximity of suppliers and customers. The available data on the stock of infrastructure in peripheral regions provide supporting evidence. Table 8-2, adapted from Biehl (1986), reports relative infrastructural levels for an aggregate of transportation, telecommunications, energy, and education, showing that the periphery countries had a substantial infrastructural deficit relative to the core EU countries in the mid-1980s.

Poor transportation infrastructure also affects economic distance from purchasing power, which is how peripherality is usually defined.

Industrial Competitiveness

R&D activity indicators provide one piece of evidence that can be used to track the level of development of firms and businesses in a region. One suspects that countries lower

TABLE 8-2 RELATIVE INFRASTRUCTURAL LEVELS IN THE COHESION COUNTRIES AS A PROPORTION OF THE EU AVERAGE, 1985–86

Country	Proportion
Ireland	67.1
Greece	56.0
Spain	74.3
Portugal	38.7

Source: Biehl 1986.

down in these rankings are also deficient in other areas of industrial and business development. Table 8-3 illustrates the position in regard to R&D over the course of the 1980s.

These three indicators, therefore, serve to illustrate some of the structural weaknesses of the cohesion economies before the emergence of the substantial SF programs.

Allocation of SF Expenditures

It comes as little surprise that these three areas of weakness were also the areas that attracted the bulk of SF expenditures, as shown in Table 8-4.

The logic of the SF programs may therefore be seen to entail expenditures in areas in which there were strong microfoundations for public intervention *and* in which the cohesion countries were found to be deficient.

Indirect Effects of SFs: Interactions with Other Developments in the Economy

Analysis of the impact of the SFs has found them to have quite moderate effects. I suggest, however, that their interaction with other concurrent developments in the Irish economy may have meant that they were particularly beneficial in that case.

TABLE 8-3 BUSINESS ENTERPRISE EXPENDITURE ON R&D AS A PERCENTAGE OF DOMESTIC PRODUCT OF INDUSTRY, RELATIVE TO THE EU AVERAGE

Country	1981	1989
Ireland/EU	0.29	0.35
Greece/EU	0.07	0.06
Spain/EU	0.14	0.29
Portugal/EU	0.07	0.12

Source: OECD 2001.

TABLE 8-4 ALLOCATION OF STRUCTURAL FUNDS IN IRELAND

Area	Allocation of total SFs, 1994–99 (%)
Physical infrastructure	36.3
Human resources	28.4
Production/investment aid to the private sector	25.8
Income support	9.5

Source: Barry, Bradley, and Hannan 2001.

Fiscal Consolidation

Successive Irish governments struggled throughout the 1980s to overcome the debt crisis that had resulted from inappropriate procyclical fiscal expansion at the end of the previous decade. The attempt to close the deficit via high taxation proved unsuccessful, due to the fact that it was by necessity procyclical (in a contractionary direction), while workers responded to the tax hikes by raising wage demands.

A new approach was tried in the late 1980s, when government expenditure, and in particular capital expenditure, was reined in as an alternative to increasing taxes still further. Barry and Devereux (1995) argue that this consolidation proved successful first because it was countercyclical, and second because it was supported by the development of the "social partnership approach," which promoted wage moderation via the promise of future reductions in income taxes.

The timing of the increase in SFs in 1989 was fortuitous in allowing the reinstatement of infrastructural projects that had been postponed as part of the necessary fiscal contraction. The infrastructural deficiencies that would otherwise have resulted would have made it more difficult to attract the levels of FDI achieved since then.

The SFs would also have facilitated the social partnership agreements by relaxing the government budget constraint, both directly (to the extent to which the principle of additionality can be sidestepped) and indirectly (through the tax revenues associated with the increased FDI inflows that subsequently emerged).[5]

Labor Market Developments

The social partnership agreements begun in 1987 brought substantial competitiveness gains and unprecedented industrial peace (Barry 2000).

This brings me to an interesting point that has not been fully appreciated in the literature on the impact of the SFs to date.[6] It concerns the effect of the labor market environment on the macroeconomic impacts of SF expenditures. To set the scene, consider the unemployment experience of three of the cohesion countries—Ireland, Portugal, and Spain—relative to the EU15 over the era from the Delors 1 Community Support Framework onward (figure 8-2).

Portugal, we see, remains at low levels of unemployment throughout, Spain's unemployment remains high, and Ireland's tumbles from very high to very low. A stark characterization of these different situations then would be to see the Portuguese labor market as extremely flexible, with the country remaining close to full employment throughout the period; Ireland's labor market might be characterized by wage rigidity, so that unemployment falls as labor demand expands, while Spain's might be characterized as an extreme insider-outsider model, where labor market insiders reap all the benefits of an increase in labor demand for themselves, so that it is all dissipated in the form of higher wages rather than greater employment.

Let us consider the effects of SFs in this context. The impact of all these spending programs can be categorized in terms of demand (short-run) and supply (longer-run) effects. The Keynesian short-run effects will be strongest where there is labor market slack (that is, Ireland and Spain rather than Portugal) and where demand can

FIGURE 8-2 IRELAND, PORTUGAL, AND SPAIN UNEMPLOYMENT RATES MINUS THAT OF THE EU15

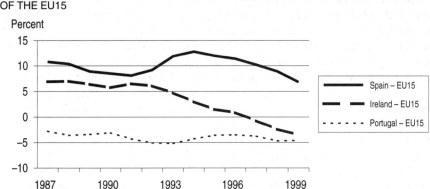

Source: Eurostat.

influence this slack (that is, Ireland rather than Spain). Thus, the short-run effects can be expected to be much larger in Ireland than in Spain or Portugal.

As to the longer-run supply-side effects, let us think of them in terms of a model with three productive factors: labor, private capital, and public capital. If the increase in public capital is the same in each case, the impact on Spain will be less than on either Portugal or Ireland—in Ireland because an increase in public capital draws more labor as well as further private capital into employment, and in Portugal because with flexible labor markets there will be a higher level of employment and a higher stock of private capital relative to the initial stock of infrastructure, so the marginal product of public capital will be higher (Barry 2002b).

In this scenario, the impact of SFs will be substantially higher in Portugal and Ireland than in Spain. Though this provides only a small part of the explanation, it is consistent with their respective convergence experiences over the period.

FDI Inflows

As mentioned earlier, Ireland's FDI-oriented strategy came to full fruition during the 1990s. It is unlikely that as much FDI could have been attracted to the economy had the extra SF-financed infrastructure not been in place.[7]

Besides the level of FDI inflows drawn to the economy, the SFs would also have affected the type of FDI that Ireland was able to attract. Over recent decades, foreign industry in Ireland has become increasingly high-tech, as figure 8-3 illustrates, and this could have come about only in conjunction with the increasing human capital stock of the labor force.[8]

Consistent with this fact, the R&D orientation of both indigenous and foreign industry has been rising, as seen in table 8-6. The overall growth in the R&D orien-

FIGURE 8-3 DISTRIBUTION OF EMPLOYMENT IN FOREIGN-OWNED INDUSTRY
IN IRELAND BY TECHNOLOGICAL LEVEL

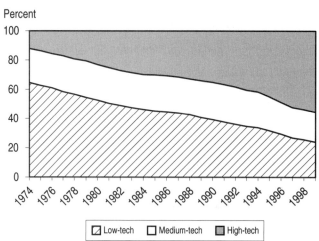

Source: Author's research.

tation of the economy, however, is primarily due to the operations of the foreign-owned sector, which carries out 64 percent of business-related R&D expenditures (BERD) in Irish industry.

Progress in Terms of Strategic Target Areas

I have argued that Ireland may have gained greater benefits from the availability of the SFs than the other cohesion economies did because of how the effects of SF spending may have interacted with concurrent developments in the economy. Let us now see how this assumption is reflected in the various peripherality indicators employed earlier.

Educational Attainment

By the end of the 1990s, with the aid of the SFs, the relative position of the EU periphery had improved. In the case of educational attainment, this can be seen by focusing on the attainment of younger members of the population, as they would have been of student age at the time of the SF disbursement (table 8-5).

Comparing the table 8-5 numbers with those for the whole population given in table 8-1, we see that in each case the periphery has converged on the OECD average in terms of educational attainment.[9]

To focus on Ireland in particular, we see that while the country continues to lag behind the OECD mean in terms of the population that has attained at least upper sec-

TABLE 8-5 EDUCATIONAL ATTAINMENT OF THE POPULATION AGES 25–34, 1998
(Country percentages are expressed as a fraction of the OECD mean)

Country	Percentage that has attained at least upper secondary	Percentage that has attained at least tertiary B (diploma level)	Percentage that has attained at least tertiary A (degree level)
Ireland/OECD	0.93	1.16	1.00
Greece/OECD	0.92	0.88	0.94
Spain/OECD	0.74	1.28	1.31
Portugal/OECD	0.40	0.44	0.50

Note: "At least tertiary B" includes "at least tertiary A."
Source: OECD 2000.

ondary education, it has converged on the OECD average in terms of those attaining at least a university degree or equivalent, and has actually gone ahead in terms of those attaining a diploma or equivalent.

This extra Irish throughput in tertiary education, furthermore, is largely concentrated in the sciences. Thus, 1995 data from the United Nations Educational, Scientific, and Cultural Organization (UNESCO 1998) reveal that 40 percent of Irish tertiary graduates are in the fields of natural sciences, agriculture, and engineering, compared with an EU average of only 28 percent. Scientific degrees and diplomas are in strong demand within foreign-owned industry in Ireland and, to this extent, Ireland's overall strategy can be seen to have influenced the setting of development priorities within the human capital domain.

Physical Infrastructure and Peripherality

While SF-supported improvements in transport infrastructure have been very substantial, it is not clear whether they have allowed the periphery to converge along this dimension. The European Commission itself suggests that "while investment in peripheral regions has improved accessibility, it has been accompanied by similar investment in neighbouring regions and more central ones, which can counteract any relative gain" (2001, volume 1, p. 132). It goes on to caution that "the overall effect of such investment depends on what other measures are taken to stimulate economic activity in the regions concerned" (ibid.), which concurs with the point made above about the interaction with Ireland's FDI-oriented industrial strategy.

Industrial Competitiveness

I used R&D indicators earlier as an illustrative measure of industrial competitiveness. Again we see, in table 8-6, that Ireland has continued to converge on core EU countries along this dimension, though the other periphery countries have not. Weakness in the R&D area is still pervasive within indigenous industry, however.

TABLE 8-6 BERD AS A PERCENTAGE OF DOMESTIC PRODUCT OF INDUSTRY, RELATIVE TO THE EU AVERAGE

Country	1991	1997
Ireland/EU	0.50	0.87
Greece/EU	0.13	0.13
Spain/EU	0.38	0.33
Portugal/EU	0.13	0.13

Source: OECD 2001.

Where Do the Central and Eastern European Countries Stand in Terms of the Strategic Target Areas?

The Central and Eastern European countries (CEECs) lag behind the rest of Europe in many of the same areas that the Cohesion Funds were instituted to address. Some brief details on this are provided below.

Educational Attainment

While the Czech Republic and Hungary are both ahead of the OECD in terms of the proportion of the younger population with secondary education, these two countries as well as Poland lag well behind in terms of third-level degrees and diplomas (table 8-7).

Some further comparisons are possible with the aid of 1995 data from UNESCO (1998) (table 8-8). They paint a slightly different picture from that emerging from the OECD. They show, for example, that the expected number of years of formal schooling for each EU country is higher than that for any CEEC, which is not what a comparison of the OECD data for Portugal and Poland would suggest. The UNESCO

TABLE 8-7 EDUCATIONAL ATTAINMENT OF THE POPULATION AGES 25–34, 1998
(Country percentages are expressed as a fraction of the OECD mean)

Country	Percentage that has attained at least upper secondary	Percentage that has attained at least tertiary B (diploma level)	Percentage that has attained at least tertiary A (degree level)
Czech Republic/OECD	1.28	0.40	0.63
Hungary/OECD	1.07	0.56	0.88
Poland/OECD	0.86	0.48	0.75
Ireland/OECD	0.93	1.16	1.00

Note: "At least tertiary B" includes "at least tertiary A."
Source: OECD 2000.

TABLE 8-8 EDUCATION INDICATORS, 1995

Country	Expected years of formal schooling	Net enrollment ratio—secondary	Gross enrollment ratio—tertiary
EU10	15.2	92	47.8
Ireland	13.6	85	37.0
Greece	13.8	84	38.1
Spain	15.5	94	46.1
Portugal	14.3	78	34.0
Czech Republic	13.1	88	20.8
Hungary	12.5	73	19.1
Poland	13.1	83	27.4
Estonia	12.5	77	38.1
Slovenia	n.a.	n.a.	31.9
Slovak Republic	n.a.	n.a.	20.2
Latvia	11.4	78	25.7
Lithuania	n.a.	n.a.	28.2
Romania	11.4	73	18.3
Bulgaria	12.1	75	39.4

n.a. = Not applicable.
Note: Net enrollment ratio refers to the percentage of the population of the age group corresponding to that level of education enrolled; gross enrollment ratio refers to total enrollment divided by the population of the age group officially corresponding to that level of education; EU10 refers to EU15 less Luxembourg and the Cohesion 4 (Greece, Ireland, Portugal, and Spain).
Source: UNESCO 1998.

source contains data for each of the CEEC economies, however, allowing one to see how they are ranked relative to each other.

These data show that the CEECs are behind even the EU cohesion countries (with the possible exception of Portugal) in terms of educational attainment.

Midelfart-Knarvik and others (2000) suggest that educational standards may be becoming increasingly important, finding: "The location of R&D-intensive industries has become increasingly responsive to countries' endowments of researchers, with these industries moving into researcher-abundant locations. The location of non-manual-labour intensive industries was and remains sensitive to the proportion of countries' labour forces with secondary and higher education" (p. 2).

Physical Infrastructure and Peripherality
Transport infrastructure plays an important role in calculations of centrality or "closeness to purchasing power." Schürmann and Talaat (2000) provide a recent ranking of EU countries and CEECs in this regard. Their index is based on a measure of travel costs between points within the overall region weighted by the purchasing power that each point represents.

The most peripheral regions at present (according to figure 4.2 in their paper, p. 44) are the Baltic states, northern Sweden and Finland, and Bulgaria and Romania. Hungary, Slovenia, the Czech and Slovak Republics, and the southwest corner of Poland are no more peripheral than Ireland, Portugal, or Spain, and less peripheral than Greece.

Interestingly, these authors also present a projection for the year 2016 based on the assumption of EU accession (with its associated reduction in border delays) and the implementation of the huge Transportation Infrastructure Needs Assessment (TINA) transport infrastructure plans for Central and Eastern Europe (TINA Secretariat 1999) (along with the Trans-European Energy Networks program for EU incumbents). In this scenario (which they plot in figure 4-14, p. 61, of their paper), some regions in Poland, the Czech Republic, the Slovak Republic, Hungary, eastern Germany, and Portugal move ahead of Ireland, with Greece left even further behind.

Industrial Competitiveness

The Czech Republic and the Slovak Republic lie between Ireland and Spain in the R&D rankings, while Hungary enters at a surprisingly low 20 percent of the EU average (table 8-9). This indicates that there is still a substantial amount of ground to be made up along this dimension.

Concluding Comments

We see that the CEECs share many of the unfavorable characteristics of the EU cohesion economies. These characteristics include relatively low levels of human capital and R&D, alongside economic peripherality. These are the kinds of disadvantages that EU regional aid sets out to redress.

TABLE 8-9 BERD AS A PERCENTAGE OF DOMESTIC PRODUCT OF INDUSTRY, RELATIVE TO THE EU AVERAGE

Country	1991	1997–99
Czech Republic/EU	1.06	0.67
Hungary/EU	0.31	0.20
Poland/EU	—	0.27
Slovak Republic/EU	1.06	0.60
Ireland/EU	0.50	0.87
Greece/EU	0.13	0.13
Spain/EU	0.38	0.33
Portugal/EU	0.13	0.13

— = not available.
Source: OECD 2001.

We have seen that the cohesion countries have converged in terms of some of these structural characteristics at least. I have argued that a benign macroeconomic environment is also important, however, specifically in terms of labor market flexibility. The tripartite Social Partnership agreements instituted in 1987 in Ireland facilitated industrial peace and a return to labor market equilibrium. Without some such steps to promote labor market equilibrium, it is doubtful that the boom of the 1990s, and the macroeconomic effects of the SFs themselves, would have been as strong. I showed specifically that an insider-dominated labor market can reduce substantially the macroeconomic benefits of SF spending. Labor market rigidities also hinder the possibilities of real convergence more directly (Barry and others 2000; Daveri and Tabellini 2000).

The chapter also illustrated how the SFs interacted strongly and positively with Ireland's FDI-oriented strategy to generate very rapid convergence when the circumstances were auspicious—that is, during the era of the Single Market and the sustained U.S. boom. Ireland adopted a low rate of corporation tax and fostered other characteristics favorable to the attraction of FDI. With the aid of SFs, educational attainment improved considerably, facilitating the shift into high-tech (though largely foreign-owned) industry. This in turn, along with targeted SF-funded aids to industry, raised the level of competitiveness of the Irish business sector. The economy would have run into infrastructural constraints much sooner, which would have impinged on its ability to attract FDI, had the SF-funded infrastructural programs not been in place.

Portugal's relatively successful convergence performance of recent years shows, however, that a reliance on FDI is not the only path to development for EU periphery economies. Again, what appears to have been crucial in the Portuguese case, relative to Spain at least, is the degree of labor market flexibility that the economy exhibits. This point has been made in a number of papers, including Barry (forthcoming a), Bover, García-Perez, and Portugal (2000), and Daveri and Tabellini (2000). Thus, Portuguese convergence has been impressive, even though, consistent with its relatively low human-capital stock, the economy has specialized in low-tech production.

This discussion suggests that there is no one route to economic development for the CEEC economies. Some, such as Hungary and Estonia, appear to be following the Irish development model, using low corporation-tax rates to attract export-oriented FDI. Others, such as the Czech Republic, though it has done well so far in attracting preaccession FDI, have not adopted the low corporation-tax strategy and may have a different development model in mind. The Portuguese experience suggests that this will not necessarily hinder real convergence possibilities (particularly since indigenous Czech industry appears to account for a substantial proportion of Czech BERD), though our simulations of a model of the Czech transition suggest that care must be taken to ensure labor market flexibility.

A further consequence of the SFs, emphasized elsewhere in this volume, is, as FitzGerald (1998) states, related to expenditure effectiveness evaluation: "The need to satisfy the donor countries, through the EU Commission, that their money is well spent has resulted in the introduction of a set of evaluation procedures which has helped change the way the administration approaches public expenditure. In the past the only question, once money had been voted by parliament, was whether it had been spent in accordance with regulations. Now there is increasing interest in assessing how effective the expenditure has been."

The introduction of more rigorous controls on the probity with which public funds are spent, as well as a more careful evaluation of the programs on which they are spent, may prove to be even more crucial in the case of the CEEC economies than it was in Ireland and the other cohesion economies.

As to regional developments in Ireland, the strength of the boom ensured that all regions of the economy expanded, though the expansion in the Greater Dublin area was much more substantial than the expansion elsewhere. By the end of the 1990s this region exhibited higher wages, lower unemployment, and greater labor force participation than elsewhere in the economy—as well as greater congestion, of course.

Once the economy reached full employment at the end of the 1990s, regional considerations came more to the fore in the deliberations of the industrial development agencies. Their recently updated Project Appraisal system places greater emphasis than heretofore on industrial dispersion across the regions (Barry, Walsh, and Murphy 2002).

Notes

1. I use gross national product (GNP) rather than gross domestic product (GDP) in this calculation to exclude the profits of foreign companies located in Ireland. GDP per capita is substantially higher.

2. I use the term Structural Funds rather loosely to include the Community Support Framework (CSF), the Cohesion Fund, and Community Initiatives. In the 1994–99 period the CSF composed over 75 percent of the total allocated to Ireland.

3. As the Organisation for Economic Co-operation and Development (1999, footnote 32) points out, however, even this apparently modest effect nevertheless represents quite a respectable internal rate of return, of 6 to 7 percent per annum, on the funds invested.

4. Before EU accession in 1973, Ireland's FDI inflows came from Europe rather than the United States, were market seeking rather than export oriented, and were relatively low-tech, characteristics that describe most Central and Eastern Europe–bound FDI inflows today (Barry forthcoming b). By the mid-1980s all these characteristics had been reversed.

5. It would nevertheless be incorrect to conclude that the SFs generated the Irish boom through facilitating income tax reductions. As mentioned earlier, corporation tax is the most important tax

relevant to the country's ability to attract FDI. This tax has actually increased over time, from the zero rating on profits stemming from manufacturing exports that was introduced in the late 1950s.

6. The literature I am referring to includes econometric work and calibration studies such as those of the Economic Social Research Institute (ESRI 1997) and Barry, Bradley, and Hannan (2001), which use the HERMIN model; the Commission's work using the Quest model (Volume 2 of the *Second Report on Economic and Social Cohesion,* European Commission 2001); and various papers by Vitor and Pereira.

7. As it was, the boom created tremendous congestion. This alone would have led to its ultimate dissipation (Barry 2002a; Dascher 2000).

8. The categorization of high-, medium-, and low-tech industries is from OECD (1994).

9. SF expenditures affect these indicators directly. Thus, apprenticeship programs affect the numbers attaining at least upper secondary education, diploma courses affect those attaining tertiary level B, and conversion courses are included in tertiary level A.

Bibliography

The word *processed* describes informally reproduced works that may not be commonly available through libraries.

Barry, Frank. 1999. "Irish Growth in Historical and Theoretical Perspective." In Frank Barry, ed., *Understanding Ireland's Economic Growth.* London: Macmillan.

———. 2000. "Convergence Is Not Automatic: Lessons from Ireland for Central and Eastern Europe." *World Economy* 23(10):1379–94.

———. 2002a. "FDI, Infrastructure and the Welfare Effects of Labour Migration." *Manchester School* 70(3):364–79.

———. 2002b. "Labour Market Structures and the Effects of EU Regional Aid." Work in progress. Processed.

———. Forthcoming a. "Economic Policy, Income Convergence and Structural Change in the EU Periphery." In Henryk Kierzkowski, ed., *Europe and Globalisation.* London: Palgrave-Macmillan.

———. Forthcoming b. "EU Accession and Prospective FDI Flows to CEE Countries." In Robert Lipsey, ed., *Real and Monetary Aspects of FDI in Industrial Countries.* Frankfurt: Deutsche Bundesbank/Springer Verlag.

Barry, Frank, and Michael B. Devereux. 1995. "The Expansionary Fiscal Contraction Hypothesis: A Neo-Keynesian Analysis." *Oxford Economic Papers* 47:249–64.

Barry, Frank, John Bradley, and Aoife Hannan. 2001. "The Single Market, The Structural Funds and Ireland's Recent Economic Growth." *Journal of Common Market Studies* 39(3):537–52.

Barry, Frank, John Bradley, Michal Kejak, and David Vavra. 2000. "The Czech Economic Transition: Exploring Options Using a Macrosectoral Model." Available at http://www.ucd.ie/~economic/staff/barry/research.html.

Barry, Frank, Brendan Walsh, and Anthony Murphy. 2002. "The Rationale for Subsidizing Jobs in a Fully Employed Economy." *Irish Banking Review* (Autumn): 38–50. Available at http://www.ucd.ie/~economic/staff/barry/.

Biehl, Dieter. 1986. *The Contribution of Infrastructure to Regional Development.* No. 2. Luxembourg: Office for Official Publications of the European Communities.

Bover, Olympia, Pilar García-Perez, and Pedro Portugal. 2000. "Labour Market Outliers: Lessons from Portugal and Spain." *Economic Policy* 30:381–428.

Dascher, Kristof. 2000. "Trade, FDI and Congestion: The Small and Very Open Economy." CEPR Working Paper 2526. London: Centre for Economic Policy Research. Available at http://www.ucd.ie/~economic/workingpapers/2000.htm.

Daveri, Francesco, and Guido Tabellini. 2000. "Unemployment, Growth and Taxation in Industrial Countries." *Economic Policy* 30:47–104.

ESRI (Economic Social Research Institute). 1997. *The Single Market Review: Aggregate and Regional Impact—The Cases of Greece, Spain, Ireland and Portugal.* London: Kogan Page in association with the Commission of the European Communities.

European Commission. 1990. *One Market, One Money.* Luxembourg.

———. 2001. *Second Report on Economic and Social Cohesion.* Luxembourg.

FitzGerald, J. 1998. "An Irish Perspective on the Structural Funds." *European Planning Studies* 6(6):677–94.

Midelfart-Knarvik, K. H., H. Overman, S. Reading, and A. Venables. 2000. *The Location of European Industry.* Economic Papers 142. Luxembourg: European Commission.

OECD (Organisation for Economic Co-operation and Development). 1994. *Manufacturing Performance: A Scoreboard of Indicators*. Paris.

———. 1999. *OECD Economic Surveys: Ireland*. Paris.

———. 2000. *Main Economic Indicators*. Paris.

———. 2001. *Main Economic Indicators*. Paris.

Pereira, Alfredo, and Gaspara Vitor. 1999. "An Intertemporal Analysis of Development Policies in the EU." *Journal of Policy Modeling* 27(7):799–822.

Schürmann, C., and A. Talaat. 2000. *Towards a European Peripherality Index*. Report for European Commission DGXVI Regional Policy. Available at http://irpud.raumplanung.uni-dortmund.de/irpud/pro/peri/ber53_gesamt.pdf.

TINA Secretariat. 1999. *Transport Infrastructure Needs Assessment (TINA): Identification of the Network Components for a Future Trans-European Transport Network in Bulgaria, Cyprus, Czech Republic, Estonia, Hungary, Latvia, Lithuania, Poland, Romania, Slovakia, and Slovenia*. Final Report. Vienna.

UNESCO (United Nations Educational, Scientific, and Cultural Organization). 1998. *World Education Report*. New York

Vitor, Gaspara, and Alfredo Pereira. 1995. "The Impact of Financial Interpretation and Unilateral Public Transfers on Investment and Growth in EC Capital-Exporting Countries." *Journal of Development Economics* 48(1):43–66.

CHAPTER 9

Does Cohesion Policy Work?
Some General Considerations and
Evidence from Spain

Angel de la Fuente

Introduction

Over the last two decades, the European Union (EU) has adopted an active *cohesion* policy aimed at reducing income disparities by subsidizing various types of investment programs in the Union's poorest regions through the so-called Structural Funds. This policy has often been questioned on at least two different grounds. Perhaps the most common argument is that it has not worked: since most of the assisted regions continue to be relatively poor in spite of these programs, EU grants are mostly a waste and should therefore be scrapped, or at least severely curtailed. The second objection, which is seldom explicitly stated but often lurks behind calls for cuts in structural programs, is based on the view that there is no reason why the EU should engage in redistribution across its constituent territories.

The European Commission's view on this second issue seems to be that such redistribution is necessary because economic integration will tend to hurt the poorer regions of the EU by facilitating the concentration of economic activity in certain core areas. As has already been said in previous chapters, this prediction seems to be based on an implicit assumption—that there are sharply increasing returns to scale—for which there is very little empirical support. Hence, I do not think one can build a solid case for cohesion policies on the basis of the divergence predictions of the "new" growth and trade theories.

But I do not think that assuming agglomeration is necessary either. In my view, the case for redistribution must necessarily be based on political and equity considerations that have to do with what a typical European citizen would consider fair and would be willing to support when it comes to EU budgetary policy. In this regard, I think we can validly extrapolate to the Community level the preferences of European electorates as manifested in the policies of national governments—provided we keep in mind that the typical taxpayer's willingness to pay for redistribution drops rapidly as his or her distance from the beneficiaries increases. While views about the desired level of redistribution vary widely across member countries, my impression is that there is fairly broad support in Europe for a moderate amount of budgetary solidarity. This consensus has been clearly visible in EU budget practices, which have consistently resulted in sizable net transfers to the poorer member countries,[1] and has been incorporated into the EU's governing treaties in the form of an explicit commitment to economic cohesion and financial solidarity among member states.

Hence, I will take it as given that a certain amount of redistribution within the EU is desirable. Given this, it probably makes sense that at least some of this redistribution should be achieved through conditional investment grants with "additionality" requirements and some sort of quality filter to make sure that the funds flowing into the poorer territories are effectively used to promote the territories' development and are not diverted for consumption purposes.

This leaves me with two questions, to which I will devote the bulk of this chapter. The first is whether we can reasonably expect that EU cofinancing of infrastructure and training programs will contribute to growth and convergence, and the second has to do with the level at which redistribution should be conducted. On the first issue, I am cautiously optimistic. I will argue that supply-oriented regional policies can work in principle and have actually worked quite well in Spain, at least when judged in terms of their stated objectives. My argument will be based on a brief review of the empirical evidence on the growth effects of investment in infrastructure and education, and on some estimates of the impact of the Structural Funds in Spain. On the second issue, I will argue that EU cohesion policy should be formulated at the national rather than at the regional level, essentially because member states already have adequate systems for internal redistribution.

Can Regional Policy Work?

There is considerable disagreement among both academics and policymakers concerning the effectiveness of the Structural Funds (and of regional policies in general) as instruments for the reduction of income disparities. Many critics of these programs argue that they cannot be very effective on the grounds that billion-dollar expenditures over two decades have not translated into clear progress in terms of regional convergence. An academic exposition of this view can be found in a recent paper by Boldrin and Canova (2001). These authors examine the evolution of the distribution of income across the EU regions over the past two decades and find no evidence that convergence is taking place or that recipients of EU transfers (with the exception of Ireland) have performed better than other regions. Like the less formal versions of the same argument, however, their analysis has the serious shortcoming that it fails to control for any factors other than EU aid.

A recent paper by Ederveen, Gorter, and Nahuis (2001) illustrates why results obtained in this manner can be extremely misleading. These authors estimate a series of convergence equations relating growth in the European regions to initial income per capita and Structural Fund transfers. When no additional variables are included in the equation, the estimated coefficient on the transfers variable is negative and significant. When regional fixed effects are introduced, however, the coefficient of EU transfers becomes positive and significant. Upon reflection, these results should not be surprising. Since the recipients of EU aid are by definition poor regions, the volume of aid works as a proxy for the omitted variables that presumably explain why these regions have below-average incomes. The estimated coefficient on the volume of aid is negative because this is the only way the specification allows one to assign to these territories a low steady-state level of income. But as soon as other factors are controlled for, even by the simple expedient of introducing a set of regional dummies, the positive impact of aid on growth becomes apparent.

A more sophisticated, although indirect, case against regional policies can be found in the regional convergence literature (see Barro and Sala i Martin 1991 and especially Sala i Martin 1996). While these authors find that the speed of regional convergence is very low in Europe and in other samples, they are also skeptical about government's ability to accelerate the process. The main piece of evidence they offer to back up this conclusion is a remarkable empirical regularity: the apparent stability of the rate of convergence, which has been found to be close to 2 percent a year in a variety of samples. According to Sala i Martin, the fact that convergence takes place at practically the same speed within groups of territories supposedly characterized by very different levels of redistributive effort implies that such policies cannot be very effective.

This conclusion seems, however, much too hasty. Governments can certainly influence the rate at which regions accumulate various productive factors—particularly infrastructures and human capital. To the extent that these factors have an effect on productivity, and on the location of mobile private inputs, there will be room for supply-side policies to influence the dispersion of regional incomes and to promote or accelerate income convergence. From this point of view, the stability of the convergence coefficient across different samples may indicate that the level of redistributive effort has been too low to have a noticeable effect on the evolution of income disparities, and/or that the policies adopted in the past have not been very effective, but it cannot be taken as evidence that regional policy per se is necessarily ineffective.

Since EU regional policy has essentially taken the form of conditional grants for the financing of training and infrastructure projects, the discussion about its effectiveness should begin with an analysis of the contribution of these two types of investment expenditures to productivity growth. Although the issue is, as we will see, somewhat controversial, I believe that the existing evidence provides reasonable support for the view that expenditure on education can have a considerable effect on productivity growth, and that the same holds true for infrastructure investment, at least in regions where the endowment of this factor is relatively low.

Academic economists have traditionally been inclined to consider educational expenditure a key component of national investment, with a substantial economic payoff in terms of output growth, and have often assigned the accumulation of human capital a central role in formal models, particularly in the recent literature on endogenous growth. This optimism seemed to be confirmed by a first round of cross-country empirical studies of the determinants of growth, where a variety of educational indicators were consistently found to have the expected positive effect. A second round of such studies (using panel data techniques), however, produced rather disappointing results and even led some researchers to question the link between education and productivity.[2] In recent years, the evidence seemed to be accumulating that such negative results were largely due to poor data and various econometric problems. The current thinking about this issue is probably well summarized by Temple (2000), who, after surveying the relevant micro- and macroeconomic evidence, concludes that "the weight of the evidence points to significant productivity effects" of educational investment. Some recent work by de la Fuente and Doménech (2002) helps support this conclusion. They find, in particular, that the amount of measurement error in the educational data sets that have been used in most growth studies is very considerable and that this error induces a large downward bias in the estimated coefficient of human capital in the aggregate production function. When this bias is corrected using an extension of the classical errors-in-variables model, the results suggest that the contribution of educational investment to productivity growth is quite sizable.

The degree of consensus on the productivity effects of infrastructure investment is probably much smaller. The issue has been the subject of a debate that is still ongoing in the literature. The available empirical evidence is problematic, and its interpretation is complicated by econometric problems that have not been fully solved. Early work on the subject, notably by Aschauer (1989), concluded that the elasticity of national or regional output with respect to public capital is large and very significant, and that the rate of return on public investment is exceedingly high. A number of more recent studies, however, have questioned these results on the basis of various econometric problems. Some of these studies find that the significance of public capital disappears when a specification in first differences is used or fixed effects are introduced to control for unobserved national or regional specificities; these studies conclude that the accumulation of public capital does not appreciably contribute to productivity growth. Other recent papers, by contrast, confirm the significance of infrastructure indicators using cointegration or panel data techniques that should in principle take care of some of the main objections to Aschauer's results. Some of them (especially Fernald 1999) also provide rather convincing evidence that causation runs from infrastructure investment to productivity growth, and not the other way around.

De la Fuente (2002b) surveys the available evidence and concludes that there are sufficient indications that public infrastructure investment contributes significantly to productivity growth, at least in countries or regions where a saturation point has not been reached. The returns to such investment are probably quite high when infrastructures are scarce and basic networks have not been completed, but fall sharply thereafter. Hence, appropriate infrastructure provision is probably a basic ingredient for a successful (regional or national) development policy, even if it does not hold the key to rapid productivity growth in advanced countries where transportation and communications needs are already adequately served. This conclusion is based in part on a comparison of results for the regions of Spain and the U.S. states. Public capital variables are almost always significant in panel data specifications for the Spanish regions and often insignificant in similar exercises conducted with U.S. data. One possible explanation for this difference is that, as Fernald (1999) notes, the data for the U.S. states start in 1970—that is, at approximately the time when the interstate highway system was completed—whereas the Spanish data refer to a sample where the stock of infrastructures is still clearly insufficient.

Some Impact Estimates for Spain

Even though the evidence on the subject is not as clear as one would like, on the whole, the literature that I have briefly surveyed in the previous section suggests that investment in education and infrastructure is an important source of productivity growth. It follows that a policy aimed at reducing regional disparities by supporting the accumulation of these factors in poor regions can work in principle.

In this section I will provide some estimates of the impact of regional policies on growth and convergence in Spain. These estimates are based on a simple supply-oriented model that has been estimated with regional panel data covering 30 years. The model has two basic ingredients. The first is an aggregate production function that relates regional output to the level of employment, the stocks of productive factors (infrastructures, other physical capital, and the educational attainment of the work force), and the level of technical efficiency. The second is an employment equation that describes the evolution of this variable as a function of changes in factor stocks and in wage rates, allowing in an ad hoc fashion for adjustment costs that generate sluggish dynamics.[3] I will also use an investment function estimated with national data for a sample of Organisation for Economic Co-operation and Development (OECD) countries to try to approximate the response of private investment to the measures financed by the Structural Funds.[4]

Before turning to the Structural Funds per se, I want to take a quick look at the evolution of Spanish infrastructure policy over the past four decades. The model I have sketched above can be used to estimate the contribution of infrastructure investment to convergence in income per capita across the Spanish regions. Figure 9-1 summarizes the results of this calculation for each quinquennium between 1955 and 1995.[5] It shows that Spanish infrastructure investment was not redistributive at all prior to 1980. After this date, by contrast, the redistributive pattern is clear and the contribution to regional convergence becomes positive and sizable. Although the policy shift actually starts a bit before Spain's accession to the EU (in 1986), there is little question that the Structural Funds have played a key role by channeling a large volume of infrastructure investment into lagging regions.

In the remainder of this section I will use the same model to estimate the contribution of the last completed Community Support Framework (CSF) to the growth of output and employment in the poorer Spanish regions.[6] The exercise is based on the assumption that investment projects that are cofinanced by the EU are no different from others of the same nature. This assumption may be a bit too optimistic because, by reducing marginal costs, EU subsidies may have made for somewhat laxer project selection standards than otherwise, but I am reasonably confident that it is not a bad approximation.

The calculations that follow attempt to quantify the contribution of all the public resources channeled through the CSF (including national cofinancing as well as EU grants) and of the induced change in private investment to growth in output and employment during the period 1994–2000. The calculation involves adding these flows of resources to observed 1993 factor stocks and using the estimated production

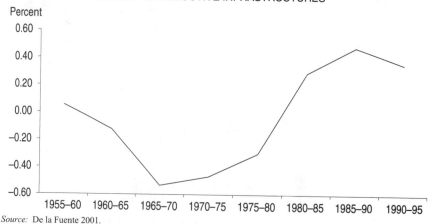

FIGURE 9-1 BETA CONVERGENCE/DIVERGENCE IN RELATIVE INCOME PER CAPITA INDUCED BY INVESTMENT IN PRODUCTIVE INFRASTRUCTURES

Percent

| | 1955–60 | 1960–65 | 1965–70 | 1970–75 | 1975–80 | 1980–85 | 1985–90 | 1990–95 |

Source: De la Fuente 2001.

and employment functions to calculate the resulting increase in the variables of interest over their observed values in the reference year. The results should be interpreted
with caution because (among many other things) they do not provide a valid response
to the question of what would have happened if the Structural Funds had not existed.
To answer this question, we would need to know how the Spanish administrations
would have reacted to the loss of these funds. It is almost certain that they would have
made up at least part of the loss using their own budgets, but it is hard to be more precise. As a rough adjustment for this and for the fact that the CSF also includes
national resources, I suggest multiplying my impact estimates by around one-half to
estimate the true marginal contribution of EU cohesion policy.

Figures 9-2 and 9-3 show the cumulative impact of the CSF on the stocks of productive factors and on the levels of output and employment of the entire set of Objective 1 regions (excluding Ceuta and Melilla) during the period 1994–2015. Figure 9-2
shows that the CSF can be seen as a large positive "shock" that, over a period of seven
years, raises aggregate factor stocks significantly above their starting levels (up to
20 percent in the case of infrastructures). Once the CSF has been executed (and assuming there are no new interventions), the stocks of physical capital and infrastructures
are allowed to gradually return to their original levels as CSF-financed investments
depreciate. The impact on the stock of human capital, by contrast, remains constant

FIGURE 9-2 CUMULATIVE IMPACT OF THE 1994–99 COMMUNITY SUPPORT
FRAMEWORK ON FACTOR STOCKS OF THE OBJECTIVE 1 TERRITORY

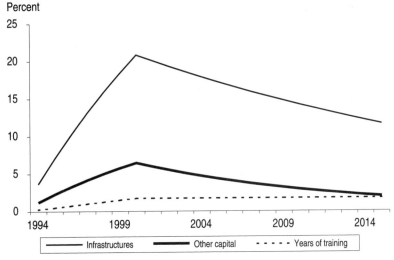

Source: Author's calculations.

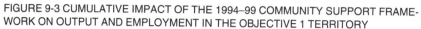

FIGURE 9-3 CUMULATIVE IMPACT OF THE 1994–99 COMMUNITY SUPPORT FRAME-
WORK ON OUTPUT AND EMPLOYMENT IN THE OBJECTIVE 1 TERRITORY

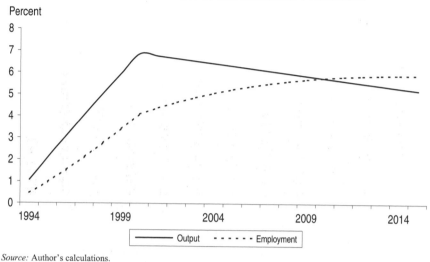

Source: Author's calculations.

until the end of the working life of the beneficiaries of training programs, which, on average, will take place after the end of the period covered in the figure.

Figure 9-3 traces the impact of these shocks on the evolution of output and employment. As may be expected, the output effect has approximately the same profile as factor stocks and begins to decline as soon as the CSF has been completely executed. The time path of employment, on the other hand, is very different from that in figure 9-2. Since this variable adjusts sluggishly over time, net job creation remains positive until about 15 years after the conclusion of the programming period.

Figure 9-4 summarizes the cumulative impact of the CSF on the output and employment of each of the Objective 1 regions in 2000. The figure shows that the growth effects of the CSF vary significantly across territories, reflecting differences in both the volume of investment and its rate of return. For the Objective 1 regions as a whole, the CSF adds 6.9 percentage points to output and 3.4 points to employment in 2000. When we take as our reference the entire country, the CSF's cumulative contributions to Spanish output and employment in the same year are 3.5 and 1.85 points, respectively.

Figure 9-5 quantifies the CSF's contribution to convergence in income per capita between Objective 1 regions and the rest of the country. It shows a *convergence ratio* that measures the fraction of the original income gap that would have disappeared as a result of the execution of the CSF (if the population of the different regions had

FIGURE 9-4 CUMULATIVE IMPACT OF THE COMMUNITY SUPPORT FRAMEWORK IN 2000

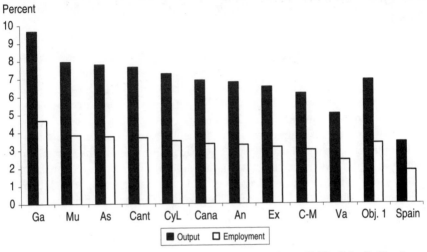

An = Andalucia; As = Asturia; Cana = Canarias; Cant = Cantabria; C-M = Ceuta y Melilla; CyL = Castilla y Leon; Ex = Extremadura; Ga = Galicia; Mu = Murcia; Obj. 1 = Objective 1; Va = Valencia.
Source: Author's research.

FIGURE 9-5 CONVERGENCE RATIOS INDUCED BY THE COMMUNITY SUPPORT FRAMEWORK

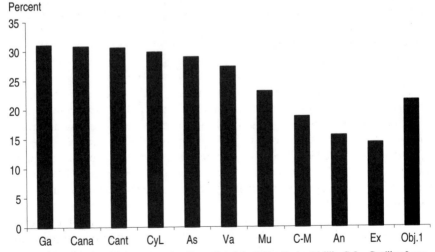

An = Andalucia; As = Asturia; Cana = Canarias; Cant = Cantabria; C-M = Ceuta y Melilla; CyL = Castilla y Leon; Ex = Extremadura; Ga = Galicia; Mu = Murcia; Obj. 1 = Objective 1; Va = Valencia.
Source: Author's research.

remained constant over the sample period and growth performance had been uniform across them except for the effects of the CSF). For the whole of the Objective 1 territory, this coefficient is a bit over 20 percent and reaches values above 30 percent for Canarias, Cantabria, and Galicia.

Should There Be Cohesion across Countries or across Regions?

The estimates in the previous section suggest that structural policies have worked quite well in Spain. They have contributed significantly to the growth of the poorer regions and to the reduction of regional disparities. It must be recognized, however, that focusing on lagging regions entails a sizable efficiency cost and may not be optimal from a national perspective. Figure 9-6 shows why. The estimated returns on public investment are much higher in some of the richest Spanish regions than in most of the territories that are eligible for assistance under Objective 1. It follows that the overall impact of EU aid would have been considerably higher (and Spain's convergence toward average EU income correspondingly faster) if efficiency considerations had been given greater weight in the allocation of these funds.

I am not sure that shifting structural assistance toward the richer regions of the cohesion countries is necessarily optimal, as it would certainly entail some

FIGURE 9-6 RELATIVE MARGINAL PRODUCT OF INFRASTRUCTURES IN THE SPANISH REGIONS, 1995

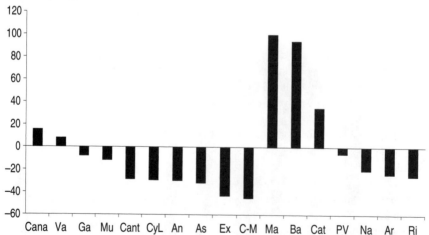

An = Andalucia; Ar = Aragon; As = Asturia; Ba = Baleares; Cana = Canarias; Cant = Cantabria; Cat = Cataluna; C-M = Ceuta y Melilla; CyL = Castilla y Leon; Ex = Extremadura; Ga = Galicia; Ma = Madrid; Mu = Muricia; Na = Navarra; PV = Pais Vasco; Ri = Rioja; Va = Valencia.
Source: Author's research.

cost in the form of greater internal inequality in output per capita. On the other hand, this cost will be substantially mitigated by the standard mechanisms for personal redistribution that operate within (but not across) countries. The social protection and tax systems of European countries will redirect a significant part of any income gains from more efficient investment policies toward the poorer segments of the population. For Spain, I have estimated that a policy shift in this direction would generate a net welfare gain (see de la Fuente 2002c). This may not be the case elsewhere, but I would argue that member countries should certainly be free to distribute EU development funds across regions as they see fit, after weighing the relevant costs and benefits. Or, to put it in a slightly different way, cohesion policy should be formulated at the national rather than at the regional level because member countries have adequate mechanisms for internal redistribution.

Notes

This chapter was prepared for a conference on income convergence and European regional policy organized by the Bertelsmann Foundation, the World Bank, and Fundación CIDOB. I gratefully acknowledge financial support from the Spanish Ministry of Science and Technology under grant SEC99-1189 and from Fundación Caixa Galicia.

1. See de la Fuente and Doménech (2001) for an analysis of the redistributive impact of the EU budget.

2. Positive results are reported by, among others, Mankiw, Romer, and Weil (1992) and Barro and Lee (1994), while Islam (1995), Caselli, Esquivel, and Lefort (1996), and other authors report the loss of significance of schooling indicators in fixed-effect specifications. Pritchett (1995) also reports negative results and argues that we should start taking them at face value.

3. See de la Fuente (2002a) for the details of the model and its estimation.

4. This function is the one estimated in de la Fuente (1997). I would have much preferred to estimate an investment function for the Spanish regions, but some of the required data are not available.

5. Figure 9-1 shows the partial convergence coefficient induced by infrastructure investment in each period. This parameter measures the rate of beta convergence that would have been observed if all regions had experienced similar growth rates except for the contribution of infrastructure investment. For further details on the parameter's meaning and construction, see de la Fuente (forthcoming).

6. This section is based on de la Fuente (2002a).

Bibliography

The word *processed* describes informally reproduced works that may not be commonly available through libraries.

Aschauer, David. 1989. "Is Public Expenditure Productive?" *Journal of Monetary Economics* 23:177–200.

Barro, Robert, and Jong-Wha Lee. 1994. "Sources of Economic Growth." *Carnegie-Rochester Conference Series on Public Policy* 40:1–46.

Barro, Robert, and Xavier Sala i Martin. 1991. "Convergence across States and Regions." *Brookings Papers on Economic Activity* 1:107–82.

Boldrin, Michele, and Fabio Canova. 2001. "Inequality and Convergence in Europe's Regions: Reconsidering European Regional Policy." *Economic Policy* 32:205–45.

Caselli, Francesco, Gerardo Esquivel, and Fernando Lefort. 1996. "Reopening the Convergence Debate: A New Look at Cross-Country Growth Empirics." *Journal of Economic Growth* 1(3):363–89.

de la Fuente, Angel. 1997. "Fiscal Policy and Growth in the OECD." CEPR Discussion Paper 1755. London: Centre for Economic Policy Research.

———. 2001. "Infraestructuras y política regional." In T. García-Milà, ed., *Nuevas Fronteras de la Política Económica, 2001.* Barcelona: Generalitat de Cataluña and Universidad Pompeu Fabra.

———. 2002a. "The Effect of Structural Fund Spending on the Spanish Regions: An Assessment of the 1994–99 Objective 1 CSF." Instituto de Análisis Económico, Barcelona. Processed.

———. 2002b. "Infrastructures and Productivity: A Survey." Instituto de Análisis Económico, Barcelona. Processed.

———. 2002c. "Is the Allocation of Public Capital across the Spanish Regions Too Redistributive?" CEPR Discussion Paper 3138. London: Centre for Economic Policy Research.

———. Forthcoming. "Convergence Equations and Income Dynamics: The Sources of OECD Convergence, 1970–95." *Economica.*

de la Fuente, Angel, and Rafael Doménech. 2001. "The Redistributive Effects of the EU Budget: An Analysis and a Proposal for Reform." *Journal of Common Market Studies* 39(2):307–30.

———. 2002. "Human Capital in Growth Regressions: How Much Difference Does Data Quality Make? An Update and Further Results." CEPR Discussion Paper 3587. London: Centre for Economic Policy Research.

Ederveen, S., J. Gorter, and R. Nahuis. 2001. "The Wealth of Regions: The Impact of Structural Funds on Convergence in the EU." Netherlands Bureau for Economic Policy Analysis, The Hague. Processed.

Fernald, John. 1999. "Roads to Prosperity? Assessing the Link between Public Capital and Productivity." *American Economic Review* 89(3):619–38.

Islam, Nazrul. 1995. "Growth Empirics: A Panel Data Approach." *Quarterly Journal of Economics* 110:1127–70.

Mankiw, Gregory, David Romer, and David Weil. 1992. "A Contribution to the Empirics of Economic Growth." *Quarterly Journal of Economics* 7(2):407–37.

Pritchett, Lant. 1995. "Where Has All the Education Gone?" Washington, D.C.: World Bank. Processed.

Sala i Martin, Xavier. 1996. "Regional Cohesion: Evidence and Theories of Regional Growth and Convergence." *European Economic Review* 40:1325–52.

Temple, J. 2000. "Growth Effects of Education and Social Capital in the OECD." Oxford University. Processed.

CHAPTER 10

Do Structural Actions Contribute to Reduced Regional Disparities in the European Union?

Antoni Castells and Marta Espasa

First of all, it is necessary to discuss some relevant points concerning regional policy in the European Union (EU). Currently, there exist two instruments of regional policy: the Structural Funds and the Cohesion Fund. They both are called Structural Actions. Since the last reform, the Structural Funds have had three main objectives:

1. *Objective 1,* the most important in quantitative terms, is the development and structural adjustment of the poorest regions in the EU—that is, the regions that have a gross domestic product (GDP) per capita below 75 percent of the EU average in purchasing power standards (PPS) terms. This objective includes the former Objectives 1 and 6.

2. *Objective 2* is focused on the economic and social restructuring of regions with structural deficiencies. This objective absorbs the former Objectives 2 and 5b.

3. *Objective 3* aims for the adaptation and modernization of education systems, training, and employment. This objective is the result of the integration of the former Objectives 3 and 4.

These objectives are carried out through four Structural Funds: the European Regional Development Fund (ERDF), the European Social Fund, the European

Agricultural Guidance and Guarantee Fund, and the Financial Instrument for Fisheries Guidance.

It could be useful to remark that Objective 1 applies to the four funds, not only to the ERDF. So it is important not to confuse EU regional aid and the ERDF, though this one is the most important instrument for achieving the reduction of regional disparities.

As will be more deeply examined in a later chapter, the implementation of the Structural Funds is relatively complex because the programming is made by objectives, while the management and the execution take place by funds.

The other instrument of the Structural Actions is the Cohesion Fund, which supports transportation and infrastructure projects. In contrast to Structural Funds, the Cohesion Fund is not allocated to the regions but to the four states with a per capita gross national product below 90 percent of the EU average: Greece, Portugal, Spain, and (temporarily) Ireland.

Tables 10-1 and 10-2 contain some key data on Structural Actions:

- Structural Actions represent around one-third of the EU budget.

- For 2000–2006, Structural Actions will amount to 213 billion euros (that is, 2.7 percent of the 1999 EU GDP).

- The yearly average amount of Structural Actions has increased from 10.6 billion European currency units (ECUs) during the period 1988–92 to 30.4 billion euros during 2000–2006. It means an increase of 5.7 percent per annum.

TABLE 10-1 KEY DATA ON REGIONAL AID IN THE EU: GLOBAL AMOUNT
AND EVOLUTION (FINANCIAL PERSPECTIVES)

Category	1988–92 (millions ECU/euro)	(%)	1993–99 (millions ECU/euro)	(%)	2000–2006 (millions ECU/euro)	(%)
Structural Actions	53,140	21.7	176,348	33.5	213,010	33.0
Structural Funds	53,140	21.7	162,248	30.6	195,010	30.2
Cohesion Fund	—	—	15,150	2.9	18,000	2.8
EU budget	244,838	100.0	529,885	100.0	646,190	100.0

— Not available.
Source: European Commission 2001.

TABLE 10-2 KEY DATA ON REGIONAL AID IN THE EU: MAIN BENEFICIARY
COUNTRIES, 2000–2006

Country	Percent of total	Percent of GDP[a]
Spain	26.4	1.4
Germany	14.0	0.2
Italy	13.9	0.4
Greece	11.7	3.0
Portugal	10.7	3.1

a. Yearly average of GDP 1999.
Source: European Commission 2001.

- Structural Funds represent around 90 percent of Structural Actions, while the Cohesion Fund represents the remaining 10 percent. The ERDF is the biggest of the four Structural Funds, accounting for 58 percent of all Structural Funds.

- The main beneficiary countries, in absolute terms, are Spain, which receives 26.4 percent of total Structural Actions; Germany, 14.0 percent; Italy, 13.9 percent; Greece, 11.7 percent; and Portugal, 10.7 percent.

- Structural Actions are specially allocated to the poorest countries of the EU: Portugal receives an amount equivalent to 3.1 percent of its GDP; Greece, 3.0 percent; and Spain, 1.4 percent.

Structural Actions and Reduction of Regional Inequalities

In this section we discuss the impact of Structural Actions on the reduction of regional disparities in the EU, focusing on two key issues[1]:

1. Does the regional aid reduce regional disparities in the EU?

2. Does the regional aid produce a progressive redistribution of income among regions?

Table 10-3 shows the most and the least benefited regions as a result of the direct impact of the Structural Actions, considering the net fiscal balance produced by these actions. By net fiscal balance we mean the amount of Structural Actions allocated to

TABLE 10-3 REGIONAL REDISTRIBUTIVE EFFECTS OF STRUCTURAL ACTIONS
(average for the period 1995–97)

Region	Amount received	Net fiscal balance	Percent of GDP	Index GDP-95 (PPS/inhabitant; EU = 100)
Most benefited regions (millions of ECUs in PPS)				
Azores (Portugal)	902.3	893.1	43.3	50
Madeira (Portugal)	662.0	648.8	28.1	52
Aegean and Crete Islands (Greece)	675.5	624.2	5.3	68
Alentejo (Portugal)	289.0	268.1	5.2	57
Algarve (Portugal)	176.0	159.1	3.8	70
Basilicata (Italy)	394.4	267.3	3.6	69
Ceuta-Melilla (Spain)	53.9	52.5	3.5	65
Least benefited regions (millions of ECUs in PPS)				
Brussels (Belgium)	4.7	−248.4	−0.9	172
Luxembourg	14.2	−91.6	−0.8	168
Rheinland-Pfalz (Germany)	46.1	−243.4	−0.4	99
Baden-Württemberg (Germany)	63.9	−782.9	−0.3	126
Stockholm (Sweden)	8.6	−122.2	−0.3	124
Nordrhein-Westfalen (Germany)	227.2	−1,160.5	−0.3	113
Schleswig-Holstein (Germany)	45.0	−162.1	−0.3	106

Note: Net fiscal balance is the amount of Structural Actions allocated to the region *minus* the contribution of the region to the financing of the Structural Actions.
Sources: Espasa 2000 and Eurostat 1998.

the region *minus* the contribution of the region to the financing of the Structural Actions—that is, the fiscal flow produced directly by the Structural Actions in this region.

What does table 10-3 show?

- The most benefited regions are clearly poor in communitarian terms.

- Excluding Azores and Madeira, which are very particular cases, the direct impact of Structural Actions in these regions is between 3.5 percent and 5.3 percent of GDP.

- The distribution among countries of the 15 most benefited regions is as follows: Spain, 6 regions; Portugal, 4; Greece, 3; and Italy, 2.

- The least benefited regions are, in general, rich regions in communitarian terms, but there is wide variation: Brussels and Luxembourg have an index of about 170, but Rheinland-Pfalz is slightly below the EU average.

- The direct impact of Structural Actions is around −0.3 to −0.4 percent of the regional GDP, except for Brussels and Luxembourg where it is close to −1 percent.

- German regions in particular contribute heavily to Structural Actions: four out of the first seven regions in the bottom half of table 10-3 are German regions.

Therefore, we can conclude that Structural Actions are allocated according to regional disparities among European regions.

Table 10-4 shows the reduction in the interregional disparities in GDP per capita due directly to the Structural Actions. We have elaborated different indicators of inequalities, some of them very elementary. We observe that the ratio of the regional GDP per capita between the top 10 percent and the bottom 10 percent is around 2.46 and becomes 2.34 after the Structural Actions. So, it is a reduction of nearly 5 percent. The reduction of the coefficient of variation is 3.62 percent. And finally, the Gini index in GDP per capita is 0.1979 before the Structural Actions and 0.1863 after. Therefore, the inequality is reduced by nearly 6 percent.

Thus, we can conclude that Structural Actions have a redistribution effect of reducing regional inequality between 3.5 percent and 6 percent, according to the inequality index we use.

TABLE 10-4 REDUCTION IN THE INTERREGIONAL DISPARITIES IN GDP PER CAPITA DUE TO STRUCTURAL ACTIONS

Category	Initial GDP per capita	Final GDP per capita	Percent variation
Maximum–minimum ratio			
One region	3.6931	3.5778	−3.12
10 percent of the regions	2.4591	2.3382	−4.92
20 percent of the regions	2.0744	1.9837	−4.37
Coefficient of variation	0.2503	0.2412	−3.62
Gini index	0.1979	0.1863	−5.87

Note: Final GDP = initial GDP *plus* net fiscal balance.
Sources: Espasa 2000 and Eurostat 1998.

Structural Actions, Income Redistribution, and Economic Growth

The negative relationship observed in table 10-4 between Structural Actions and GDP per capita should be more systematically tested. Can we show the existence of a negative and significant relationship between the level of GDP per capita and the net fiscal balance produced by Structural Actions in the different regions?

Table 10-5 answers this question. There is a negative and strongly significant relationship between both variables. The lower the GDP per capita, the higher the positive impact of Structural Actions. Row 1 of table 10-5 indicates that the elasticity of the ratio of net fiscal balance to GDP in relation to the GDP per capita is around −6.5 percent, which means that an increase of 10 percent in GDP per capita produces a reduction of 0.65 percent in the ratio of net fiscal balance to GDP. This is an important redistributive impact, considering that funds represent only 0.4 percent of the EU GDP. Comparing, for instance, with national funds, the equivalent coefficient would be around −35 percent to −40 percent, but they represent 40 percent to 50 percent of GDP (that is, 6 times more impact but 100 times greater size).

In the same sense, row 2 of table 10-5 indicates that the elasticity of final GDP in relation to initial GDP is 0.935. This means that an increase in GDP of 10 percent becomes an increase of only 9.35 percent because the remaining 0.65 percent is redistributed toward poor regions through Structural Actions.

Finally, we are especially interested in the effect of Structural Actions on regional growth. Does regional aid produce a significant effect on growth of regional

TABLE 10-5 RELATIONSHIP BETWEEN NET FISCAL BALANCE AND GDP PER CAPITA ($n = 122$)

Dependent variable	Constant	Independent variable: ln Y	R^2	F
ln NFB	0.0029	−0.0655	0.1916	29.7
	(0.836)	(−5.448)	(0.03647)	
ln YF	0.0029	0.9345	0.9804	6,039.3
	(0.836)	(77.713)	(0.03647)	

Note: NFB = net fiscal balance due to Structural Actions (in the regression this variable is specific as 1 + NFB/GDP); YF = final GDP (YF = Y + NFB), where Y = regional GDP per capita (expressed as an index with respect to the average and in PPS).
Source: Castells and Espasa 2002.

GDP? A preliminary result was obtained when testing this relationship. Row 2 of table 10-5 shows a strongly significant and positive effect of Structural Actions on regional growth. The elasticity between both variables is around 0.02.

However, the results change dramatically if we take account of a convergence process. If we introduce the variable GDP per capita, then the significance and the coefficient of the variable Structural Actions are sharply reduced. This reduction occurs because Structural Actions may have an effect on regional growth but may actually overlap a process of convergence/divergence that would have taken place even without the Structural Actions.

The reverse is also true. The intensity of the process of economic convergence is dramatically reduced if we introduce the factor Structural Actions (table 10-6). The coefficient of regression (β-convergence coefficient) is reduced, in absolute terms, from −0.0950 (row 1) to −0.0617 (row 3), and its significance is reduced from 99 percent to 95 percent. The conclusion is that when studying economic convergence, it is particularly important to specify the explicative function, introducing the appropriate variables for controlling nonconsidered effects.

Finally, we would like to mention that different models have been used for simulating the macroeconomic effects of Structural Actions. The European Commission has published some of the most important results. It is difficult to compare these models because they use different methodological approaches and consider different channels of the impact of the Structural Actions on GDP. Some of them mainly consider the demand effects, while others pay special attention to effects on productivity (table 10-7).

TABLE 10-6 EFFECTS OF THE STRUCTURAL ACTIONS ON REGIONAL GROWTH, 1995–97 (n = 122)

Dependent variable	Constant	Independent variable: ln GDP pc95	Independent variable: ln SApc	R^2	F
ln (GDPpc98/GDPpc95)	1.0789 (5.608)	−0.0950 (−4.771)		0.1525 (0.060400)	22.767
ln (GDPpc98/GDPpc95)	0.1960 (20.780)		0.0190 (4.526)	0.1387 (0.060889)	20.485
ln (GDPpc98/GDPpc95)	0.7735 (2.584)	−0.0617 (−1.930)	0.0089 (1.328)	0.1578 (0.060209)	12.338

Note: GDPpc = GDP per capita expressed in PPS; SApc = expenditure per capita on Structural Actions.
Source: Castells and Espasa 2002.

TABLE 10-7 MACROECONOMIC IMPACT OF THE STRUCTURAL FUNDS: COMPARISON OF THE RESULTS OF THE SIMULATION MACROECONOMETRIC MODELS
(percent of additional growth with respect to the basic situation)

	Pereira	Beutel		Hermin 4			QUEST II	
	1994–99	1989–93	1994–99	1994	1999	2020	1989–93	1994–99
	Annual average (%)	Annual average (%)	Annual average (%)	Total effects (demand effects)	Total effects (demand effects)	Total effects (demand effects)	Annual average (%)	Annual average (%)
Greece	0.4–0.6	0.8	1.0	1.2 (1.1)	9.4 (4.8)	9.5 (1.5)	0.3	0.1
Ireland	0.4–0.6	0.9	0.6	6.2 (6.2)	9.3 (5.9)	12.4 (4.0)	0.3	0.3
Portugal	0.6–0.9	0.9	1.1	7.0 (7.0)	9.2 (8.1)	8.9 (7.6)	0.3	0.2
Spain	—	0.3	0.5	1.9 (1.9)	4.3 (2.9)	8.7 (1.9)	0.1	0.1
EU4 average	—	0.5	0.7	—	—	—	—	—

— Not available.
Source: European Commission 1999.

Concluding Remarks

This chapter contains three main points:

1. The direct impact (that is, the transfer impact generated by the flow of income directly produced by the EU budget) of Structural Actions has a positive and significant effect in the reduction of regional disparities (around 5 percent).

2. This impact is limited because of the small size of these funds relative to the EU GDP (0.4 percent).

3. While this direct impact is very clear, it is much more difficult to evaluate the medium- and long-term effects of the regional aid with regard to stimulation of endogenous growth.

Finally, we should raise two specific issues about the future of Structural Actions.

Direct Income Transfers or Medium- and Long-Term Effects on GDP Growth

Theoretically, the Structural Actions produce two kinds of effects on regional income: (a) a direct income transfer from some European regions to other European regions; and (b) a positive impact on the medium- and long-term GDP growth of beneficiary regions. Although the second of these two effects is the specific target of regional policy, it must be noted that while the first effect is very clearly tested, the results concerning the second one are much less conclusive.

Specifically, a sharp reduction in disposable income inequalities (that is, the income after the budgetary action of the government) can be verified (for instance, in Spain), but a much more moderate reduction in GDP inequalities is also verified. However, it is also true that this reduction could have been slighter (or even negative) in the absence of Structural Actions.

We have to stress the special difficulties in evaluating the specific impacts of regional policy on the endogenous factors of growth (and, in the end, on the GDP) because of the multiple causal relations that are involved for both variables. However, this is a problem of not just the Structural Actions but all regional policy. Over the years it has been difficult to obtain conclusive results about the real effects of domestic regional policies on regional growth in any country. Thus, we should not blame the regional EU policy for a problem that has to be attributed to our own limitations.

Territorial Scope of Structural Actions

What should be the eligible territories for Structural Actions: poor regions or poor states? As is well known, regions are now the eligible territories for Structural Funds (which amount to around 90 percent of all Structural Actions), and states are now the eligible territories for the Cohesion Fund.

Territorial scope is a relevant issue for two reasons. First, if Structural Actions were allocated to more productive regions of the poorest states, there would be a greater effect on the global growth of these states. Second, the most important redistributive effect among regional income comes from the national budget (which represents around 50 percent of GDP) rather than from the European budget (which is around 1 percent of GDP). Therefore, at the end of the day a higher GDP in the richest regions of the poorest states spreads, via the national budget, to their poorest regions.

There is still an additional reason to be considered: the general condition of co-financing of the Structural Actions obliges the beneficiary countries to allocate a very important share of "domestic" public investment to the poorest regions, which means that in a situation of budgetary discipline, only a limited amount of public investment is allocated in the richest regions of the poorest states.

Obviously, all these reasons would not be valid if Structural Actions were something more than a plain transfer of income—that is, if it were proved that they have a relevant effect on medium- and long-term GDP growth of beneficiary regions.

Note

1. The tables and the results that we are going to comment upon are based on data from the Ph.D. thesis of Marta Espasa (2000), who has estimated the detail of the allocation of Structural Actions at the regional level. A first presentation of the results appeared in Castells and Espasa 2002.

Bibliography

Castells, Antoni, and Marta Espasa. 2002. "Desequilibrios territoriales y políticas de cohesión en la Unión Europea en la perspectiva de la ampliación." *Papeles de Economía Española* 91:253–78.

Espasa, Marta. 2000. "The Redistributive Power of the European Union Budget: Analysis through Fiscal Regional Flows." Ph.D. diss., University of Barcelona, Department of Public Finance.

European Commission. 1999. *Sixth Periodic Report on the Social and Economic Situation and Development of the Regions of the European Union.* Luxembourg.

———. 2001. *Second Report on Economic and Social Cohesion.* Luxembourg.

Eurostat. 1998. *Statistiques en bref.* Region 1. Luxembourg.

CHAPTER 11

Impact of Regional Aid on Catalonia

Alexandre Muns

Catalonia does not qualify for Objective 1 resources, as its gross domestic product (GDP) per capita is higher than 75 percent of the European Union (EU) average. Per capita gross national product (GNP) in Catalonia (purchasing power parity, or PPP) in 1996 was only 1 percent below the EU average, while per capita GNP in Spain remained 21 percent below the EU average. Income convergence of Catalonia with the EU has been achieved through high rates of economic growth and the adoption of policies that have enhanced competitiveness and have been supplemented by funding from the EU. The liberalization of services markets in accordance with the Single Market Program has also contributed powerfully to GNP growth considering the relative decline of the industrial sector.

By the end of the 2000–2006 period, Catalonia's per capita GDP is expected to rise to 110 percent of the EU average, thanks to growth rates that will continue to surpass the EU average. Catalonia *does* qualify for Objective 2 resources. Its solid traditional industrial base, which nonetheless has experienced a considerable decline since the 1970s, enables it to qualify for Objective 2 given the relatively high percentage of the work force employed in the industrial sector. Catalonia is also experiencing structural difficulties in the agricultural sector that make it eligible to receive funding under Objective 2. Most of the Catalan territory is eligible to receive EU Structural Funds under Objective 2. The amount of money that Catalonia obtains from the EU Structural Funds is comparable to the resources it raises through its tax on the registration of vehicles.

Priorities for the 1994–99 Period

Execution of the projects approved for this period was deemed satisfactory by the regional authorities. The projects were executed through the European Regional Development Fund (ERDF), the European Social Fund (ESF), the Cohesion Fund, the European Agricultural Guidance and Guarantee Fund-Guidance (EAGGF-G), and the Financial Instrument for Fisheries Guidance (FIFG) according to the following objectives:

Territorial:

- Objective 2: Restructure regions that suffer from industrial decline.

- Objective 5b: Foster development of rural areas.

Horizontal:

- Objective 3: Tackle long-term unemployment.

- Objective 4: Support the adaptation of workers to industrial transformations.

- Objective 5a: Speed up the modernization of the agricultural and fishing structures.

- Additionally, some of the actions carried out by the Structural Funds in Catalonia were executed through 13 different EU initiatives: Interreg, Retex, Urban, Pime, Rechar, Konver, Leader, Pesca, Adapt, Integra, Now, Horizon, Youthstart.

ERDF

The subsidies that flowed from the ERDF to Catalonia in the 1994–99 period amounted to €912 million, which is the equivalent of €226 per capita. In the 1993–96 period, Catalonia received an annual average of €87.3 million from the ERDF, placing it among the last regions in Spain because it does not qualify for Objective 1 funding. The focus of the ERDF funding has been in the following areas:

- Improvement in the production environment

- Improvement in the environment

- Research and technological development and innovation

- Transport and communications infrastructures

- Local development and quality of life.

Cohesion Fund
The Cohesion Fund has supported projects in infrastructure (transportation and services) and the environment. In 1993–96, Catalonia placed first among regions of Spain in terms of funding obtained from the Cohesion Fund (Andalucia and Madrid ranked second and third). Catalonia received an average of €109.7 million per year from the Cohesion Fund in this period.

Priorities for the 2000–2006 Period

The EU's structural and cohesion policy will be implemented in Catalonia in the 2000–2006 period through the following instruments: The Structural Funds (ERDF, ESF, EAGGF-G, FIFG), the Cohesion Fund, and the part of the EAGGF-G earmarked for rural development.

The Structural Fund actions will be channeled through the following objectives:

- Objective 2: Economic and social transformation of areas with structural deficiencies. This objective will be financed by the ERDF and the ESF.

- Objective 3: Adaptation and modernization of educational and training policies and systems. This objective is financed by the ESF.

Community initiatives:

- Interreg: Cross-border, transnational, and interregional cooperation (ERDF).

- Urban: Economic and social revamping of cities and neighborhoods affected by crises (ERDF).

- Equal: Promotion of measures to combat inequalities and discrimination in the labor market (ESF).

- Leader: Fostering rural development (EAGGF-G).

Innovative actions:

- Advancing projects related to the information society (ERDF).

- Structural actions in fisheries in areas not included in Objective 1.

Examples of Projects Financed in Catalonia

One recently financed project is construction of the high-speed train route that links Spain to the French network through Catalan territory (Train a Grande Vitesse, or TGV). This project has been considerably sped up by Cohesion Fund support. Another project involves expanding the port of Barcelona so that it can double its capacity by 2006. This project is also cofinanced by the Cohesion Fund. A water purification plant on the Besès River is also under way. The ground-breaking ceremony for this project was held in October 2002 and attended by Prime Minister José María Aznar and Catalan president Jordi Pujol. Another water purification plant is being built on the Llobregat River. Finally, under consideration is a project involving construction of a new metro (underground) line that would reach the Barcelona airport and the city's main exhibition area. It would be one of the longest metro lines in Europe.

Perverse Effects

Since Catalonia does not qualify for Objective 1 resources, EU cofinancing on regional aid projects cannot exceed 50 percent. There is thus no danger that excessive dependency on EU subsidies will be created. The projects cofinanced by the EU's regional policy in Catalonia would have been undertaken and finalized even without EU financing. The main difference is that as a result of the Structural Funds the projects are being carried out in a shorter period of time. To meet the deadlines set by the EU, the timetables for completing the projects have been accelerated.

However, various perverse effects of the funding have been noted:

- The creation of dependency on subsidies (retirees returning to Andalucia).

- The opportunity cost of not providing funds to richer regions and thus not fostering the growth potential of these regions (such as Catalonia) that contribute funding through national mechanisms toward the development of the poorer regions in the nation.

- The promotion of the establishment of economic activities that may be inefficient and for which the region offers no competitive advantage (for example, agriculture in Murcia through Common Agricultural Policy [CAP], which lacks the necessary labor pool and water resources).

Experience on an Institutional Level

The requirements for providing information to the Commission after the monies have been assigned are too cumbersome and time-consuming. The Commission demands a lot of information and the execution of many audits. These procedures require too much of the regional administration's time and resources. There is widespread consensus on the part of most existing EU member regions on the need for simplification, as was expressed in the conclusions of a May 2002 seminar on regional policy held in Brussels and attended by Commissioner Michel Barnier. Seminar attendees agreed that regional aid implementation needs to be simplified. This conclusion is especially significant for the accession countries, since their administrative machinery—especially at the regional level—is less developed than that of existing member states and will thus be unable to cope with the current information requirements of the Commission.

CHAPTER 12

Real Convergence in the Slovak Republic and European Union Regional Funds

Martin Bruncko

With the approach of European Union (EU) accession, regional development—a major EU policy concern—is fast becoming a top policy issue in the Slovak Republic. The magnitude of the funding potentially involved is considerable (up to 4 percent of gross domestic product [GDP] in EU transfers plus counterpart funds) and could conceivably help fuel the country's convergence toward EU standards. In the absence of a carefully thought-out strategy, however, this potential could easily be squandered.

This chapter suggests that while substantial regional disparities exist in the Slovak Republic in terms of output per capita, their significance for policy and planning purposes should not be misjudged. First, there is little indication that these disparities are particularly large by European standards. Second, these disparities are not widening. Third, they are hardly reflected in disparities in household income. This is due in part to the way labor market structures operate (centralized collective bargaining and single wage tariff at the national level) and to the impact of uniform social transfers. The combination of those two factors unfortunately contributes to the persistence of wide regional disparities in terms of unemployment. The first section below takes stock of these various dimensions of regional disparities and the related policy implications.

The experience of other low-income countries in joining the EU seems to indicate that rapid income convergence may be associated with an initial widening of regional differences in GDP per capita, as growth first takes hold within localized "growth poles." The second section discusses how that experience applies to the Slovak Republic.

The final section draws the contours of what a regional convergence strategy might involve for the Slovak Republic. One aspect might be to focus investments on a limited number of growth poles—starting with Bratislava—where external effects on productivity are likely to be highest, and then gradually spread externalities toward the east. In view of fiscal consolidation objectives, such public intervention policies would need to be pursued by redirecting, rather than expanding, government programs toward those key strategic objectives (regions, sectors). To be successful, such a strategy would require both labor and social welfare reform in order to give people a greater incentive to move to where the jobs are being created and to induce firms to establish themselves outside of the Bratislava growth pole.

Level and Sources of Regional Disparities

As most observers of the Slovak economy have stressed, a significant cleavage exists between the modern and well-performing Bratislava region and the much less prosperous rest of the country. With less then 12 percent of the Slovak population, Bratislava produces more than 22 percent of the Slovak GDP. If we use a regional decomposition into eight Nomenclature des Unités Territoriales Statistiques (NUTS) 3 regions (following the nomenclature used by the Eurostat), we find that the GDP per capita in the Bratislava region reaches twice the national average and more than three times that of the poorest Slovak region, Prešov (see table 12-1).

TABLE 12-1 REGIONAL GDP PER CAPITA AT PURCHASING POWER STANDARDS, 1996–99

Region	Percent of EU average				Percent of Slovak average			
	1996	1997	1998	1999	1996	1997	1998	1999
Bratislava	92	100	99	100	203	203	202	197
Trnava	51	51	50	55	106	106	103	109
Trenčín	44	44	44	46	92	93	91	92
Nitra	37	39	40	42	82	82	83	83
Žilina	38	40	41	42	84	84	84	83
Banská Bystrica	42	43	44	45	91	91	90	90
Prešov	30	31	32	32	66	66	66	65
Košice	44	44	47	50	93	93	97	99
Total	46	48	49	50	100	100	100	100

Sources: Statistical Office of the Slovak Republic, Eurostat, and author's calculations.

These disparities arise from differences in both productivity levels and employment rates (see table 12-2). Bratislava comes out ahead of the rest of the country on both counts.

Many factors combine to make Bratislava more productive than the rest of the country: its productive structure; its many small and medium enterprises (SMEs); its higher investment rates; its greater attractiveness to foreign direct investment (FDI), linked in part to its proximity to EU markets; and its concentration of university graduates. The two richest regions, Bratislava and Košice, are also those that have made the greatest progress toward a service-based economy and that currently have the highest share of services in output among all Slovak regions. Services account for almost three-quarters of value added and employment in Bratislava. At the other extreme are large parts of the southern and eastern Slovak Republic that have suffered from substantial declines in agricultural production, as well as industrial towns that were hit by the collapse of military production. SMEs have typically driven the transformation process. Again, although Bratislava accounts for 11 percent of the Slovak population, more than 32 percent of all Slovak small enterprises with less then 50 employees are based there.

The larger part of the country's capital stock is concentrated in Bratislava. Its investment-to-GDP ratio has consistently reached almost twice the national average. In per capita terms, investment in Bratislava has been 6.4 times higher than the average for all other regions and 14 times higher than for Prešov. One factor behind such high investment rates is that Bratislava has attracted the bulk of the incoming FDI. By the end of 2001, 51.4 percent of FDI stock in the corporate sector was concentrated in Bratislava. The only region that has come close has been Košice, following the purchase of VSŽ by U.S. Steel Corp.

TABLE 12-2 REGIONAL DIFFERENCES IN PRODUCTIVITY AND EMPLOYMENT

Region	Productivity[a] (% of average)	Employment rate[b]
Bratislava	158.7	60.2
Trnava	105.5	50.1
Trenčín	88.9	50.2
Nitra	89.7	44.9
Žilina	82.3	48.9
Banská Bystrica	95.3	45.8
Prešov	67.8	46.5
Košice	109.6	43.8
Total	100.0	48.5

a. Regional value added per person employed, 1999.
b. As of 2001.
Sources: Statistical Office of the Slovak Republic, Eurostat, and author's calculations.

As in other economies in Central and Eastern Europe, the Slovak geography has played an important role in shaping FDI decisions. Empirical studies of investment patterns confirm that foreign investments are motivated by market proximity (Boeri and others 2000; Döhrn 1996). Regions situated in the west and along major transportation corridors perform much better than those situated along the eastern borders with Hungary, Poland, and Ukraine. Western European centers situated close to borders with the accession countries exercise a particular influence on the neighboring border regions (Gorzelak and Zarycki 1995). Bratislava has a particular advantage in its proximity to Western markets, access to decisionmakers, good infrastructure, and network economies. Proximity to Bratislava and Austria may explain to a large extent the high FDI inflow into the Trnava region. The eastern regions face an opposite situation. They border similarly poor and economically problematic regions in the neighboring countries and are quite far from their main future markets in the EU and from deep-water ports such as Rotterdam and Hamburg. Potential investors in the region, in agricultural processing and light industry as well as in tourism, are also deterred by poor roads.

Another reason why investors choose Bratislava over other locations is its high concentration of university graduates. Bratislava has an almost 2.5 times higher share of university graduates in the labor force than the national average. This fact helps to account for the high productivity and low unemployment rates in Bratislava. Even in regions with very high unemployment, someone with a university degree is approximately three times less likely to be unemployed.

Mitigating Factors

Nevertheless, the significance of these regional differences should be not exaggerated. There are good reasons to believe that the existing statistics (although fully consistent with the Eurostat methodology) overstate the underlying reality. First, regional GDP per capita statistics record, in Bratislava, the value added generated by the large work force that commutes from outside the region. Dividing the regional output by the number of residents (irrespective of the number of people employed) inflates the output per capita figures in the region of Bratislava accordingly. Furthermore, statistics on regional GDP per capita at purchasing power standards (PPS) are calculated on the basis of a single set of prices for the whole country. The prices are taken from a survey in Bratislava only, where prices are higher than in the rest of the country, thereby leading to the underestimation of comparative GDP levels in outlying areas.

Second, leaving aside the outliers of Bratislava and Prešov, the regional variation in GDP per capita is actually fairly small. All other regions range between 42 and 55 percent of the EU average. Third, it is worth noting that regional differences in GDP per capita have been narrowing, not widening, in recent years. Fourth, the gap observed between the capital city and the rest of the country is not exceptional in Europe. The gap between the GDP per capita in Prague or Inner London and the respective national averages is even greater than that in the Slovak Republic (see table 12-3). Actually, the magnitude of the gap between the capital city region and the rest of the country depends crucially on the size of the statistical region that includes the capital city. The smaller the capital region, the higher its GDP per capita gap is likely to be, reflecting a growing density of economic activities as one moves toward city centers. In Poland and Hungary, the gap in GDP per capita between the capital region and the rest of the country may look narrower, but this is in part because the NUTS 3 regions of Bratislava, Prague, and Inner London are very small, while the NUTS 3 regions of Warsaw and Budapest include a number of surrounding areas.

Furthermore, reflecting the impact of social safety nets as well as labor market outcomes, there is much less disparity in household income across regions than there is in output per capita (see table 12-4). Barely 34 percent separates the average disposable incomes at the top and bottom of the range. It would be surprising if regional differences in cost of living were much smaller.

However, the mechanisms at play exacerbate the one truly worrisome form of regional disparity: that in (un)employment rates. Reflecting the impact of centralized collective bargaining (and of the nationwide wage tariffs collective bargaining arrangement set) and of a uniform minimum wage, there is far less wage variation across regions than the underlying differences in productivity would warrant. The case is particularly stark in the industrial sector: while industrial productivity varies by a factor of 3.5 between the most and the least productive regions, the difference in industrial wages between these two regions is less than 50 percent (table 12-5).

The net result is that higher unit labor costs price out the most depressed regions, irrespective of transport costs and other aggravating factors. Conversely, it comes as

TABLE 12-3 RELATIVE LEVEL OF GDP PER CAPITA IN SELECTED CAPITAL
REGIONS, 1999
(percent of national average)

Region	Relative level of GDP per capita
Inner London[a]	238
Prague	212
Bratislava	198
Brussels[a]	152
Warsaw	151
Budapest	149
Vienna[a]	146

a. Data for 1998.
Sources: Statistical Office of the Slovak Republic, Eurostat, and staff calculations.

TABLE 12-4 GROSS AND NET INCOME PER PERSON PER MONTH, 2000
(percent of national average)

Region	Gross income	Net income
Bratislava	125	122
Trnava	96	96
Trenčín	97	97
Nitra	98	100
Žilina	93	93
Banská Bystrica	99	99
Prešov	90	91
Košice	102	101
Total	100	100

Source: Statistical Office of the Slovak Republic.

little surprise that the employment rates we observed at the outset of this discussion (see table 12-2) are highest in regions where the wage/productivity ratio is most favorable, or that those regions also attract the most FDI (table 12-3). The presence of large social transfers to the unemployed makes the situation tolerable and limits its impact on household disposable income.

TABLE 12-5 REGIONAL DIFFERENCES IN PRODUCTIVITY AND WAGES
(percent of national average)

Region	Economy		Industry	
	Productivity[a]	Average wage[b]	Productivity[a]	Average wage[b]
Bratislava	159	138	205	132
Trnava	106	98	124	93
Trenčín	89	96	93	94
Nitra	90	89	80	93
Žilina	82	94	71	90
Banská Bystrica	95	91	100	90
Prešov	68	84	61	84
Košice	110	103	104	103
Total	100	100	100	100

a. Regional value added per person employed, 1999.
b. As of 2001.
Source: Statistical Office of the Slovak Republic.

Nevertheless, this uniform approach to labor relations and social welfare contributes to entrenching regional unemployment and therefore to exacerbating, rather than lessening, regional disparities. While the unemployment rate has consistently remained relatively low in Bratislava and significantly below the national average (see table 12-6), it increased dramatically in all other regions between 1997 and 1999. The unemployment rate in the region with the worst-performing labor market was 4.4 times higher than in Bratislava.

Impact of EU Accession

The experience of existing EU members suggests that the Slovak government may face some stark choices in fueling convergence toward EU levels while dealing with interregional equality. Indeed, while all cohesion countries (Greece, Ireland, Portugal, and Spain) have experienced at least some degree of income convergence at the national level, convergence at the subnational level has been meager. In countries that have converged very rapidly, national growth has tended to be driven by growth poles (usually around capital cities and major agglomerations), with the relatively lower growth in other parts of the country resulting in widening regional disparities. The trade-off between economic efficiency (that is, rapid convergence at the national level driven by a small number of growth poles) and interregional equality has been confirmed and quantified in several studies (see, for example, de la Fuente 1996).

This observation is in line with the findings of the "new economic geography" models that analyze how spatial patterns of agglomeration of economic activities may lead to differences in income levels. These models predict that more advanced economies (including regional economies) will benefit more from a partial integration, as firms will exploit economies of scale by concentrating in those economies.

TABLE 12-6 REGIONAL UNEMPLOYMENT RATES, 1997–2001
(percentages)

Region	1997	1998	1999	2000	2001
Bratislava	4.1	5.1	7.2	6.4	5.8
Trnava	10.6	12.5	16.3	14.9	15.5
Trenčín	8.3	10.8	13.5	12.7	12.7
Nitra	14.3	17.6	21.5	21.7	23.1
Žilina	10.8	14.1	17.7	16.8	16.4
Banská Bystrica	14.9	19.7	23.1	21.8	23.6
Prešov	17.8	22.1	26.0	22.1	24.0
Košice	17.1	20.8	25.1	24.4	25.6
Total	12.5	15.6	19.1	17.9	18.6

Source: Statistical Office of the Slovak Republic.

However, as integration advances beyond a certain threshold, industries will move to regions where they can benefit from labor cost advantages, enabling poorer economies that have retained such advantage to catch up.

The Slovak Republic appears to be at the stage at which relatively low trade costs induce firms to exploit economies of scale by concentrating their production in or close to the Bratislava region, where there are more customers and suppliers, knowledge spillovers, and other location-specific benefits. This results in a process of endogenous concentration in which more and more firms and workers are attracted to the region. The benefits that these firms derive from their location in this agglomeration boost productivity and outweigh higher (absolute) wage levels, giving rise to a growth pole syndrome in Bratislava. The models suggest that as the economic integration deepens, and trade costs become lower and tend to disappear, higher wage costs in Bratislava should lead industries to move to other regions that have preserved their lower labor cost advantages. In the initial stage after the Slovak Republic joins the EU, however, the economic importance and concentration of economic activities in Bratislava may increase rather than decrease. Situated only 65 kilometers from Vienna and with a new highway connecting the two cities scheduled to be completed by 2005, Bratislava will probably experience rapid economic integration with Vienna. Conversely, as most of the neighboring eastern regions in Poland and Hungary are as depressed as the Slovak areas, EU accession is not likely initially to boost the local demand for Slovak firms situated in the east. Although economic integration with the EU should provide major economic benefits and should stimulate the convergence of the Slovak Republic as a whole, it may also, if not properly addressed, exacerbate economic disparities between the capital and the rest of the country.

Outline of a Regional Development Strategy

The appropriate response is not to suppress the growth potential of the capital region (for example, by diverting resources away from it) but to maximize that potential while facilitating the diffusion of the convergence process to other regions, first of all through labor markets (to improve the wage competitiveness in poorer regions) and social welfare reforms (to help poorer regions and to stimulate labor mobility). Improving transport access between Bratislava and the east would help make Bratislava a springboard toward regions that establish or maintain wage competitiveness.

Investment Priorities

The EU Structural Funds have the potential to help the country make the transition. As a candidate for EU membership, the country has already benefited from EU grant funding through its access to the preaccession funds. When the country enters the EU, the amount of funding from the Cohesion Fund and the Structural Funds could increase substantially. While the current inflows of EU grant assistance amount to less than 1 percent of the Slovak GDP, they could eventually reach up to 4 percent of the Slovak GDP.

In planning for the use of the Structural Funds, two important considerations should be kept in mind. First, *the country should seek to maximize the related supply (as different from demand) effects.* The inflow of Structural Funds may lift demand and disposable income in the short term, but without supply-side effects (arising from the improved stock of human and physical capital, physical infrastructure, and broader market environment) the impact of Structural Funds will be ephemeral. In the short term, the magnitude of demand effects may be higher (close to the amount of actual spending), but it is their ability to help lift the recipient country's potential growth rates that will make a lasting difference in the longer run. Various studies suggest that the supply-side effects added approximately one-half of 1 percentage point to the real GDP growth rate in Ireland and Portugal over the course of the 1990s.[1]

How large these effects will turn out to be will depend crucially on the strength of the economic rates of return that the related investments are going to generate. The higher the economic return is, the higher the supply effect will be. In practice and in light of the discussion above, *it may well be that many of those high-return investment opportunities lie in the richer Bratislava region.* This should not be a reason to ignore them.

On the contrary, the government would be well advised to reconsider the recent decision to exclude Bratislava from the benefit of EU funding under Objective 1 (which has the largest allocation of Structural Funds). Even though support of the Bratislava growth pole might initially lead to some exacerbation of regional disparities in output per capita, the increased regional variation should be socially sustainable in the short term.[2] Perhaps the simplest way to achieve this would be to revise the NUTS 3 structure of the country to subsume Bratislava within its surrounding region.

In addition to Bratislava, the government may wish to explicitly foster the later development of other growth poles. There are some signs that a growth pole may be emerging around Košice. In addition to a relatively fast shift to a service-based economy, the regional economy has been growing more rapidly since 1997 than any other region in the Slovak Republic. Košice has a relatively good endowment of human capital, thanks to several major universities and a relatively high stock of FDI.

An important aspect of stimulating the regional economies and the outflow of economic activities from Bratislava to other regions will be to reduce trade costs through *significant improvements in transportation infrastructure* (including a high-speed road connecting the eastern part of the country and Bratislava). Building on the experience that the Slovak authorities have already acquired in the preaccession period with the Structural Instrument of Pre-Accession Fund, this could be the main focus of Cohesion Fund resources.

The second priority area of public investment should be *human capital.* The importance of investment in human capital has been confirmed by several recent empirical studies and experiences of the current EU members (Alesina, Danninger, and Rostagno 1999; European Commission 1993). A major focus on education policy is particularly important in order to create the appropriate conditions for generating endogenous growth processes and attracting industries with leading technologies. While medium- and high-tech industries are expanding toward the periphery in the EU, studies find that their location remains sensitive to countries' endowments in terms of researchers. Although the Slovak Republic has a fairly good endowment of researchers in technical disciplines, government support of research and development is currently very low compared with the level of support in other European countries considered technological leaders. With full accession to the EU, researchers will face further strong incentives to relocate to other EU member countries. This could lead to an accelerated "brain drain" process, with a strong negative impact on long-term growth prospects in the Slovak Republic.

Labor Market and Social Welfare Reforms
In order to foster national and interregional convergence, the government should implement labor market reforms that will decrease the disparities in employment and unemployment rates across regions, particularly between Bratislava and the rest of the country. The specific reforms should strive for two main goals: to increase the employment rates in regions outside of Bratislava and to increase the outflow of labor from depressed regions to regions with better employment opportunities. Raising the employment rates in poor regions would decrease the gap in regional output per capita levels by boosting production in poor regions. Improving labor migration would decrease the regional disparities in unemployment levels and per capita output by decreasing the nonproductive population in poor regions.

Fiscal Sustainability
To be viable, this investment strategy will need to fit within the overall fiscal consolidation strategy. In other words, *the utilization of Structural Funds will need to fit within a declining overall expenditure envelope.* This is the objective the country has set itself in the context of its preaccession economic program. The discussion in Chapter 1 highlights just how central that objective was to the entire development scenario.

The role of this overall budget constraint can hardly be exaggerated. Depending on the assumptions about macroeconomic variables and about the rate of utilization of EU funds, the Slovak Republic could be receiving funding equal to 1.6 to 1.8 percent of GDP in 2004. Together with cofinancing from the Slovak sources, the structural operations supported by the EU funds may amount to 2.5 to 2.8 percent of GDP in 2004 and 3.0 to 3.5 percent in 2006. By that time, the government plans to reduce its expenditures outside of subsidies and transfers to about 12 percent of GDP. The implication is that, by that time also, *more than one-quarter of the monies spent on government consumption and investment will need to come from EU Structural*

Funds. To put it another way, if the government decided to apply Structural Funds to finance investment only, *the entire projected public investment program would need to be financed from that source* to absorb the amounts discussed.

The Slovak government should avoid the temptation of using EU funding on newly created spending programs. On the contrary, what is required is *a massive redirection of existing government programs that would meet the eligibility criteria for EU funding* (including the so-called additionality criteria). The financial resources from the Structural Funds should be viewed as additional revenues that should be fully integrated into the existing public investment planning.

Conclusions

The experience of the cohesion countries suggests that it would be wrong to direct regional development funds away from the regions with the best growth potential on the basis of the assumption that they are already more productive. Instead, to achieve the most rapid overall convergence possible, the government should target public investment to those areas in which such investment generates the highest returns, even if that involves an initial widening of regional GDP differences.

Three strategic priorities have emerged from the discussions above. The actions they would entail are listed below:

1. Foster the development of a limited number of growth poles, starting with that of Bratislava, where external effects are highest, focusing public investment, including the EU funds, on *human capital* and *productive public infrastructure,* particularly transport infrastructure.

2. Improve the functioning of the labor market to facilitate a rapid diffusion of the induced growth.

3. Redirect, rather than expand, the existing expenditure programs to meet the eligibility criteria for Structural Funds financing.

Notes

1. These estimates are based on conservative assumptions, and the true magnitude of the supply-side effects of the Structural Funds may actually be larger (see, for example, Pereira and Gaspar 1999; Barry, Bradley, and Hannan 2001).

2. In the post-2006 programming period, which should also coincide with a full integration of the Slovak Republic into the Schengen area, Bratislava may increasingly benefit from an economic integration with Vienna. At this point, a focused public development initiative may no longer be justified in Bratislava.

Bibliography

Alesina, A., Stephen Danninger, and Massimo Rostagno. 1999. *Redistribution through Public Employment: The Case of Italy.* IMF Working Paper 177. Washington, D.C.: International Monetary Fund.

Barry, Frank, John Bradley, and Aoife Hannan. 2001. "The Single Market, the Structural Funds and Ireland's Recent Economic Growth." *Journal of Common Market Studies* 39(3):537–52.

Boeri, T., G. Bertola, M. Burda, F. Coricelli, J. Dolado, J. Jimero, K. Köllö, M. Lubyove, M. Makovéc, D. Munich, R. Portes, and G. Saint-Paul. 2000. *The Impact of Eastern Enlargement on Employment and Labour Markets in the EU Member States.* Report for European Commission's Employment and Social Affairs Directorate, European Integration Consortium (DIW, CEPR, FIEF, IAS, IGIER), Berlin/Milan, Germany/Italy.

De la Fuente, Angel. 1996. *Inversión pública y redistribución regional: el caso de España en la década de los ochenta.* Papers de Treball, 50.96, Barcelona.

Döhrn, R. 1996. "EU Enlargement and Transformation in Eastern Europe: Consequences for Foreign Investment in Eastern Europe." *Konjunkturpolitik* 42(2–3): 113–32.

European Commission. 1993. *The Economic and Financial Situation in Italy.* Office for Official Publications of the European Communities, Luxembourg.

Gorzelak, Grzegorz, and G. Zarycki. 1995. *Regional Development and Policy in Poland after 1990.* EUROREG, University of Warsaw.

Pereira, Alfredo, and Vitor Gaspar. 1999. "An Intertemporal Analysis of Development Policies in the EU." *Journal of Policy Modeling* 21(7):799–822.

CHAPTER 13

The Role of EU Regional Aid in Economic Convergence in Slovenia

Igor Strmšnik

Integration of each new country into the geographical and socioeconomic area of the European Union (EU) is somewhat different because each new country has its own characteristics. One of the Republic of Slovenia's special characteristics is its extreme natural and cultural diversity. It is situated at the crossroads of four European geographical areas: the Alps, the Pannonian plain, the Dinaric Alps, and the Adriatic Sea. As a result, Slovenia is characterized by a large number of natural regions, naturally formed borders, many different types of terrain, great biodiversity, border regions, national minorities, and dispersed settlement. At the same time, the landscape is quite ecologically fragile. The result of all these factors is limited access to some areas, difficult settlement conditions, and difficult organization of economic activities.

A second characteristic is the positive macroeconomic results that Slovenia has achieved during its transition to a market economy. Among transition countries, Slovenia passed relatively quickly through its period of crisis. Its gross domestic product (GDP) started to rise in 1993 and by 1998 had reached the level of economic activity recorded in 1987, when economic growth initially started to decline, heralding the economic and political crisis of the former Yugoslavia (figure 13-1). During 1993 to 1998, Slovenia's economy underwent many structural changes, achieving basic macroeconomic stabilization (reduction of inflation to single-digit levels) and introducing the main elements of a market system. All these results were achieved without any balance of payments or general government deficits. In 2001, the country's relative economic development reached 70 percent of the average GDP per

FIGURE 13-1 SLOVENIA'S GDP, 1992 FIXED PRICES, 1987–2001

Billions of Slovenian Tolars

Source: Statistical Office of the Republic of Slovenia, Institute of Macroeconomic Analysis and Development estimates.

capita at purchasing power parity in the EU (table 13-1). It has almost caught up with the least developed member states of the EU, Greece and Portugal.

On the other hand, the situation in the area of internal socioeconomic cohesion is less satisfactory. The concentration of economic activity and population in only some parts of the country has led to great disparities in terms of distribution of jobs, the unemployment rate, and the educational structure of the population; inadequate transport links between regions; and uneven access to social infrastructure within regions. The problems are particularly pressing in the structurally less developed, economically weaker, and predominantly agrarian regions; demographically endangered areas; areas with low income per capita; economically and socially unstable areas with an obsolete industrial structure and high unemployment rate; and border regions. With the transition to a market economy in the 1990s, these structural problems became even more obvious, and in some areas they even deepened.

TABLE 13-1 SLOVENIA'S GDP, 1995–2001

	1995	1996	1997	1998	1999	2000	2001
GDP-Slovenia (% growth)	4.1	3.5	4.6	3.8	5.2	4.6	3.0
GPD-Slovenia/EU15 purchasing power parity (%)		64	66	67	68	69	70

Accession to the EU will increase the level of spatial, economic, and communication integration and openness in all areas. The free movement of persons, goods,
capital, and services as well as information; the promotion of domestic and foreign
investment; and the integration into the system of euro regions will lead to a number
of development benefits. On the other hand, certain disadvantages are also expected,
such as transformation of Slovenia into a transit area, further concentration of economic activities around the capital, centralization, further depopulation, and increasing regional development discrepancies (figure 13-2). The problems of regional
development will thus gain new dimensions that can be solved only by the priority
engagement of development policy and increased budgetary funds for these purposes. Budgetary resources in the Republic of Slovenia are already rather limited
because of the many tasks relating to approximation to the *Acquis Communitaire* (a
set of requirements common to all EU countries) and implementation of structural
reforms. Financial requirements are greatest in the fields of infrastructure, environmental protection, and agriculture. According to the National Programme for the
Adoption of the *Acquis,* in the few years after Slovenia's accession to the EU, the projects directly related to this event will call for cofinancing of the budget in the amount
of 4 percent of GDP per year.

Upon accession to the EU, the Republic of Slovenia will further endeavor to
build upon the advantages of its geopolitical position and to provide for solid infrastructural integration into the wider European area. At the same time, the Republic
of Slovenia would not want to become merely a transit country. It seeks to take
advantage of its coastal position and its maritime orientation and, simultaneously, to
preserve its national spatial and cultural identity. By pursuing an active policy, it
wishes to enable balanced and endogenous regional development and to overcome
existing regional disparities. The aim of regional policy is to promote interregional
cooperation within and beyond the Republic of Slovenia and inclusion into the European regional network. The preservation of at least minimum settlements in the
mountainous and difficult-to-access regions is a precondition for the preservation and
development of the cultural landscape. These goals of regional and spatial development are in fact identical to the goals of the cohesion and structural policies of the
EU; therefore, Slovenia expects to be able to continue pursuing them also after accession to the EU.

In the preaccession period, Slovenia is receiving support from Poland Hungary
Aid for the Reconstruction of the Economy (PHARE), Structural Instrument of
Pre-Accession, and Special Accession Program for Agriculture and Rural Development (SAPARD) programs; the support amounts to around 0.3 percent of Slovenia's GDP. With the preparation of the National Development Plan, Slovenia
ensured that it had in place the strategic basis for the Structural Funds that will
become available to Slovenia as a member state for promotion of sustainable development (2004–2006). In the preaccession period, Slovenia is also establishing (with
financial support from PHARE) administrative structures for managing, imple-

FIGURE 13-2 SLOVENIA: REGIONAL DISPARITIES

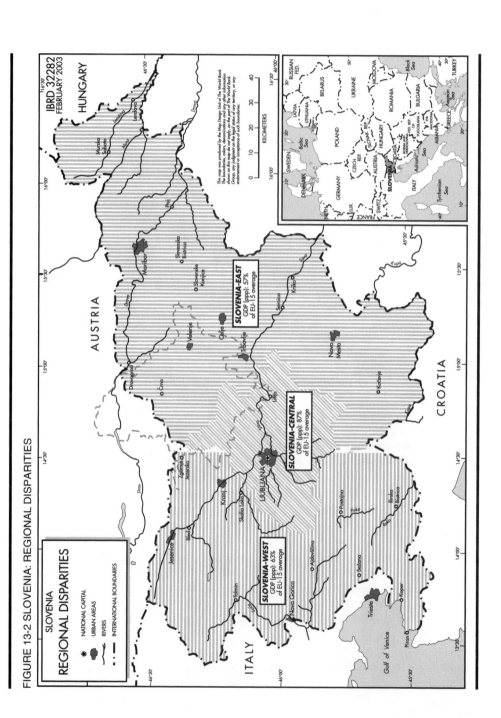

SLOVENIA
REGIONAL DISPARITIES

- ⊛ NATIONAL CAPITAL
- ▮ URBAN AREAS
- RIVERS
- INTERNATIONAL BOUNDARIES

SLOVENIA-WEST
GDP (ppp): 63%
of EU-15 average

SLOVENIA-CENTRAL
GDP (ppp): 87%
of EU-15 average

SLOVENIA-EAST
GDP (ppp): 57%
of EU-15 average

IBRD 32282
FEBRUARY 2003

This map was produced by the Map Design Unit of The World Bank.
The boundaries, colors, denominations and any other information
shown on this map do not imply, on the part of The World Bank
Group, any judgment on the legal status of any territory, or any
endorsement or acceptance of such boundaries.

0 10 20 30 40
KILOMETERS

AUSTRIA

HUNGARY

ITALY

CROATIA

Gulf of Venice

198

menting, monitoring, and supervising the measures eligible for financing from the Structural Funds.

There are considerable regional disparities between the most developed city, Ljubljana (the capital) and most other portions of Slovenia, which have the statistical characteristics of regions with low economic development. After accession to the EU, additional development problems are expected to arise, especially in the country's border areas, which will also constitute a new external border of the EU. To address these problems, at least the less developed parts of the country will have to be eligible for measures under Objective 1.

When preparing the experts' materials for the preparation of the National Development Plan, Slovenia had to make certain estimates as to the financial outflows and inflows between the EU's and Slovenia's budget in the period after accession. Slovenia prepared a study that discussed a number of possible scenarios, depending on the assumptions as to the number of new member states, the outcome of negotiations on EU accession, and the interpretation of the Berlin conclusions. In the preparation of the National Development Plan 2001–2006, Slovenia presented the variant according to which on the expenditure side there would be a transitional period for all payments into the EU budget in the period 2003–2006 (except for the EU's own traditional resources), whereas on the revenue side, there would be a gross inflow amounting to 3 percent of Slovenia's GDP from the EU Structural and Cohesion Funds. Slovenia expects to be on an equal footing (allocation of funds per capita) with the EU member states with a similar level of economic development—such as Portugal and Greece—during their negotiations regarding financing in 2000–2006.

Bibliography

IMAD (Institute of Macroeconomic Analysis and Development). 2001. *Slovenia in the New Decade: Sustainability, Competitiveness, EU Membership, Strategy of Economic Development of Slovenia 2001–2006. Summary.* Ljubljana.

———. 2002. *Analysis of Economic Developments in 2001 and Prospects for 2002 and 2003.* Spring Report. Ljubljana.

Ministry of Economy. 2001. *Pre-Accession Economic Programme of the Republic of Slovenia.* Ljubljana.

Republic of Slovenia, Ministry of the Economy. 2001. *National Development Plan 2001–2006.* Ljubljana.

CHAPTER 14

Managing European Union Funds in the Candidate Countries: Administrative Organization and Resource Distribution

Vitalis Nakrosis

The European Union (EU) cohesion policy is the second largest public policy in the EU in terms of its budgetary size. In the period 2000–2006 its total budget will account for one-third of the EU budget (€213 billion). The main aims of the EU cohesion policy are to reduce regional disparities between the levels of development of the various regions and the backwardness of least-favored regions or islands, including rural areas.

In order to achieve these aims, financial support is allocated to the EU member states from four Structural Funds—the European Regional Development Fund (ERDF), the European Social Fund (ESF), the Guidance Section of the European Agricultural Guidance and Guarantee Fund (EAGGF), and the Financial Instrument for Fisheries Guidance (FIFG)—as well as the Cohesion Fund.

In the current programming period, 2000–2006, the Structural Funds are channeled to the EU member states through national programs and four community initiatives (Interreg, Urban, Equal, and Leader). National programs vary according to three main objectives:

1. Exactly 70 percent of the funding goes to regions whose development is lagging behind the EU average (Objective 1).

2. Exactly 11.5 percent of the funding assists economic and social conversion in areas experiencing structural difficulties (Objective 2).

3. Exactly 12.3 percent of the funding promotes the modernization of training
    systems and the creation of employment (Objective 3) outside the Objec-
    tive 1 regions.

After their accession to the EU, the candidate countries will benefit from the Structural and Cohesion Funds. For instance, in the period 2004–2006, Lithuania is likely
to receive about €1.5 billion, of which €579.52 million will come from the Cohesion
Fund. At present, the candidate countries are involved in the preparation of programming documents (National Development Plans [NDPs] or Single Programming
Documents) to receive EU support in the period 2004–2006.

In addition, since 2000 the candidate countries have had access to the Poland
Hungary Aid for the Reconstruction of the Economy (PHARE) Social and Economic
Cohesion Program (supporting productive environment, human resources, and small-
scale business-related infrastructure), the Special Accession Program for Agriculture
and Rural Development (SAPARD) (supporting agriculture, rural development, and
fisheries), and Structural Instrument of Pre-Accession (ISPA) (supporting environment and transport). Their annual budgets in Lithuania are about €14–16 million,
29 million, and 50–70 million, respectively. The EU's preaccession instruments were
designed to promote economic development in the candidate countries as well as
facilitate their accession to the EU cohesion policy.

The primary purpose of this chapter is to explain—drawing on the experience of
Lithuania—how the candidate countries prepare for the Structural and Cohesion
Funds. Two main topics are considered: administrative and territorial organization,
and resource distribution. The chapter will devote more attention to the former set of
issues because of their prevalence in the agenda of Lithuania's government.

This chapter is organized into two main sections. The first section discusses
administrative and territorial organization. A framework for analyzing administrative, economic, and financial systems for the management of the Structural Funds is
presented and applied to explain the dynamics and state of Lithuania's preparations
to manage the Structural Funds. The second section discusses resource distribution.
The main question addressed in that section is how to balance efficiency and equity
in the distribution of resources.

Administrative and Territorial Organization

There is no uniform approach to the management of EU funds among the EU member states. Therefore, the EU candidate countries can develop their own systems, taking into consideration several alternative approaches to the management of EU funds.

Alternative systems for the management of EU support can be formulated on the
basis of two main principles:

1. Integrated/unintegrated management of the Structural Funds, defining the
    extent to which the Structural Funds are managed through existing national

administrative, economic, and financial systems or systems set up specifically for the Structural Funds

2. Centralized/decentralized management of the Structural Funds, defining the extent to which the management of the Structural Funds is centralized or decentralized in the territorial-administrative sense.

Integrated/Unintegrated Management
This principle can be defined according to three main criteria:

1. Low or high administrative integration[1]—that is, the Structural Funds are managed by existing national administrative systems or by administrative systems set up specifically for the Structural Funds (for example, project selection is carried out by competent national institutions or committees or by institutions or committees set up specifically for the Structural Funds).

2. Low or high economic integration—that is, whether existing national development programs and projects are cofinanced by the Structural Funds or new programs and projects are developed in order to absorb the Structural Funds, and whether development programs and projects cofinanced from the Structural Funds are coordinated with existing national strategic documents.

3. Low and high financial integration—that is, the extent to which the Structural Funds are integrated into the national financial system (budget, treasury, financial control, and so forth).

For instance, integrated administrative systems were used by Austria, Germany, Portugal, and Spain; unintegrated systems by Belgium, Denmark, the Netherlands, Sweden, and the United Kingdom; and mixed systems involving elements of both other types of systems by Finland, France, and Italy (Taylor, Batchler, and Rooney 2000).

Centralized/Decentralized Management
This principle can be defined according to three main criteria:

1. (De)centralization of programs—that is, programs (and projects) cofinanced from the Structural Funds can be centralized (for example, sectoral operational programs under the Community Support Framework or the Single Programming Document for the whole country with centralized priorities and measures) or decentralized (regional operational programs under the Community Support Framework, Single Programming Documents for different territorial-administrative units, or one Single Programming Document with decentralized priorities and measures).

2. (De)centralization of decisionmaking—for example, centralized or decentralized project selection by central, regional, or local institutions/committees.

3. Use of central or regional/local institutions for the implementation of the Structural Funds.

The application of centralized or decentralized systems for the management of the Structural Funds depends significantly on the type of program (Objectives 1, 2, and 3). Also, it depends on the territorial-administrative unit benefiting from the Structural Funds (the whole country or a particular territorial-administrative unit). The EU member states whose territories received assistance under Objective 1 of the Structural Funds (for example, Greece, Ireland, and Portugal during the 1994–99 programming period) used more centralized systems.

Four alternative systems can be formulated on the basis of these principles and criteria (table 14-1).

It should be noted that these systems are extreme alternatives, unlikely to be found in practice because existing systems usually involve elements of several different systems. However, they provide a good framework for analyzing the preparation of the candidate countries for the management of the Structural Funds.

TABLE 14-1 ALTERNATIVE SYSTEMS FOR THE MANAGEMENT
OF THE STRUCTURAL FUNDS

	Centralized: • Centralized programs • Centralized decisionmaking • Central institutions	*Decentralized:* • Decentralized programs • Decentralized decisionmaking • Regional and local institutions
Integrated: • High administrative integration • High economic integration • High financial integration	**Integrated-centralized**	**Integrated-decentralized**
Unintegrated: • Low administrative integration • Low economic integration • Low financial integration	**Unintegrated-centralized**	**Unintegrated-decentralized**

Every alternative system has strengths and weaknesses. For instance, centralized systems can be more absorptive, but decentralized systems can be better suited for local community development. Integrated systems can be better at coordinating national and EU investments, but unintegrated systems can have higher visibility among the public.

However, it is assumed in this chapter that the appropriateness of various alternative systems to the candidate countries is determined by the characteristics of national administrative, economic, and financial systems. For instance, it was concluded that the integrated-centralized system will be the most effective in absorbing the Structural Funds in the period 2004–2006 in Lithuania, which will benefit from Objective 1 of the Structural Funds as a single Nomenclature des Unités Territoriales Statistiques (NUTS) 2 region (see Nakrosis 2002). Since about 90 percent of investment expenditure that may be eligible to cofinance the Structural Funds is managed by sectoral ministries at the central level, the introduction of the integrated-centralized system would entail less administrative reorganization and lower costs.

On the basis of this analytical framework, the following section attempts to determine which system will be used for the management of the EU funds in Lithuania after its accession to the EU. It is likely that Lithuania will use the integrated-centralized system for the management of the EU funds.

DYNAMICS OF LITHUANIA'S ACCESSION TO THE EU FUNDS:
TOWARD THE INTEGRATED-CENTRALIZED SYSTEM

In the period 1997–2000, Lithuania made a number of policy and institutional decisions establishing a decentralized framework for the management of the EU funds. For instance, the preparation process was coordinated by the Ministry of Public Administration Reforms and Local Authorities (responsible for the territorial administration; merged with the Ministry of Interior in 2000). According to the regional development law adopted in 2000, the EU funds were to be channeled on a decentralized basis in 10 countries (through regional development plans implementing the NDP).

However, since 2001 Lithuania has changed the orientation of its preparations for the Structural Funds toward a more integrated-centralized system. In February 2001 the Lithuanian government adopted a key decision, the NDP Concept Paper, involving two major policy and institutional decisions:

1. The NDP coordinating the EU preaccession assistance (PHARE, ISPA, and SAPARD) was integrated into the budget and the State Investment Program.

2. The Ministry of Finance (coordinating the budget and the State Investment Program) became a coordinating authority for the Structural Funds and the Cohesion Fund, replacing the Ministry of Interior (responsible for the territorial administration).

The section below assesses the present situation of Lithuania with regard to the management of the Structural Funds.

INTEGRATED/UNINTEGRATED SYSTEMS

Low Administrative Integration. The Ministry of Finance, which is a coordinating authority for the budget and the State Investment Program, is a competent authority for the preparation of the Single Programming Document and will become a Managing Authority for its implementation.

Three Paying Authorities will be set up to carry out functions defined in the Structural Fund regulations. One new Paying Authority for the ESF will be set up in the Ministry of Social Security and Labour, while the National Fund (set up under the Ministry of Finance for the decentralized management of the PHARE program) and the National Paying Agency (set up under the Ministry of Agriculture for the management of SAPARD) will be reorganized to carry out functions of the ERDF and EAGGF (Guidance Section) Paying Authorities, respectively.

Functions of intermediate and implementing bodies will be carried out by existing national institutions. However, two new implementing bodies (the ESF Agency and the ISPA Implementing Agency) remain to be established for the management of the EU preaccession instruments (the PHARE Economic and Social Cohesion and ISPA).

Low–Medium Economic Integration. Many measures of the Single Programming Document have been designed on the basis of existing budgetary programs and the State Investment Program in order to cofinance their implementation from the Structural Funds. On the other hand, several new measures were proposed specifically for the Single Programming Document. Their implementation should be cofinanced from the budget, the State Investment Program, or other sources.

Some sectoral inputs into the Single Programming Document were prepared on the basis of long-term sectoral documents. Also, a loose strategic framework during the programming process is provided by the economic development strategy and other wider national strategic documents until 2015. The extent to which the Single Programming Document will be embedded into, and coherent with, a national strategic framework remains to be seen.

Low–Medium Financial Integration. The existing budgetary framework is already suitable for the management of the Structural Funds in a flexible way. The EU funds are likely to be channeled through the treasury, but methods of their integration into the budget are still under consideration.

The existing internal audit system (consisting of internal audit units and an audit department inside the Ministry of Finance) will be used to ensure sound financial management of financial support. The EU funds will be cofinanced primarily from the budget and the State Investment Program.

CENTRALIZED/DECENTRALIZED SYSTEMS

Centralized Programs. Since support of the Structural Funds to Lithuania will not exceed €1 billion during the period 2004–2006, it will be channeled to the Single Programming Document covering the whole country. The Ministry of Finance proposed a centralized structure for the Single Programming Document involving no regional or local priorities and measures (even in the Ignalina target region, where the negative socioeconomic consequences of decommissioning the Ignalina nuclear power plant need to be addressed).

Centralized Decisionmaking. (De)centralization of decisionmaking was still under consideration at the time of this writing, but centralized decisionmaking is likely to be used for the management of the EU funds. For instance, centralized project evaluation and selection procedures are likely to be followed during the implementation of the Single Programming Document.

Centralized Implementation. Central-level institutions (sectoral ministries and other public administration institutions) dominate the preparation of the Single Programming Document. However, one county administration and the Association of Local Authorities are represented in the Single Programming Document working group, and socioeconomic partners are being consulted during the programming process.

All intermediate (ministries of economy, social security and labour, transport, environment, and agriculture) and implementing bodies (the National Labour Exchange, the ESF Agency, the Small and Medium Enterprise Development Agency, the Transport Investment Directorate, the ISPA Implementation Agency, the Central Financial and Contracting Unit, the National Paying Agency) proposed in the Concept Paper concerning the administrative system for the management of the Structural Fund assistance are central-level institutions.

EU INFLUENCE ON PREPARATION FOR STRUCTURAL FUND MANAGEMENT
The assessment above does not mention the dynamics of Lithuania's accession to the Structural Funds or the impact of various actors involved in this process of preparation. A combination of external and internal factors can explain the dynamics of Lithuania's preparation for the Structural Funds and the introduction of an integrated-centralized approach. One of the most important internal factors was slow preparations to implement the PHARE 2000 Economic and Social Cohesion and the abolishment of a coordinating authority for the Structural Funds, the Ministry of Public Administration Reforms and Local Authorities, in 2001.

However, it is the impact of the EU that is examined in the following section. This emphasis will reveal the powerful role the European Commission played in the candidate countries during the preaccession period. The EU exerted its influence on the process of preparation for the Structural Funds in the candidate countries through several instruments, outlined below.[2]

Models: Provision of Legislative and Institutional Templates. In 2000 the European Commission provided an informal working document to the candidate countries. The document, which defined the main requirements for the administrative capacity of the candidate countries, provided a guiding framework for the candidate countries during the process of preparation for the Structural Funds. These requirements are presented in box 14-1. Lithuania has already implemented

---

BOX 14-1 ADMINISTRATIVE CAPACITY REQUIREMENTS FOR STRUCTURAL FUNDS

- Capacity to prepare adequate statistical data (gross national product/cap/purchasing power standards [PPS], unemployment rates) at NUTS 2 and 3 levels for the determination of eligible areas by the Commission; and data required for programming, monitoring, and evaluation
- Clear ministerial responsibilities and responsibilities of other state bodies for Structural Funds and the Cohesion Fund, in particular for preparation of Objective 1 programs
- Establishment of an interministerial coordination body and elaboration of coordination procedures
- Designation of a Managing Authority for each program
- Partnership: involvement of regional/local authorities, and socioeconomic and other partners
- Existence of adequate budgetary procedures, including procedure for multi-annual commitments and cofinancing procedure
- Requirement that member state can show that additionality has been respected
- Designation of a payment agency and elaboration of payment procedures
- Establishment of monitoring committees
- Elaboration and appraisal of indicators for monitoring and evaluation
- Capacity to perform independent (ex ante) evaluation of programs
- Functioning financial control, independent of final beneficiaries
- Compliance with other community policies (competition, state aids, public procurement, environment, equal opportunities)
- Elaboration of procedures for the certification of expenses and for correcting irregularities
- Independent auditing capacity
- Capacity to prepare projects for the implementation of Structural Funds and the Cohesion Fund ("project pipeline")

---

some requirements. Other requirements should be implemented before or after Lithuania joins the EU.

Agenda Setting and Monitoring. The European Commission influenced the preparation for the Structural Funds by setting the agenda of the candidate countries and monitoring their accession progress. The most important tools of agenda setting and monitoring are the European Commission's Regular Reports and the Accession Partnerships. In its annual Regular Reports the European Commission identifies institutional or policy problems in the candidate countries and recommends solutions.

For instance, in its 2000 Regular Report the European Commission emphasized that "it is of the utmost importance that the necessary structures for coordinated programming, management, monitoring, evaluation and financial management and control of Structural Fund assistance are established at a central level, before a stand is taken on whether a further decentralization is feasible or advisable" (Commission of the European Communities 2000, p. 77).

Two main factors affected the Commission's selection of a centralized model: limited administrative capacities of the candidate countries on the regional and local level, and the short duration of the programming period (2004–2006). In order to implement this recommendation, the Lithuanian government prepared a number of policy and institutional decisions, including the NDP Concept Paper.

Gatekeeping: Access to Negotiations. The EU can influence the preparation of the candidate countries for the Structural Funds by giving access at different stages in the accession process, in particular starting and concluding negotiations on Chapter 21 of the Structural Funds. For instance, in February 2001, during technical consultations with the second-wave candidates, the European Commission requested information about the institutional setup of programming and implementing the Structural Funds in Lithuania. More specifically, the European Commission (in its comments on the NDP Concept Paper) welcomed a clear distinction between Lithuania's own regional policy, put under the responsibility of the Ministry of Interior, and the programming and preparation for the Structural Funds, put under the authority of the Ministry of Finance.

Technical Assistance and Twinning. Technical assistance and twinning projects financed by the PHARE program and other bilateral programs are important sources of information, advice, and technical assistance to the candidate countries. For instance, to prepare candidate countries for the management of the EU funds, the European Commission proposed a Special Preparatory Program (SPP). The most significant outputs of the PHARE SPP I in Lithuania included the preparation of a National Paying Agency for accreditation, the development of a training program on the Structural Funds, and the preparation of the NDP.

A few Irish experts employed in the Lithuanian SPP I promoted a centralized method of managing the EU funds. Their advice was derived from the successful experience of Ireland, which followed a centralized approach in the period 1994–99. Under the 1994–99 Community Support Framework, funding from the Structural Funds was allocated to eight sectoral and only one regional operational program in Ireland.

Preaccession Assistance Instruments. From 2000, the candidate countries became eligible to receive assistance under the PHARE Social and Economic Cohesion component (for business and human resource development), ISPA (for environment and transport infrastructure), and SAPARD (for rural development) programs. The European Commission set a framework for the programming of the PHARE Economic and Social Cohesion component (precursor of the SERDF and the ESF) by issuing guidance notes to the candidate countries.

According to the first guidance note, support of the PHARE Economic and Social Cohesion 2000 component was to be concentrated in a few target regions. In Lithuania, three target regions (Klaipeda-Taurage, Utena, and Marijampole) were identified to receive assistance from this component in business and human resource development. However, in the PHARE 2000 Review, the European Commission proposed to introduce more sectoral approaches similar to the Objective 1 approaches of the Structural Funds (European Commission 2001a). Therefore, support of the PHARE 2001 in Lithuania was concentrated primarily on a sectoral basis in the business and human resource sectors. In addition to the PHARE 2001 programming exercise, this decision facilitated the reorientation of Lithuania's preparations for the Structural Funds toward a more integrated-centralized model.

Resource Distribution

Economic Development Policies in Candidate Countries: Plentiful Ends, Limited Means

After the reestablishment of independence, Lithuania, together with other transitional economies, started to dismantle the system of public interventions in the economy and accorded higher priority to macroeconomic stability, liberalization, privatization, and other important issues of economic transition. A combination of overloaded agendas and fiscal deficits prevented the introduction of active economic development policies in the transition economies.

The stabilization of the economy and the increasing pace of accession to the EU allowed the candidate countries to start introducing economic development policies. In the past three years there has been a proliferation of various development strategies and programs in Lithuania. One can distinguish between two sets of strategic documents that overlap to a certain extent. Since 1998 Lithuania has adopted national development programs and strategies for such sectors as industry, small and medium enterprises, exports, quality management, business innovation, the information society, tourism, and research and development.

There are about 80 strategic documents in Lithuania, most of them of national origin. At the end of 2001 the government attempted to establish a hierarchy of strategic documents. The Government Resolution divided all strategic documents into long-term planning documents (the state long-term development strategy, the spatial development plan, sectoral long-term strategies); midterm intersectoral, sectoral, and horizontal planning documents (including the economic development strategy, the NDP); and short-term planning documents (strategic business plans). Also, the government prepared the long-term economic development strategy until 2015. However, because of loose interministerial or intergovernmental coordination it represents only a collection of sectoral development strategies with 19 sets of competing objectives rather than a coherent development strategy.

A second set of development plans and strategies was created as a result of Lithuania's preparation to manage the EU preaccession support instruments. The Lithuanian government prepared three multiannual strategic documents (the NDP for PHARE, the Rural Development Plan for SAPARD, and Transport and Environment

Strategies for ISPA). In order to launch annual programming of the PHARE Economic and Social Cohesion component, the Lithuanian government prepared three preliminary NDPs for 2000–2002, 2001–2003, and 2002–2004. Although the Structural Funds represented an important learning process, their preparation revealed several important weaknesses:

- Owing to their formal nature, the preliminary NDPs mainly served the purpose of unlocking annual assistance under the PHARE Economic and Social Cohesion component.

- Preliminary NDPs were not linked to national processes of budgeting and investment planning in the candidate countries.

- Preliminary NDPs in the candidate countries failed to meet some requirements of the Structural Funds, in terms of both process (for example, involvement of socioeconomic partners) and content (for example, absence of ex ante evaluation, quantified targets, and indicators) (European Commission 2001b).

Two sets of strategic documents illustrate that the Lithuanian government is running two parallel investment management processes, one for national investments and another for EU funds. Because of growing amounts of national expenditure to meet EU funds requirements, having two parallel processes is not sustainable. Although in 2001 the Lithuanian government decided to integrate the preparation of the NDP as well as the budget and the State Investment Program into a single framework, this decision has not been fully implemented.

Despite the proliferation of strategic planning documents, Lithuania's economic development policies are lacking well-defined support instruments, public interventions, and implementation structures through which the Structural Funds can be channeled. Support instruments and interventions, which can be supported by the Structural Funds and the Cohesion Fund, are particularly underdeveloped in the business sector. Industry- and business-directed expenditure incurred in 1999–2001 and eligible for the EU funds amounted to only 1.5 percent of all national eligible expenditure (Brozaitis and Nakrosis 2002).[3] There is a need to redirect business support from interventions ineligible under the Structural Funds (for example, tax support) to eligible interventions. The candidate countries are in the process of designing state aid schemes to be cofinanced by the Structural Funds.

The EU preaccession instruments facilitated Lithuania's creation of new development instruments. Some new instruments were downloaded from the EU documents (for example, several fields of intervention most appropriate to Lithuania from the SAPARD regulation); other instruments resembled those of other EU member states. In addition, the preaccession instruments allowed the country to develop appropriate monitoring and evaluation systems (for example, the Rural Development

Plan for SAPARD was subject to ex ante evaluation; its midterm evaluation is being organized). However, in contrast to the programs cofinanced by the EU, the remaining national programs are not subject to monitoring and evaluation procedures.

STRATEGIC CONTENT OF NATIONAL PROGRAMMING DOCUMENTS: EFFICIENT, EQUITABLE RESOURCE DISTRIBUTION

The Lithuanian government committed to presenting the Single Programming Document to the European Commission at the beginning of 2003. Its preparation is being coordinated by the Ministry of Finance through the Single Programming Document working group, which involves not only sectoral ministries but also socioeconomic partners. Unlike previous NDPs, the Single Programming Document will be made operational in a program complementing and implemented with support of the Structural Funds. An essential part of the programming documents is a development strategy defining development objectives, priorities, and measures.

During the programming process, the candidate countries need to balance efficiency and equity in the distribution of resources (Pires 2002). On the one hand, the candidate countries can concentrate support of the Structural Funds in "motor" regions and expanding sectors of the economy (for instance, the information technology sector of the Lithuanian economy, which is concentrated in the capital region). This strategy would aim at reducing the development gap vis-à-vis the EU average.

On the other hand, the candidate countries can concentrate support from the Structural Funds in regions that are lagging behind and in contracting sectors of the economy (for example, Lithuanian rural areas, whose economic structure is dominated by agricultural activities). This strategy would aim at reducing internal regional development disparities as well as the backwardness of least-favored areas (see table 14-2).

It is likely that the programming documents of most candidate countries will propose mixed development strategies biased toward equity and distributing benefits from the Structural Funds to various territorial entities, sectors of the economy, or socioeconomic groups. Although efficiency is favored by the Structural Funds' philosophy aiming at the reduction of development disparities between poor member states and the EU average, the philosophy's impact is offset by several factors favoring equity in the distribution of resources.

First, in the preparation of programming documents, the candidate countries should take into account the priorities outlined in the European Commission's guide-

---

TABLE 14-2 TERRITORIAL AND SECTORAL CONCENTRATION OF THE STRUCTURAL FUNDS: DISTRIBUTION OF RESOURCES

Type of regions	Expanding sectors of the economy	Contracting sectors of the economy
Motor regions	Growth poles	Mixed
Regions lagging behind	Mixed	Disadvantaged areas

lines (Commission of the European Communities 1999). Some common policies and funds of the EU favor specific sectors of the economy (the Common Agricultural Policy and the EAGGF, favoring farmers and processing plants, respectively) or territorial areas (the Common Fisheries Policy and the FIFG, favoring zones of fisheries).

Second, the partnership principle of the Structural Funds brings the development needs of different sectors (infrastructure, human resources, and productive sectors); authorities (central, regional, and local); and socioeconomic partners to the process of programming for the Structural Funds. The involvement of various institutions in the consultation process favors equity rather than efficiency in the distribution of resources.

The bias toward equity in the allocation of resources is likely to produce shopping lists of interventions eligible under the Structural Funds, rather than coherent development strategies. For instance, the European Commission criticized the Lithuanian programming documents (both preliminary NDPs and a first draft of the Single Programming Document) as lacking a strategic focus. There is a risk that insufficient attention to efficiency in the distribution of resources may produce the phenomenon of "chasing the money" and limit the degree to which EU cohesion policy objectives can be achieved.

Finally, the short programming period (2004–2006) and the limited experience of the candidate countries in managing the EU funds constrain their capacity to implement very wide and ambitious strategies. Therefore, the European Commission suggested that the candidate countries design a clear set of priorities and measures for the period 2004–2006. Also, Lithuania is considering the introduction of various pilot projects and technical assistance measures to build necessary capacity for the next programming period.

RISK OF NEGATIVE DISTRIBUTIONAL EFFECTS AND MARKET DISTORTIONS
A considerable amount of EU funds will be available to the candidate countries after their accession to the EU. As mentioned above, in its draft financial proposal the European Commission estimated that total assistance to Lithuania in 2004–2006 will amount to €1,485 billion, or about €500 million annually. The annual volume of EU support will be about twice as large as the total Lithuanian State Investment Program.

However, in the preaccession period the candidate countries are preoccupied primarily with the following issues:

- How to complete all preparations needed to receive EU assistance

- How to draw down as much support from the EU funds as possible and manage the funding without fraud, abuse, and irregularities.

The effective and efficient management of EU support is not very high on the agenda of the candidate countries. Therefore, high volumes of EU support coupled with insufficient attention paid to their effective and efficient management may produce negative distributional effects and market distortions during the implementation period.

Negative distributional effects and market distortions of the Structural Funds can be minimized by designing public interventions aimed at creating positive externalities or public goods whose benefits are widely distributed (for example, public infrastructure), addressing common business development needs (as opposed to development needs of individual enterprises), reducing entry barriers, and minimizing the amount of imperfect information and uncertainty (Nakrosis and Vilpisauskas 2000). A good list of rationales for public interventions was proposed in the midterm evaluation of Ireland's Community Support Framework:

- Spending on public goods (for example, infrastructure)

- Corrective subsidies (interventions designed to alter relative prices so as to correct for general ongoing externalities [for example, grants and subsidies for job creation])

- Targeted subsidies designed to overcome specific externalities (such as information barriers) or to alter behavior (for example, in-company training and research and development)

- Spending with a distributional motivation (for example, social housing) (Honohan 1997).

However, although the distortionary effects of the Structural Funds can be minimized, it is very difficult to avoid them altogether.

CAPACITY TO COFINANCE THE STRUCTURAL FUNDS
After the accession of the candidate countries to the EU, large sums of public or equivalent expenditure will be required to cofinance support of the Structural Funds and the Cohesion Fund. Since an average rate of cofinancing in the cohesion countries amounts to about two-thirds of the total eligible cost, Lithuania would need to allocate about €731.44 million of national cofinancing to absorb the EU funds in 2004–2006.

Some authors argue that there seems to be a clear risk of the lack of national cofinancing potentially leading to sizable underuse of the preaccession funds available from the EU. However, recent analysis of Lithuania's capacity to absorb the EU funds found that the amount of state and municipal expenditure incurred in 1999–2001 and potentially eligible as cofinancing for the EU funds stands at €1,556 million, exceeding the minimal cofinancing requirement by about two times (Brozaitis and Nakrosis 2002).

However, the distribution of eligible expenditure according to sectors of the economy is not in line with the situation of the EU member states benefiting from the Cohesion Fund. For instance, the cofinancing capacity in Lithuania is least sufficient in the sectors of industry and business as well as the environment (Brozaitis and Nakrosis 2002).

These discrepancies can result in the need to redistribute public expenditure after EU membership. Two main types of redistribution are likely to occur:

1. Redistribution among sectors of the economy ineligible (public adminis- tration, law and order, social security, defense, and so on) and eligible (the productive sector and services, human resource development, and socio- economic infrastructure) under the Structural Funds

2. Redistribution from ineligible to eligible expenditure inside eligible sectors of the economy (for example, from ineligible expenditure of maintaining existing roads to eligible expenditure of constructing new roads in the trans- port sector).

The redistribution of resources, although not socially or economically optimal, may be inevitable for the absorption of the EU funds. In order to absorb the EU funds, Por- tugal needed to shift public resources in its first years of EU membership from social areas to areas covered by the Structural Funds (Pires 2002).

Finally, in order to match the EU funds with national expenditure, the candidate countries need to overcome at least two formidable problems: designing measures in the programming documents matching their existing expenditure and developing a sufficient "project pipeline." For instance, in order to draw down assistance from the Structural Funds programmed in the Single Programming Document, Lithuania will need to prepare about 1,000 projects. However, the country's capacity to prepare projects for the Structural Funds is insufficient (Commission of the European Com- munities 2000); the culture of project management in the Lithuanian public sector is still in its infancy. For instance, considerable support is allocated to finance various public administration institutions rather than separate economic development projects.

Conclusion

In the period 2001–2002, the agenda of the candidate countries was dominated primar- ily by the establishment of adequate administrative structures to manage the Structural Funds. The European Commission affected the preparation of the candidate countries for the management of the Structural Funds through several instruments discussed above. Lithuania will use the integrated-centralized system to manage the EU funds.

It was argued that a centralized model promoted by the European Commission to all candidate countries, regardless of their territorial-administrative and other characteristics, can have negative effects (for example, on the processes of decentralization) (Pires 2002). However, it should be stressed that the introduction of the integrated-centralized approach in Lithuania has been relatively successful so far. It significantly contributed to increasing the scope and speed of preparations for the Structural Funds. For instance, Lithuania was among the first few candidate countries to close preliminary negotiations on Chapter 21.

This impressive scope and speed were possible because the European Commission's recommendations were quite similar to the existing characteristics of administrative, economic, and financial systems in Lithuania. The integrated-centralized system of managing the Structural Funds was more appropriate than the alternatives because 90 percent of investment expenditure that may be used to cofinance the Structural Funds is managed by sectoral ministries at the central level. During a discussion with me in October 2002, in explaining the recent progress of Lithuania on Chapter 21, one Lithuanian official concluded that the function of coordinating the EU funds had finally "found its home."

However, resource distribution received less attention in the candidate countries in the preaccession period. Despite plentiful objectives of economic development policies, the candidate countries need to develop support instruments and public interventions through which the Structural Funds can be channeled.

Also, the candidate countries need to balance efficiency and equity in the distribution of resources in their programming documents for the Structural Funds. Most candidate countries are likely to propose mixed development strategies biased toward equity rather than efficiency. Equity in the distribution of resources is favored by the fact that the candidate countries should take into consideration various national priorities as well as EU priorities in the preparation of their programming documents.

Notes

1. This criterion was borrowed from Taylor, Batchler, and Rooney (2000). According to the degree of administrative additionality, this article distinguished between "differentiated" and "subsumed" systems. I have defined the other criteria.

2. Instruments are drawn from Grabbe 2001.

3. To compare, in Portugal assistance to private businesses only under state aid schemes amounts to about 25 percent of all expenditure by the EU funds.

Bibliography

Brozaitis, H., and Vitalis Nakrosis. 2002. *Lithuania's Capacity to Absorb the EU Structural and Cohesion Funds Assistance.* Summary. Vilnius: National Regional Development Agency.

Commission of the European Communities. 1999. *The Structural Funds and Their Co-ordination with the Cohesion Fund: Guidelines for Programmes in the Period of 2000–2006.* Working Paper. Luxembourg.

———. 2000. *Regular Report on Lithuania's Progress towards Accession.* Luxembourg.

European Commission. 2000. *The Main Administrative Structures Required for Implementing the Acquis.* Luxembourg.

———. 2001a. *PHARE 2000 Review—Strengthening Preparations for Membership.* Luxembourg.

———. 2001b. "Preparations for the Structural Funds in the Candidate Countries." Synthesis paper presented at the Twinners Seminar, Brussels, March 15 and 16.

Grabbe, H. 2001. "How Does Europeanisation Affect CEE Governance? Conditionality, Diffusion and Diversity." *Journal of European Public Policy* 8(4):1013–31.

Honohan, P., ed. 1997. *EU Structural Funds in Ireland: A Mid-Term Evaluation of the CSF, 1994–1999.* ESRI Policy Research Series, No. 3, July.

Nakrosis, Vitalis, and R. Vilpisauskas. 2000. "Adapting to EU Transfers: The Case of Lithuania." Paper presented at the conference on EU Structural Support: Its Macroeconomic and Distributional Effects and Social Environment, Prague, November.

Nakrosis, Vitalis. 2002. *Assessment of the Effects of the EU Regional Policy on Lithuania's Public Administration* (in Lithuanian). Vilnius: National Regional Development Agency.

Pires, L. M. 2002. "Discussion Paper for the Session 'Managing the Increased EU Aid in the Central and Eastern European Countries.'" Barcelona, October 11.

Taylor, S., J. Batchler, and M. L. Rooney. 2000. "Implementing the New Generation of Programmes: Project Development, Appraisal and Selection." *IQ-Net Bulletin* 7(September):5.

CHAPTER 15

Managing European Union Regional Aid in Central and Eastern European Countries: Do the Countries Need Development Aid?

Jan Szomburg

In the past 12 years of transformations, Central and Eastern European Countries (CEECs) have had to cope with the historically unprecedented culmination of four major challenges:

1. Systemic transformation—a transition to utterly new market rules that required CEECs to modify their behaviors and philosophy as well as to acquire new skills

2. Far-reaching structural changes

3. Swift opening of economies and globalization

4. A technological revolution (information technologies).

Confronted with those four challenges, CEECs proved their enormous adaptive capacities and learning skills. However, this very intense adjustment period has been accompanied by high social costs. Unemployment in most CEECs is much higher than in the existing member states. A part of their human capital has become depreciated. Societies accustomed to the system of socialist egalitarianism now face increasing social and regional differentiation (World Bank 2002). Transformation-related fatigue, and disappointment with the market economy and democracy, are deepening. They find expression in the relatively common conviction that in the old days (that is, in the times of socialism) people were better off, although—in objective terms—living standards have much improved in all CEECs since socialism ended.

The years 2003–2006 appear very difficult for CEECs. They can expect the following:

- Very demanding conditions of European Union (EU) membership

- High adjustment costs to the *Acquis Communitaire*

- Strong competition from abroad, ensuing from—among other things— support (subsidies) to investments in EU member states from national budgets and Structural Funds, which are many times higher than appropriations for investment support in CEECs

- High cost of a nominal convergence policy in preparation for the European Monetary Union—reduction of inflation, budget deficit, and public debt.

Comparison with Cohesion Countries

The situation of CEECs on the eve of accession is frequently compared with the situations of the so-called cohesion countries—the current EU members Greece, Portugal, and Spain. Some have argued that CEECs are slightly better off than the cohesion countries were before accession and that the new enlargement will not be substantially different from previous ones (chapter 3). However, regardless of all econometric analyses, it is worthwhile to consider how certain aspects of the CEECs' history might make their experience different. One aspect is related to human capital, even more so to social capital, the sphere of mentality and culture as well as institutions. The former German Democratic Republic provides the most telling example of the significance of that historical background. The fundamental difference between the CEECs and the triad Greece, Portugal, and Spain is that the former had a 50-year break in their market economies. Therefore, formal educational background does not reflect the actual level of human capital expressed in terms of very practical skills and behaviors of entrepreneurs, managers, employees, bureaucrats, and households. The break in continuity of functioning under a market economy has also a very significant adverse impact on the functioning of various public institutions that greatly affect an economy's efficiency and investment-related attractiveness, including courts, notary offices, and various bodies regulating and monitoring market operations (offices regulating the telecommunications market, securities and exchange commissions, and so forth). They are either utterly new institutions or old institutions fulfilling new functions. Quite naturally, those institutions learn from their own mistakes and try to build up their ethos and operating models. The process of reforms and maturing of such institutions is not yet complete, which adversely affects the certainty of business operations, protection of ownership rights, and abidance by contracts—so-called systemic competitiveness in general. Central and local government administrations are only learning to get by in the new market economy—they are not yet excelling.

The distinct features and experiences of CEECs have also led to an absence of continuity in the sphere of ownership. Although a certain process of primary accumulation of capital has been completed, it is not the solid backbone of national capitalism that exists in the cohesion countries. The historically unprecedented scale of sale to foreign investors of enterprises—including such entire key sectors as banking—is reflected in the subsidiarization of CEECs' economies, where major undertakings in given economic sectors become subsidiaries of foreign companies. As a result, there are adverse changes in the economies' functional structure: research and development, marketing, strategic planning, and so on are frequently transferred to foreign seats of strategic investors, with only production-related functions remaining in the country.

At the same time, the endogenous development of small and medium enterprises (SMEs) encounters various obstacles, including capital weakness (absence of continuity in capital accumulation). Financial markets are not mature enough to facilitate this development. Paradoxically, privatization of the banking sector with the participation of large strategic investors impaired the support provided to SMEs. As an example, in Poland there is a clear gap between the financial market's supply and demand (loans or ownership capital) at the level of 1 to 5 million euro.

A thorough analysis of the differences between CEECs and cohesion countries in the preaccession period is beyond the scope of this chapter. There are many more distinct features, including the heritage of socialism in the form of costly public social services, whose share of gross domestic product (GDP) is much higher than in the cohesion countries in the preaccession period.

One should also mention the fundamental fact that CEECs are poorer than the cohesion countries. There is an obvious conclusion: CEECs need development aid, although the aid itself cannot guarantee success. Adequate internal policies will need to be in place to put that aid to good use.

Four Perspectives on Structural Fund Use

Structural Funds can be viewed from four different perspectives:

1. The absorption perspective

2. The impact perspective

3. The institutional perspective

4. The macroeconomic perspective.

From the absorption perspective, the major question concerns the utilization rate of Structural Funds appropriated to a given country. It takes little effort to find out how much of the appropriated money a given country or region used. This information is easily accessible and easily understood by the general public. Therefore, this perspective is of utmost importance for politicians and bureaucrats. If appropriated funds are not used, the leaders have to explain why. From this perspective, it is most important to develop the largest possible supply of projects and focus on big, simple projects that can safely ensure use of the allocated resources. If the absorption perspective dominates, less importance is attached to programs ensuring the coherence of interventions and their possibly large impact upon social and economic cohesion (long-term supply effects).

From the perspective of Structural Funds' impact upon an economy, the question of whether all appropriated resources have been used is less important. The major issue becomes the impact of Structural Funds on economic competitiveness and productivity and/or on bridging regional development gaps—that is, medium- and long-term supply and structural effects. Cohesion and relevance of entire programs count much more than individual projects. Because the effects of Structural Funds with regard to their impact upon social and economic cohesion are not as easily evaluated as the rate of funds utilization, and hence they are less comprehensible for the public at large and also outlast the political cycle, there is much less pressure on politicians and bureaucrats to adopt this perspective.

The institutional perspective has two aspects. One concerns the direct impact of institutional arrangements upon allocation of control over Structural Funds (the decisionmaking process). This is a very sensitive issue for politicians and bureaucrats since it directly defines the scope of their influence and the strength of their position. A more or less open struggle concerning the form to be assumed by Structural Funds' management system is raging between ministries or between central and regional levels, and so forth. Solutions reached in this regard are difficult for the public at large to assess. The other aspect of this perspective concerns the impact of Structural Funds management on a country's institutional order (administrative system) and the shape that order will assume in the future. Structural Funds can be, for instance, a stimulus for the desirable decentralization of a country or for the undesirable disintegration of its administrative system.

This kind of partly indirect influence is quite significant for a country's long-term administrative efficiency and systemic competitiveness. However, there are not too many incentives for politicians to take account of this criterion. The meaning of their efforts in this respect is not easily discerned, and the effects are naturally delayed. Moreover, those effects can be incompatible with the requirements of swift and complete absorption.

Given the entirety of the background conditions and all four perspectives for viewing Structural Funds, one can identify two extreme approaches:

1. The approach targeting short-term absorption

2. The approach targeting development.

The first approach takes absorption efficiency—that is, a given country's ability to consume as much of the appropriated funds as possible in a given period (for example, 2004–2006)—as a dominant criterion for the organization and management of Structural Funds. Attention is focused on ensuring the largest possible number of technically mature projects. This approach naturally favors large infrastructural investments—for example, motorways—which do not necessarily yield the best possible outcome from the point of view of a country's development in a given period (Chapter 2). Needs of local and regional development and needs of endogenous potential are rather poorly addressed under this approach. With a view to forgoing old ministerial structures and old procedures for spending public funds, new structures and new procedures are established alongside the old ones. Thus, fast decisionmaking paths are created that are free from the "redundant" burden of the operations of legislative bodies: the parliament and regional councils as well as the central administration. This "shortcut" approach can indeed bring about the best short-term absorption outcome—for instance, in the years 2004–2006—but in a later period, say 2007–2012, it can prove a trap, diminishing the capacities for full absorption at the level of 4 percent GDP, particularly in such areas as human resources, SMEs, or regional innovative systems.

The approach targeting development from the very start is a long-term one. It is founded upon an awareness of the macroeconomic costs of using external assistance and appreciation of the fundamental role of institutional settings. It focuses not so much on individual projects as on programs aiming at ensuring their cohesion. It treats the challenges of Structural Funds as an opportunity to reform administration, decentralize it, and improve general procedures for spending public money, while avoiding fragmentary organization and management. It better addresses the needs of endogenous development and "soft" investments. Paradoxically, in the long run this approach yields better absorption capacities than the first approach, not to mention a larger positive influence upon social and economic cohesion.

The macroeconomic perspective is usually completely ignored in considerations regarding Structural Funds. However, a mass inflow of Structural Funds can decrease macroeconomic stability if not well used. It can stimulate increased external imbalance through excessive increase of internal demand and foreign exchange rates.

Bibliography

World Bank. 2002. *Transition: The First Ten Years.* Washington, D.C.

CHAPTER 16

Managing Regional Aid in Latvia

Janis Kruminš

Regional policy in Latvia, like regional policy in many other candidate states, is a new approach to solving the country's socioeconomic problems. It demands the breaking of many stereotypes that represent traditional politicoeconomic thinking; it also demands the creation of a totally new scale of values.

Important groundwork has already been done in Latvia:

- The National Development Plan and the National Territorial Plan have been elaborated.

- The Law on Regional Development has been adopted.

- Five planning regions and the institutional structure for the management of the European Union (EU) resources are currently being established.

However, some decisions made to date have not been good because of the existing stereotypes.

Unlike most Latvians, I believe that regional policy should be oriented toward the development of lagging and depressed territories, and that the planning and implementation of the regional policy should take place at a decentralized level. Existing statistics confirm that this is the best approach.

Intensification of significant development differences between Riga and Ventspils—the capital and the biggest transit port in Latvia—and the rest of the state territory can be observed in Latvia. In 1996, incomes of the rural population were approximately 93 percent those of the urban population, but by 2000, this figure had dropped to 73 percent. This means that the growth of the national economy can be seen in only the biggest cities, while the situation in the rural areas declines more and more. A single working person in Ventspils pays seven times the income tax paid by all the inhabitants of the average small rural district.

Therefore, it is obvious that Latvia is seeing the development of "economically empty" territories. Investors do not find them attractive, no new workplaces can develop in them, and their residents cannot create a satisfactory tax base to maintain or develop the territories' infrastructure.

It is no wonder then that in Latgale—the eastern region of Latvia, which shares a border with Russia—only 9 percent of residents want their children to stay in their native town or village after they graduate from school. The rest see no prospects for their offspring there.

For that reason, I am convinced that the EU Structural Funds should be guided territorially, rather than in a sectoral manner, through the ministries. The financial aid needs to reach the planning regions; there should be as little mediation and bureaucracy as possible.

I am a defender of the decentralized approach. More than ever, regional institutions need to be involved in the planning and implementation of regional development policy; they need to be entrusted with higher responsibilities. The situation can be managed best at the regional level, where decisions about the support for existing projects should be made. Of course, clear programming and strict fiscal control are still needed.

Let us follow the principle of subsidiarity in regional policy as well.

Finally, our experience indicates that structures of political management and responsibility need to be strengthened in the regions.

The local governments have established development agencies for their regions. However, coordination is still lacking. There is no consensus on the responsibilities in planning the development of regions, on the level of participation in projects, and on the necessary amount of cofinancing.

Therefore, two-level regional municipalities should be established that would fall within the territories of the planning regions and that could take full responsibility for the development of their regions, including the use of the EU resources. Latvia has already started preparing the regional reform.

A year ago, leading economists in Latvia concluded that "Latvia will become a monocentric state with a fragmented regional structure." We hope that effective help from the EU funds will prevent development of this unfavorable situation and will promote balanced long-term development for Latvia. We must contribute our wisdom, our will, and our daily efforts to these ends. It all depends on us.

CHAPTER 17

Discussion Notes

Luis Madureira Pires

Three main topics were to be discussed at our session regarding management of Structural Funds after accession: institutional arrangements, financial absorption capacity, and the development policy priorities.

As a background to this discussion, there are, of course, issues such as the relationship between the European Union (EU) regional policy and domestic regional policies, the effectiveness of domestic regional policies and decentralization processes, the participation of regional players in allocating and managing EU funds, and the impact of additionality and fund absorption on the priorities of national development policy.

The institutional topic received the most attention from our speakers. We were very lucky to hear excellent lectures on the advantages and disadvantages of centralized/decentralized management of the EU Structural Funds and the significant and contradictory role played by the European Commission in this area.

Although I do not fully agree with Szomburg when he says that the "regionalized concept of the Structural Funds is not fully adequate to CEEC [Central and Eastern European Countries]" just because the Central and Eastern European countries' territories are, for now, entirely eligible for Objective 1 of the Structural Funds, I do agree that the special arrangements imposed by the Commission on the candidate countries for the implementation of the first programming period (2004–2006) favor neither the strengthening of the regional and local tiers of government nor a fair involvement of regional and local players in fund allocation and management.

It is true as well that we have not sufficiently discussed the European Commission's main concern: to justify a centralized implementation model even in regionalized countries like Poland—that is, the technical and financial capacity of regional and local authorities to handle the EU funds and to guarantee their sound management.

However, this assessment and decision of the model to choose—a topic that is quite politically sensitive in countries where the first steps toward decentralization have just been made—should in my opinion be made by each candidate country itself, which will thus take the risks of potential lower financial absorption.

Among the CEECs we can observe very different situations, from large regionalized countries like Poland to medium-size centralized countries where some steps have been taken toward decentralization (for example, the Czech Republic, Hungary) to small countries where one hardly can talk about regionalization (for example, the Baltic countries, Slovenia), even though decentralization to lower tiers of government is still an issue.

Doubtless, in small countries using a Single Programming Document the current Structural Funds framework favors a very centralized approach both horizontally and vertically. Regarding larger countries with several Nomenclature des Unités Territoriales Statistiques (NUTS) 2 regions and with very deep territorial disparities, there is no reason to defend such an approach other than to increase potential efficiency (at the expense of some effectiveness) in the use of the funds (in order to ensure full absorption) or in response to the fear of fund misuse.

As Szomburg has underlined, the European Commission should not take a uniform approach to all those situations because the political message that is now being sent to the regional players is contradictory and may jeopardize domestic efforts to create a modern and more efficient public administration and a more participatory model of development.

It should be stressed that over the first three years of accession the challenge for the CEECs will be huge. Several factors could in fact hinder full absorption up to 2006 and reduce the chances and the speed of catching up, as Nakrosis has mentioned. I would recall some factors I deem to be crucial at this stage: the suitability of programming documents to the real needs of the country; the adaptation of policy instruments to the Structural Fund requirements, namely to support private initiatives; an adequate, efficient, and skilled administration to handle the EU grants; a wide mobilization of potential project providers; and the availability of a sufficient amount of ready-to-launch investment projects.

A second topic I would like to discuss is related to the matching funds and the budgetary capacity to meet the needs of the incoming EU funds. The situation described by Nakrosis for Lithuania, where the EU transfers will amount to several times the public investment budget of the country, will necessarily affect the strategic choices of the government regarding development policies. This will indeed be a major issue for the new member states.

Even in Portugal, where the EU funds represent around the same amount as the domestic allocations for the state investment plan, very significant shifts could be noticed over the first years after the Delors Reform from noneligible to eligible expenditure. Some areas—mostly social—were disregarded in favor of others covered by the Structural Funds assistance, thus making absorption a major criterion in the allocation of domestic taxpayers' money. And when political and social considerations obliged the government to pay more attention to those almost-forgotten areas, the budgetary deficit increased steadily, rising to unacceptable levels, as is the case today.

Finally, let us discuss the efficiency/equity issue. Should the new member states give full priority to a fast-catching-up process by betting on the growth poles—that is, the regions or centers where a higher yield from investment in development terms can be expected? Or should they instead mainly ensure that the whole population and territory will benefit from the new opportunities offered by the EU structural assistance?

The answer is not simple, and the balance between those two extreme options will be different from country to country, based on political and social considerations. However, it is clear that the Structural Funds philosophy after 1988 stresses the need to reduce the development gap between poor member states and the EU average rather than to decrease internal regional disparities.

It should therefore surprise no one if the European Commission pays more attention to economic and social cohesion between states rather than between regions, the latter becoming more and more a domestic issue. This means that the new financial resources made available by the EU will not necessarily lead to an increase of the regional policy budget; if the national priority for using the Structural Funds is to achieve a faster but probably less sustainable development, domestic resources as well will be concentrated on that objective, and the route to regional development could be narrower.

I hope these short remarks will fuel the debate on the challenges for the new member states and their regional policies and structures resulting from access to Structural Funds.

CHAPTER 18

What Future for EU Regional Policy?

Christian Weise

Enlargement will without a doubt bring new and severe challenges to European Union (EU) regional policy. The income gap between old and new members is substantial, and quick and automatic convergence of per capita incomes is not expected. Even more pronounced are the disparities at the regional level. That is why achieving a balance between national catching up (which has to be the undisputed top priority in the new member states) and regional development requires diligent and efficient policymaking at all administrative levels in the Central and Eastern European countries.

This chapter concentrates on the future of EU regional policy. It discusses the budget that will be necessary for Structural Funds' work after enlargement, offers a closer look at future burden sharing and at the question of whether or how the principle of equal treatment of all member states is going to be applied, and lists ways to improve the efficiency of EU regional policy. The analysis starts with some remarks on guiding principles for the funds in an enlarged EU.

Principles for Structural Funds in an Enlarged EU

The first principle may sound a bit odd in these times of savings and budget tightening: "Policies first, budget second!" This means that we should first discuss what kind of objectives we should try to achieve at the European level, which policies we want to pursue, and how to do this efficiently. Only in a second step should we look at the budgetary implications and decide whether our wish to implement a policy is worth the money. I will illustrate this with two examples. It is not really convincing to claim that under all circumstances the EU budget should not exceed 1.27 percent of the EU gross domestic product (GDP), which is currently the upper limit. If we want, say, to organize defense and security solely at the European level, which might be sensible, we will probably need more money than 1.27 percent, but that would not necessarily be a crisis. On the other hand, the claim (voiced by some representatives of the European Commission, among others) that we need to spend at least 0.46 percent of the EU GDP on combating regional disparities (which is the current amount) is a nonstarter. In an EU with a growing GDP and convergence there is less need for this policy, and the absolute amount of money spent here should be reduced, not raised.

Second, it is poor policy to consider unequal treatment of the member states. The principle of equal treatment is for good reason an absolutely basic principle in the Union. Departing from it would be hazardous. This does not exclude, of course, transition periods during which the *acquis* is not completely implemented in new member states.

Third, we should accept what is called the "statistical effect." This term denotes the phenomenon that the average GDP per capita in the EU will fall if very poor new members join the club, which will make today's poor EU regions richer compared with the EU average. As a consequence, some current recipients of transfers will no longer be eligible for substantial aid from the Structural Funds. The affected regions argue that they would not be richer in absolute terms and that therefore, they should get as much transfers after enlargement as before. This is wrong. The funds aim at reducing disparities, not at tackling absolute poverty (which exists in, for instance, Sub-Saharan Africa but not in the EU). Therefore, relative income should be kept as the main criterion for eligibility. Generous phasing-out payments for affected regions are sensible, of course.

Fourth, it is convincing and necessary to take absorption capacity into account when allocating transfers to member states. You can do too much of a good thing. Experience with the implementation of transfers in today's poor EU members shows that it is not always easy to spend the transfers from the funds in a sensible way. This is also the case with the preaccession aid the candidate countries are getting now. The regulation that no member state should get more than 4 percent of its GDP in Structural and Cohesion Funds transfers is, therefore, absolutely justified. However, this also has a very severe and limiting impact on the transfers to the new members. Critics may point out that new members will get per capita transfers that are far below those of the current cohesion countries if this rule is applied and that this amounts to unequal treatment of member states, but the 4 percent rule applies to all members, and no current EU member has ever gotten as much support as the new members will get if transfers are expressed as share in GDP.

Fifth, the EU needs to concentrate its funds more on the neediest recipients. The principle of subsidiarity (as it is put in Article 5 of the European Community Treaty) says that the European level should do only what member states cannot do on their own. That means that there should be no or at least no substantial Structural Funds transfers to member states with an average GDP per capita. Figure 18-1, however, shows that the only three current members that have a GDP per capita that is clearly below the EU average (Greece, Portugal, and Spain) get less than half of the funds. This is the main problem of today's EU structural policy.

Financing Structural Policy after Enlargement

There are two major topics when arguing about financing enlargement. The first is how much money will be needed for the east, and the second is how the resulting burden will be shared between today's recipients and today's net payers. Both questions will be addressed in turn.

The necessary amount of money for the new members can be estimated in four steps (explained in more detail in Weise 2002a). First, some assumptions about the growth of GDP in the new members are needed. I applied conservative estimates based on the experience of convergence of per capita GDP in European market economies since World War II. Second, I followed the rule that the lower a recipient's per capita GDP, the higher its per capita support should be. I used the relation between both per capita figures for today's main recipients of structural aid and calculated the likely per capita support for new members. Third, I checked whether this

FIGURE 18-1 ALLOCATION OF STRUCTURAL FUNDS IN EU15, 2000–2006

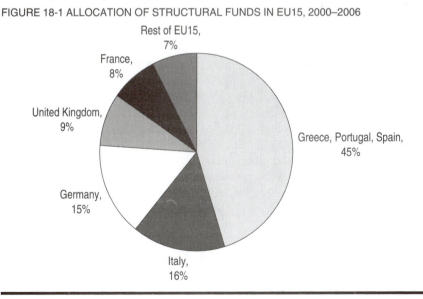

result would be more or less than 4 percent of GDP. Apart from the Czech Republic, Slovenia, and Cyprus, the figure was higher than this absorption limit. Fourth, I took the lower one of each figure for all countries. Figure 18-2 shows the amount of support the individual new member states can expect after a gradual phasing in of the transfers. Poland will receive by far the biggest share, with 9.5 billion euro in 1999 prices. The Czech Republic and Hungary will get the same amount as much poorer and much more populous Romania. This is the logical consequence of the application of the absorption limit. In total, the EU will spend some 22 billion euro in Structural Funds transfers to the 12 new members. These are gross transfers. The contributions of the new members will be somewhere in the range of 1 percent of their GDP. So, net transfers will be substantial. It might be noteworthy to point out that these countries got only 3 billion euro in 2000 and 2001 in preaccession aid. It already proved difficult for them to absorb this sum.

The next topic is who will pay for these net transfers. The payers will be either today's rich members (in the form of higher contributions) or the poor ones (in the form of lost subsidies). First of all, I took a closer look at future Objective 1 regions. These regions get the most substantial support from the funds. A region qualifies for Objective 1 if its per capita GDP in purchasing power parities is below 75 percent of the EU average (that is, the "statistical effect" comes into play here). My point of departure was the 1999 figures. I extrapolated them to 2002 assuming a standard value for the speed of convergence; 2001 to 2003 will be the relevant period for the

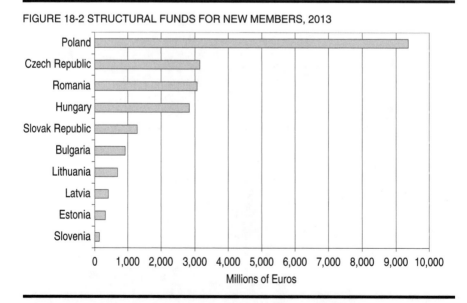

FIGURE 18-2 STRUCTURAL FUNDS FOR NEW MEMBERS, 2013

check of a region's eligibility for Objective 1 support after the end of the current planning period in 2006. Having done this, I could see whether a region would qualify under different scenarios. Figure 18-3 shows the results for the most important recipients of aid. All results are expressed relative to the size of today's population in Objective 1 regions (100 percent). You can see that even without any enlargement and with an unchanged threshold for eligibility (75 percent, EU15), regions with almost 25 percent of the current population of all Objective 1 regions will lose eligibility. This happens because of successful convergence of these regions. Eligibility loss will take place mainly in Greece and in Spain. An additional 30 percent of the current Objective 1 population will lose aid when 10 new members are included (75 percent, EU25) and 20 percent more when Bulgaria and Romania join (75 percent, EU27). In the last scenario I assumed a higher threshold in an EU27 (80 percent) in order to guarantee ongoing support for more of today's recipients. According to these results, Germany will be the country most affected by the inclusion of 10 new members, while Italy will have a very close eye on the membership of Bulgaria and Romania. Two words of caution are in order, however. First, the database is quite shaky; data for regional GDP in purchasing power parity (PPP) are not overly reliable. Second, I applied the same rate of convergence for all EU regions. GDP growth for the *länder* of the former German Democratic Republic, however, is lower than that for western Germany, and the German GDP growth is the lowest in the EU. That means that the *länder* might very well stay eligible for support because of their low growth.

FIGURE 18-3 OBJECTIVE 1 POPULATION POST-2007, ALTERNATIVE CRITERIA
(percent of current Objective 1 population)

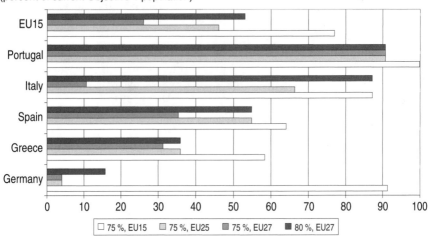

Furthermore, I calculated four different scenarios for the development of the Structural Funds budget after 2006. Only the basic idea and the results for the EU in total can be presented here:

1. In a "status quo EU15" scenario, I assume that there will be no enlargement and no change of the rules for allocating the budget. The "statistical effect" will be active and there will be some phasing out for regions that lose support.

2. In a "status quo EU25" scenario, I analyze the effect of inclusion of 10 new members in an unchanged structural policy.

3. In a "moderate reform EU25" scenario, I assume that Objective 1 support will amount to 90 percent of the funds (instead of two-thirds—its share today).

4. In a "substantial reform EU25" scenario, I concentrate 90 percent of the funds on poor member states (defined here as having a per capita GDP below 90 percent of the EU average) instead of poor regions.

Figure 18-4 shows the results of my calculations. The support for the new members (applicant countries) is not affected by the various reforms. The transfers to the east will be lower in 2007 than in 2013 because the new members will not get full support in year 1 of their EU membership. This is done to allow their administrations to adjust gradually to the new task of implementing these funds responsibly and efficiently. The EU15 will lose support in this period in all scenarios because the gradual phasing out of regions that no longer qualify for support will end in 2013. Enlargement by 10 new members (that is, without Bulgaria and Romania) will reduce initial support for recipients in the EU15 from 30 billion euro to some 22 billion euro. In 2013, the EU15 would get 22 billion euro without enlargement and some 12 billion euro with enlargement. More concentration on the neediest recipients would, of course, lead to smaller amounts of total transfers.

The scenarios show what could be achieved with sensible reforms that would not harm the current recipients most in need of support. For obvious reasons, any statement on the likelihood of these scenarios depends on political assumptions. The EU leaders have to choose between making minor changes to the current system and making more significant, efficiency-oriented reforms. In the short term, the first option certainly is more attractive for them. However, this would turn the structural policy into a second version of the Common Agricultural Policy and would seriously endanger support for the European integration process. EU member states would be forever bargaining over ill-founded subsidies.

FIGURE 18-4 STRUCTURAL FUNDS, VARIOUS SCENARIOS, 2007–13

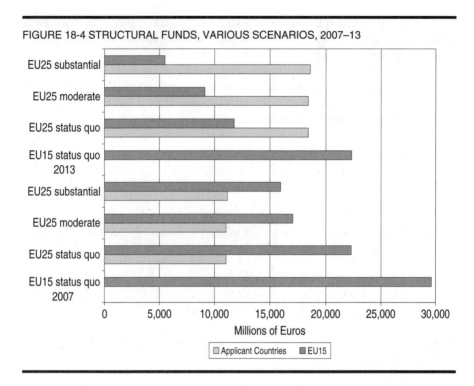

Improving the Efficiency of the Structural Policy

First of all, we should take stock of the positive elements in the current procedure. Two main positive features are the programming approach and the involvement of the regional administrative level. Programming has enforced consistency of the support policy and made transparent what is happening with the funds that are channeled to poor regions. Some critics propose to change the system into an unconditional payment system between rich and poor member states because the recipients know best what is good for them and their government is directly responsible to the target group of the support programs. Precisely for these reasons unconditional transfers would, however, be most likely also spent for distributive purposes. Therefore, taxpayers in rich member states probably would not accept unconditional payments. They require a degree of integration that has not yet been achieved in the EU.

Smaller changes in the current support policy system might prove helpful to obtain a more efficient policy without extensive reform. Sensible steps could include a higher degree of national cofinancing, perhaps depending on the national GDP per capita. Support should come in the form of loans instead of grants. Improvements might also be possible in the area of evaluations, control mechanisms, and sanctions in the case of misused transfers.

More important and promising are three more radical reform proposals. First, support should be concentrated on poor member states instead of on poor regions. This would be compatible with the principle of subsidiarity, it would rest the policy on a more reliable database, and it would be much easier to implement and to control. In addition, growth poles in a poor member state would be eligible for support. Lisbon is excluded from substantial support today, and under today's approach Athens, Prague, Bratislava, and Budapest will be excluded in the future.

This proposal does not amount to a renationalization of support policies, as is often claimed. The EU would still be active in poorer member states, and its competition control would still monitor national support policies in richer countries. It is not the end of solidarity in the EU. On the contrary, this approach would mean a concentration of the Union on the most pressing problem: catching up by the new member states. Support of, say, the Ruhrgebiet in western Germany by "Brussels" is not a convincing example of solidarity in Europe.

Second, we should take into account that the new members are not only poor but numerous. Today, it is not very clear how the budget is allocated among member states. Negotiation tactics seem to be at least as influential as socioeconomic indicators. The European Council of March 1999, which dealt among other things with the allocation of Structural Funds for the years 2000–2006, agreed on special rules for 11 out of the 15 EU members. That kind of muddling through is not an option with 25 members. What is needed are clear and binding rules for allocating the budget for the funds, such as the following:

- You get support only if the national GDP per capita in PPP is below X percent of the EU average.

- Your support per capita increases by the factor Y, the lower your national GDP per capita in PPP is.

- Your total support is limited to a maximum of Z percent of your GDP in euro.

Values for X, Y, and Z have to be decided politically and then applied to all EU members.

Third, we should think about conditionality for Structural Funds (see Weise 2002b). This discussion will be on the agenda sooner or later. The recipient governments are not necessarily focusing their economic policy clearly on growth. If the national economic policy is not oriented toward achieving growth, any EU transfers for this purpose are wasted. The difficult thing is to define what elements of "growth-oriented economic policy" are under the influence of the government, can be expressed in quantitative terms, and are comparable across EU members. The solution is probably to be found in structural fiscal policy indicators such as the share of the public sector in GDP or the share of unproductive expenditure in the public sector.

Conclusions

Enlargement can be financed. We have to accept some current recipients' loss of eligibility for Objective 1 support due to the lower EU per capita GDP after enlargement (provided there is a meaningful phasing out). The national catching up of the new members is the most important task for their economic policy and for EU structural policy.

With many more participants in the "great budget haggling," we have to act like grownups. The current "something for everyone" approach is no longer an option. If the EU is to remain strong, we need clear, convincing, and binding rules for allocating its budget.

Bibliography

Weise, Christian. 2002a. "How to Finance Eastern Enlargement of the EU." Deutsches Institut für Wirtschaftsforschung Discussion Paper 287, Berlin. Available at http://www.diw.de.

————. 2002b. Strukturfondstransfers in einer zukunftsfähigen EU—Konzentration, Subsidiarität und Kopplung an die nationale Wirtschaftspolitik, Nomos Verlagsgesellschaft. Baden-Baden (available in German only).

CHAPTER 19

Discussion Notes

Vasco Cal

Although an academic, Christian Weise agrees with the finance ministers of Germany and Holland. But a debate is going on in Germany and in Holland. In Germany, some *länder* or some ministers of *länder* do not agree with the finance minister's approach. In Holland, the regions also do not agree with the approach of their finance minister.

The reason is very simple. It could be very logical to ask why the European Union (EU) should give subsidies to the regions that are better off than the less-developed countries of the EU. Many people advocate concentrating on the less-developed areas and the poor countries.

In fact, if you concentrate on the poor areas of the poor countries, you will save between half and two-thirds of the current budget. You will save it for the finance ministers. But, of course, the regions will not get the money because the finance ministers will not give the money to their regions as the EU does now.

So the debate on this issue is not simply about the right approach. It is also a problem of redistribution and political aims. What are the political aims of the EU in this issue of regional development? Is this just a redistribution effect, with the EU sending money to the poor countries as it was sent to the African countries, for example, for years and years, without getting any results in the end? Or can this EU regional policy approach now show that it got some results and it paid off because the approach was different from the one that involved just sending money to the underdeveloped countries of Africa?

Previous chapters of this book contain many criticisms about the analysis of the effect of EU regional policy. But I will show that some of this criticism is not valid.

The Cohesion Report is a report that the European Commission is required to produce every three years. Every three years the Commission has to analyze economic and social cohesion in the EU and the contribution of Community policies— not only structural policies but all the Community policies and national policies.

The first Cohesion Report was adopted in 1996, and it gave birth to Agenda 2000. The second Cohesion Report, adopted in 2001, is the first EU report to analyze what an enlarged union with 27 member states would be like. All the other Commission reports analyzed the situation of the 15 member states and the 12 candidate countries, asking, What should the 12 candidate countries do to arrive at the level of the 15 members? But the global approach that looked at the 27 member states of the future EU asked, How should the policy change to cope with the new situation? The report had three main conclusions:

1. Compared with those today, regional disparities will more than double in an enlarged EU:

    *   Almost the entire population of 105 million in the applicant countries will be living in regions with a per capita gross domestic product (GDP) of less than 75 percent of the Community average, which will itself be roughly 18 percent less than the present level.

    *   The standard of living in the least-developed regions of the enlarged EU will be equivalent to about 31 percent of the Community average, compared with 61 percent at present.

2. There will be three groups of member states in the enlarged EU:

    *   A group comprising the majority of the current applicant countries, which will have a per capita GDP (expressed in purchasing power standards [PPS]) of 45 percent of the Community average

    *   A group comprising the majority of the current member states, with an average GDP per capita of 120 percent of the Community average

    *   An intermediate group comprising the cohesion member states (Greece, Portugal, and Spain) plus some of the applicant countries (Cyprus, the Czech Republic, and Slovenia), with a standard of living averaging around 80 percent of the Community average.

3. In spite of the progress, in particular in terms of economic growth, that the regions and member states that have benefited most from the cohesion pol-

icy have achieved, many EU regions are still lagging behind or are suffering from shortcomings in terms of real convergence and the availability of factors of competitiveness. Eurostat gives the figures for regional and national prosperity, employment, and unemployment for every region of the enlarged EU.

That is the main reason why the second Cohesion Report launched a huge debate on the future of cohesion policy, not only about the effects and the results of the past policy but also about what should be the future orientations and how the enlarged union should be handled.

The impact of this report on the Council, the European Parliament, and the regions was relatively high, so the Council asked the Commission to prepare interim reports every year to update the data from the Cohesion Report.

I will talk now about the first progress report, which was adopted in January 2002. Map 19-1 shows the GDP per capita in PPS of the enlarged EU with 27 member states. And today in the EU there is only one region with less than 50 percent of GDP. I think that Epirus in Greece has 47 percent of the current EU average.

So the range of income levels within what is called Objective 1 today is between 50 and 75 percent, but most of the regions range from 65 to 75 percent. There is a very small gap between the less-developed of the current regions and the ones that are in the upper limit of eligibility of Objective 1.

In the future, enlarged EU, most of the poorest regions from the candidate countries will have an income below 50 percent of the future average, and the future average for 27 member states will in itself be 18 percent lower than the current average. We will pass from €22,600 per capita to about €18,500 per capita (year 2000).

So income in the regions that are less developed in the future EU will range from 30 percent or even less, as in some regions in Romania and Bulgaria, to 75 percent. Of course, this is a major change in the regional situation, and the Commission is preparing to make major reforms in the regional policy to cope with it.

In this first progress report, which was in January 2001, the European Commission decided to analyze the situation on the basis of the EU average of 25 member states, because it was already clear that Bulgaria and Romania would not become members until the end of 2006. So they will not count for the future Community average that will define the 75 percent threshold in the future. The future average will fall 13 percent, not 18 percent.

So the statistical effect that worried Christian Weise so much will be less than was anticipated in the second Cohesion Report.

These are the summaries of the statistical effect. How many regions now fall below the 75 percent threshold? The population of these regions in the current EU as a proportion of the European population is 18 percent, and the average GDP per capita is 65 percent, or 21,000.

MAP 19-1 GDP PER HEAD BY REGION (PPS), 2000

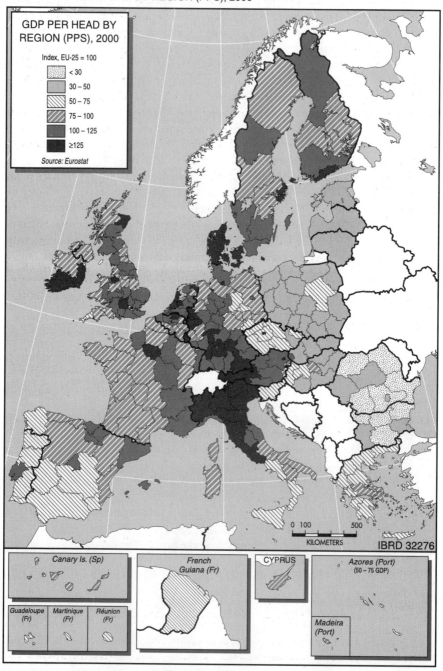

GDP PER HEAD BY REGION (PPS), 2000

Index, EU-25 = 100

- < 30
- 30 – 50
- 50 – 75
- 75 – 100
- 100 – 125
- ≥125

Source: Eurostat

Canary Is. (Sp)

French Guiana (Fr)

CYPRUS

Azores (Port) (50 – 75 GDP)

Guadeloupe (Fr)

Martinique (Fr)

Réunion (Fr)

Madeira (Port)

0   100   500
KILOMETERS

IBRD 32276

In a scenario of a 25-member EU, as shown in table 19-1, part of the population that is eligible today will no longer be eligible. This group, which numbers about 18 million, will no longer be eligible on the current Objective 1 regions because of what was called the statistical effect of lowering the Community average. But probably the lowering will be coupled with a phasing-out process for the current regions that will be more important than the current phasing-out process from 2000 to 2006.

So in the future EU, the main priority of the EU regional policy will be in any case the less-developed areas of the less-developed countries. Today we have already concentrated about 70 percent of the funds on Objective 1 if you account for everything that is going to these regions. In the future, this percentage will probably be even higher. That is the first aspect.

The second aspect that I will not develop now is why the regional policy of the EU should also deal with other regions that are not so underdeveloped in Community terms. The primary answer is, for political reasons.

If you discuss the situation now and you announce that for the future enlarged EU you will concentrate on only the less-developed areas and that in some years this

TABLE 19-1 SUMMARY STATISTICS FOR REGIONS FALLING BELOW THE 75 PERCENT THRESHOLD
(based on GDP per capita in purchasing power standards, 2000*)

Index used	In the EU15	In the EU25		In the EU27	
	EU15 = 100 €22,577	EU15 = 100 €22,577	EU25 = 100 €19,647	EU15 = 100 €22,577	EU27 = 100 €18,516
Number of regions falling below the 75 percent threshold	50	87	69	101	70
of which in EU15	50	50	32	50	20
Population in those regions (millions)	69	139	115	169	122
of which in EU15	69	69	45	69	24
Population as a percentage of EU15/25/27	18%	31%	25%	35%	25%
EU15 regions as a percentage of EU15 total	18%	18%	12%	18%	6%
Average GDP per capita (PPS) of regions falling below the threshold	65	53	55	48	46
of which in EU15	65	65	69	65	68

*Provisional GDP estimates.
Source: Eurostat, calculations, Regional Policy Directorate-General.

will mean that there will be only the candidate countries' regions, all the support that the EU gave to the regions of the current EU will disappear.

If the Structural Funds were limited to the regions and countries that most needed them, and if the citizens of the other countries, even if there were problems that could justify a Community approach, did not agree with that Community approach, that would have a major negative political impact, and in some years' time, even the money for the less developed areas would disappear.

Look at the recent example of the floods in Austria, the Czech Republic, and Germany. If the EU had not been able to come up with some solutions to this emergency situation immediately, what would have been the reaction of the Austrian, Czech, and German citizens? Would they have accepted the answer that the EU could give the money to only the Baltic countries or to Bulgaria and Romania, no matter what the crisis in other regions? This is a political aspect, and you have to consider it, even if in academic terms you can ask whether it would be helpful.

I will now very rapidly present some issues that have been discussed regarding the future cohesion policy. The first is that the future cohesion policy will give priority to the less-developed regions. That is something that is very clear today, and so I have already discussed this topic.

The second issue concerned whether a regional or a national approach should be used. I think that Carole Garnier will pick up on this subject in Chapter 20, because DG Economics and Finance is working on this issue. I remind you only that the treaty says that the cohesion policy deals with the disparities among regions and not the disparities among countries, and that the cohesion policy should address this problem.

The third issue is that we need to address the statistical effect of which of the regions will no longer be eligible for aid because the Community average will decrease.

The fourth issue is the support for the intermediate regions. I stressed before that intermediate regions are supported mainly for political reasons, but I could also have developed the technical arguments on which kind of regions the Community should support, and why. In the past, regions in industrial or rural restructuring were supported by Structural Funds to compensate for some of the negative short-term effects of the internal market process. In the future, the approach followed for these intermediate regions will be completely different.

Alexandre Muns's chapter discusses a map of Barcelona that indicates areas that are eligible for aid. But it was not the EU that led to that map; it was the political situation of Barcelona, of the *generalitat* of the Catalonia and of Madrid. Commissioner Barnier has already announced that the EU will not interfere with zoning for these intermediate areas. It is up to each member state to define which areas should be helped by the Structural Funds in the future. And then there will be discussion about what kind of projects should be financed by the Structural Funds. But these subjects are too large to address in this chapter.

Christian Weise said that 0.45 percent is an arbitrary figure. Indeed it is. But, by coincidence, in 1999, 0.45 percent of EU GDP was the total cohesion policy expenditure. In 2006, it will be the total amount of the cohesion policy, including the candidate countries, according to the Berlin conclusions in 1999.

So the question is also political. If the EU were enlarged, with many more regions and many more millions of persons in eligible areas, and if the gap between these regions became wider, would it be possible to justify that the solidarity effort in the future would be lower than it was in the past—in other words, with the current EU?

Anyway, we have a limit. It was already decided in Berlin. Each country can receive no more than 4 percent of its GDP from Structural Funds and the Cohesion Fund.

The candidate countries, the 10 acceding countries, have 4.5 percent or 4.6 percent of the Community GDP. This means that they have a threshold of 4 percent of 4.6 percent, and that 0.18 percent of the EU's current GDP will be the limit for the support of Structural Funds and the Cohesion Fund to the new member states.

Another subject that has been discussed is the simplification of the procedures. When the Commission talks about simplification, everybody becomes worried because it means that things will become more complicated, I heard once. EU Commission's Director Riera stated yesterday in a very direct and simple way that most of the complications of the current regulations were introduced in the negotiations of the council that prepared the decisions in Berlin. In some ways that is true.

What happened was very simple. In Berlin, it was decided to decentralize the management of the Structural Funds and give more responsibility to the member states. But an article in the treaty still specifies that the Community is responsible for the good management of the EU budget. So the European Parliament, mainly led by German deputies and a court of auditors, puts the responsibility with the Commission if anything appears anywhere in the EU that suggests fraud because the article of the treaty says that the Commission is responsible for Structural Funds management. But the regulation said that the management of the Structural Funds was decentralized to the member states, and in many, many member states with a federal structure, it was decentralized to the regional level.

So there was a problem. How did the member states solve this problem? They increased their control, they increased the number of reports requested from the beneficiaries, and they increased the amount of information needed for decisions. The member states made sure that they are covered if something goes wrong.

Last Monday in Brussels, Commissioner Barnier convened a meeting of ministers in charge of Structural Funds to discuss this problem of simplification. It was amazing to listen to the minister in charge of Structural Funds in one member state recognizing that the complications of the current procedures of the Structural Funds were introduced by the central government and not by the Commission, and that the Commission's current simplification effort for 2000–2006 should be followed by a bigger effort from the member states themselves. The government, when assuming responsibility for managing the funds, was afraid of all the potential problems, and so it increased all the demands for data, reports, and so on.

So when we talk about simplification—well, there are different levels of responsibility for the current situation. That is the first matter.

The second one is this: Does everybody speak about simplification in the same way when talking about Objective 1 or when talking about other intermediate areas of the European region? No. Because everybody says that the approach to Objective 1, the regions lagging behind—the programming effort, the evaluation, the financial stability—are the qualitative values of the Structural Funds approach. This approach allowed many member states and regions to improve management not only of Structural Funds but also of national funds. And there was an upgrading of the public administration of the recipient countries and regions.

So when we talk about simplification, sending a check to Objective 1 regions will not solve the problem. On the contrary, we need to have this multiannual programming effort because it can stabilize the investment and the macroeconomic environment of the less-developed regions of the EU and has already helped those regions catch up.

A different aspect is the simplification for the intermediate regions. Here, there is a point, of course, because the amounts of aid for Objective 1 regions and intermediate regions are completely different. For Objective 1 regions, the amount stands at 220 euros per capita. For the intermediate regions, it stands at 40 euros per capita. So it does not make sense to ask the intermediate regions to have the same heavy programming procedures that are required for the less-developed regions.

So this question of simplification will probably allow the Commission to take a proportional approach in the future, but a proportional approach means that for the less-developed areas of the Community, the current approach will mainly be maintained in the future.

Last but not least—and very important mainly for the candidate countries—is the link to the other policies. Structural policy and cohesion will not be attained only through subventions and transfers of money. The impact on cohesion from the other policies—Common Agricultural Policy, competitiveness policy, and so on—is much higher than most people realize. The decisions—for example, on trans-European networks—have a major impact in the countries, and, of course, sometimes this impact reduces cohesion. So in the future I think that the other policies should contribute more to cohesion and allow the financial burden to be lower.

CHAPTER 20

Conclusions of the Conference

Carole Garnier

It is difficult to conclude a seminar devoted to such complex issues as long-term growth and convergence—issues whose mechanisms are not fully understood. Let me just make a few remarks on policy matters.

There are strong limitations in the help that currently available theories, models, and empirical evidence can provide to our understanding of long-term growth determinants and the potential for policy to influence income levels. However, as different as they may be, both the augmented neoclassical Solow model and the new endogenous growth theory indicate that an increase in the rate of accumulation of human and physical capital can have strong effects on the rate of growth. Whether these effects are permanent or transitory is relatively unimportant compared with the common conclusion that policy can play a role.

The European Union (EU) cohesion policy is geared toward the accumulation and improvement of factors of production. This includes access to knowledge and technological progress since it is now widely agreed that contrary to the neoclassical assumption, differences in technical efficiency are substantial and persistent across economies and may explain the dispersion of income levels. The EU assistance does not take the form of income support through unconditional transfers but of cofinancing grants to be used for specific investment purposes.

There is evidence that this policy has had a positive impact on national growth and convergence. Statistics show that there has been significant convergence in gross domestic product (GDP) per capita in the four cohesion countries (Greece, Ireland,

Portugal, and Spain), even if one excludes the impressive performance of Ireland. Isolating (with the help of modeling) the effect of the Structural Funds from that of other factors that also influence growth reveals that the Structural Funds have a positive and significant impact. For instance, the Hermin model simulations for the period 2000–2006 indicate that the impact on real GDP—compared with its baseline level of the combined demand and supply-side effects of the Structural Funds—reaches some 6 percent in Greece and Portugal and 4 percent in eastern Germany (figures 20-1 and 20-2).

In addition to their impact on growth, the Structural Funds have had a beneficial impact on social and institutional capital, which is often overlooked. Through their planning, partnership, monitoring, evaluation, and control requirements or through specific programs, the Structural Funds have been instrumental in increasing efficiency in public administration. This contribution to governance is not to be neglected since it is a condition for efficient use of any assistance for regional or overall economic development policies.

However, the impact of such proactive policies, be they conducted at the EU or the national level, can be highly variable. The reason is not differences in the amount of financial assistance. Though granted similar amounts of Structural Funds expressed as a percentage of GDP, some countries have performed better than others. This fact means that proactive aid is unlikely to lead to significant

FIGURE 20-1 HERMIN SIMULATION RESULTS ON THE IMPACT OF STRUCTURAL FUNDS PROGRAMS, 2000–06
(percent deviation of real GDP level from baseline)

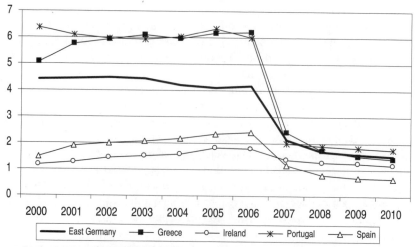

Source: Community Support Framework Objective 1.

FIGURE 20-2 QUEST II SIMULATION RESULTS ON THE IMPACT OF STRUCTURAL
FUNDS PROGRAMS, 2000–06
(percent deviation of real GDP level from baseline)

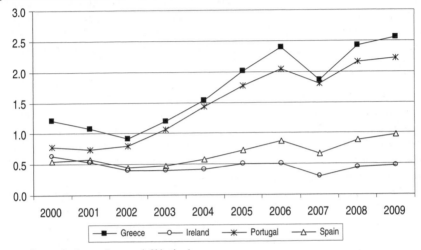

Source: Community Support Framework Objective 1.

results if it is not inserted in a context and a strategy that are themselves conducive
to growth and employment. Merely injecting resources into an area is doomed to
fail. Thus, the issue is not how to be granted a considerable share of available funding, which is often given high priority, but how to define and implement an appropriate strategy.

The strategy is threefold. The first step is to ensure that national policies are
conducive to the objectives of structural aid. Macroeconomic stability—and, more
generally, predictability—is a prerequisite. Without necessarily inferring causality,
one can note that experience shows that in Ireland or Greece, convergence has
occurred simultaneously with the implementation of stability-oriented economic
policies. Structural reforms, in particular labor market reforms, also need to be considered. Labor utilization is an important component of growth. Policies and institutions play a strong role in determining the degree of employment of the working-age
population. Policies that can positively influence regional development also include
a wage formation process that takes account of differences in labor productivity and
equity-driven implicit interregional transfers designed to avoid dependency.

The second element of the strategy is to define the territorial level—national or
regional—to be targeted for convergence. This is an issue worth considering for the
Central and Eastern European countries. The Williamson hypothesis (1965), according to which there may be a trade-off between national growth and the reduction of

regional disparities during the first stage of catching up, finds some empirical confirmation in the EU15. High national growth in the 1990s in Ireland has been accompanied by a widening of regional disparities. This has also been the case in Spain. Regional dispersion fell in the mid-1980s and remained rather static until the early 1990s, but a gradual rise has occurred since 1993. Conversely, Greece experienced low national growth in per capita income (0.2 percent) during 1980–96, leading to divergence from the EU15, but had low interregional disparities. Since 1996, Greece has converged toward the EU average and regional disparities have increased.

Behind such evolution is the fact that national growth is driven by regions with higher potential because of either the exploitation of agglomeration economies or better endowments in factors considered essential for growth. However, the fact that there are increasing regional disparities within catching-up countries does not mean that economic development is a zero-sum game and that some regions are losers. Ireland is a good illustration, as until 2000 it followed a purely national approach that did not attempt to direct capital toward the least-favored areas. These areas (border, midland, and western Ireland) have seen their GDP per capita compared with the national average decline from 79 percent in 1991 to some 73 percent at the end of the 1990s. But during the same period they have converged very significantly to the EU average: from 60 to more than 80 percent, as illustrated in table 20-1. Similarly, in Spain, all regions (except Asturias and Cantabria) that were above the Spanish average at the beginning of the period have converged toward the EU15 average.

Except in Ireland, the issue of whether to give predominance to national development or to the reduction of regional disparities has been solved through sequencing by the catching-up member states of the EU15. From 1989 to 2000, approximately 75 to 80 percent of the total Structural Funds and national cofinancing was devoted to national and interregional programs, while the remainder was allocated to specific regional programs. It is only since 2000 that Portugal and

TABLE 20-1 NATIONAL GROWTH AND REGIONAL CONVERGENCE IN IRELAND, 1991–99

	1991	1992	1993	1994	1995	1996	1997	1998	1999
Border/midland/western									
IRL = 100	79.2	79.2	77.2	76.9	75.3	75.8	73.1	74.0	72.8
EU15 = 100	60.2	62.6	63.3	67.7	70.0	71.3	76.0	80.0	81.6
Southern/eastern									
IRL = 100	107.7	107.6	108.3	108.5	109.0	108.8	109.7	109.3	109.7
EU15 = 100	81.8	85.0	88.8	95.4	101.4	102.2	114.1	118.1	122.9

Source: Ireland's National Statistical Office 1999.

southern Italy have shifted toward more specifically regional spending by allocating some 50 percent of the total to regional programs.

A third issue in any development strategy is to define which types of investments should be considered for support. Theory provides little guidance in this regard. It does highlight some broad categories of investments that are more conducive to growth. But even when there is consensus, such as on the key role of human capital, most studies are far too aggregated to be of use in selecting the specific kinds of measures to be financed. In some cases—for instance, transport infrastructure—there may even be contrasting views on the effects on lagging regions.

However, the only proactive policy that seems to have had very limited impact, if any, is state aids. They have been used in the Mezzogiorno and eastern Germany with no discernible benefits. They have probably been more instrumental in Ireland because they were inserted into very comprehensive packages, including human capital, access to knowledge, and networking. However, even in Ireland, estimates made in the 1990s (Honohan) indicate that some 80 percent amounts to dead weight—that is, investors would have invested without support.

Thus, apart from these very broad indications, the investment mix and specific measures have to be selected on the basis of the specificities, needs, and potential of the country or region concerned. A good diagnosis of the situation, an assessment of weaknesses, and an assessment of potential are prerequisites to define the objectives and priorities of the development strategy.

To conclude, there is no unique and simple causality between proactive development policies such as the Structural Funds and long-term growth and convergence. Action is required on several fronts, which include a series of national policies as well as adequate elements of strategy. A very comprehensive policy package such as the one implemented in Ireland is needed to enhance the positive impact of Structural Funds–like policies and measures. In other words, structural assistance calls for self-help to be efficient.

Index

Note: *b* with page number refers to boxes, *f* refers to figures, and *t* refers to tables.